The Sales. Promotion Handbook

CHRIS
BROWN

KOGAN
PAGE

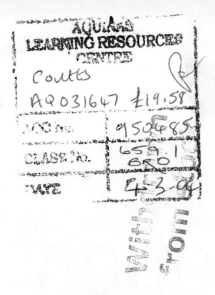
First published in 1993
Reprinted in 1997 and 1999

Kogan Page Limited
120 Pentonville Road
London N1 9JN

British Library Cataloguing in Publication Data

A CIP record for this book is available from the British Library.

ISBN 0 7494 0998 3

Printed and bound in Great Britain by
Biddles Ltd, Guildford and King's Lynn

Contents

Acknowledgements   **8**

1 Introduction   **9**
Purpose of the handbook   9
Content   9
Intended audience   11
Structure of the handbook   11

2 Promotions and Total Quality – Perfect Partners   **13**
What is sales promotion   13
A changing world   17
Principles of Total Quality promotions   20

3 Setting Objectives   **27**
Promotional goals and objectives   27
Planning promotional strategy   35

4 Principles Governing the Decision-Making Process   **42**
Planning   42
Creativity   43
Knowing your customer and the environment   44
Five promotional drivers   45
The dynamics of participation and response   48
Budget setting   50
Choosing the right promotion   52
Promotional law and codes of practice   53

5 Rewards – Introduction and Price-Based Techniques   **65**
Introduction   65
Better price   66

6 Rewards – Better Value Without Discounting   **90**
Free (or nearly free) gifts   90
Prizes   100
Emotional benefits (image)   105

7	**Media and Applications**	**111**
	One-to-one contact	111
	Mass communication	114
	Point-of-purchase promotions	122
	Communicating to known consumer types	127

8	**Application Principles Explored**	**138**
	Trial gaining	138
	Targeting	140
	Information technology led promotions	149
	Joint promotions	152
	Redemption levels (including coupons)	156
	Buy-outs and fixed-fee promotions	161
	Promotion types to match objectives	162

9	**Creativity**	**166**
	The creative process	166
	Buying in creativity	170
	Managing creative resources	174
	Executional hints and tips	178

10	**Review the Selected Promotion – Check**	**181**
	The four key check questions	181
	The implications of the chosen promotion	185
	Promotional standards	196
	Modelling redemption costs and promotional efficiency	197
	Pre-promotional research	201

11	**Implementation Processes**	**211**
	Planning the implementation	212
	Design, artwork and print	216
	Sourcing	219
	Agreements with other parties	229
	Implementing targeting systems	230
	Handling and fulfilment	231
	Insurance	241

12	**Implementation Checklists**	**243**
	General checklists and notes	243
	– overview	243

– restrictions and conditions	245
– protection against copying	246
– proofs of purchase	248
– application and entry forms	249
Specific activity checklists and notes:	249
– price promotions	249
– coupons	252
– sendaways	257
– gift with purchase and container premiums	262
– banded packs	262
– prize promotions	263
– joint promotions	270
– press promotions	271
– sampling	273
– direct marketing	273
– database building	275
– telemarketing	278
– door drops	280
– charity promotions	281
– in-store demonstrations, roadshows and exhibitions	282
13 Evaluation	**283**
The principles and scope for evaluation	284
The responsibility for evaluation	286
An evaluation checklist	288
Evaluation measures explored	288
Learning – completing the circle	301
Appendices	
Glossary	303
Useful organisations	307
Some useful suppliers	311
Further reading and useful publications	312
Index	**315**

Acknowledgements

There are innumerable people, colleagues, agency personnel and other members of the industry, who have contributed to my understanding and knowledge of promotions and have in some way helped in the creation of this book. It is impossible to give individual credit to all of them here. I have restricted my thanks to a few individuals who have offered specific help, information, encouragement or allowed me to reproduce their material in putting this handbook together. They can rest assured that I do not hold them responsible for any errors I am bound to have made in representing their part of the promotions industry.

I would like to offer particular thanks to: David Blackler at BBL; Susie Franklin; Graham Griffiths at Promotional Campaigns; Ian Hewitt; Peter Holloway; Alan Kahya at Supremia; Richard Lewis at Granby representing the PHA; Ed Lyons; Judy Middleton at NCH; Sue Short at the ISP; Peter Sleight; Mike Slipper; and Nick Wells at Circular Distributors. Specific thanks also for allowing me to use their material to: John Farrell at IMP; Jeanette Hull at the DMIS; John Segar at Harris International Marketing; and Terry Skelding at Promotional Insights.

Extra special thanks go to Oona Hains for all her exceptional hard work and tolerance, well beyond the call of duty, in helping to create the manuscript and the look of the book. It is deeply appreciated.

My thanks also go to everyone I know in the industry who are bound to have contributed in some way. My apologies go to anyone I have not mentioned by name.

Thanks also to all at Kogan Page for their patience, particularly Philip Mudd and his cheerful encouragement, even in the face of deadlines being postponed yet again.

Lastly a very special thank you to my wife, Fleur, for her help, support, understanding and forbearance. I certainly could not have finished the task without her.

This book is dedicated to the memory of Catapult, who kept me company while I was writing by insisting on making a nest in my papers and sitting on the keyboard.

Chris Brown
May 1993

1

Introduction

PURPOSE OF THE HANDBOOK

The purpose of the *The Sales Promotion Handbook* is to provide a practical reference to help create and implement quality promotions of all types. It is hoped that it will help improve the standards of promotional practice, and make life better and easier for all those involved in promotions, be they promoter, outlet, resource supplier or, not least, the consumer.

The handbook is intended to enable promotional practitioners to plan and implement activities more effectively in a structured, quality way. In particular it seeks to provide tools to help:

- ❏ identify brand needs and translate them into meaningful objectives for the situation in hand;
- ❏ confidently plan promotional strategy, selecting relevant and effective promotional techniques to meet the identified objectives;
- ❏ derive the best creative solution;
- ❏ progress promotions practically;
- ❏ evaluate and learn from running these promotions;
- ❏ provide a reference for some of the various terminologies, organisations and codes of practice within the industry.

For all the above to happen efficiently in a quality way, some understanding of Total Quality (TQ) thinking is essential. This book will demonstrate how promotions, and all those involved with them, can benefit from this approach.

CONTENT

The emphasis of the book is on the practical rather than the esoteric or theoretical. Real-life examples that may make an interesting read but would cloud the issue and create a diversion are kept to a minimum, chiefly being used to illustrate the application of different techniques. The focus is maintained on providing a book that can be used more easily on a frequent and regular reference basis. It is not just a 'good read' for those used to running promotions, it is designed to make things happen.

This practical emphasis does not mean it merely provides a list of actions to perform. It also seeks to offer clarity by providing structure and a degree of explanation for the reasons behind the recommendations. Only by understanding the thinking will it be possible to make maximum use of the handbook within the broad diversity of the readers' marketplaces.

This handbook does not intend to supplant the role of marketing service agencies. On the contrary, it should help good suppliers to work more closely and effectively with their clients to produce better quality results that will lead to more business for them and more time freed up for the client to devote to other key tasks, such as identifying new markets.

It will never be possible to cover every practical issue or provide a list of all the solutions to the great diversity of businesses that promote their products. For this reason no responsibility can be accepted for errors, omissions or the effects of promotions derived and implemented using this book. The responsibility must lie with the promoter, who should be in the best position to understand the needs and peculiarities of their marketplace. It is the principles that are important and these will usually remain valid even though the marketplace may be highly dynamic and laws, codes of practice and the appeal of different promotional techniques are all subject to change.

The book often approaches issues from the standpoint of a fmcg (fast moving consumer goods) promoter but a little thought will see their application for service companies, retailers and other manufacturers alike.

It is important to grasp one element of terminology. The book is customer focused, and references to customers and consumers are made. The consumer is the person on the street, the end user. Customers are generally taken as meaning intermediary customers (eg retailers) who have to be served on the way to delivering the message to the consumer. Sometimes 'customers' will be used to describe all parties in the communication chain including the end consumer, such use should be obvious at the time.

It should also be noted that all the views expressed in the book are the personal opinions of the author and should not be construed as fact, or as the opinion of any companies or organisations.

In conclusion, I hope the book will help readers plan and implement promotions in a quality way, remove some of the drudgery from promotions, and give a robust framework in which ideas and creativity can flourish.

INTENDED AUDIENCE

This guide to promotions has value at all levels within any organisation that promotes, large and small, and whether or not TQ practices are already part of company life.

For the hands-on practitioner it is intended to be a constant guide and companion through the highly complex steps that should culminate in effective activity, yet so often fail for unworthy reasons. It is hoped that marketing managers, brand assistants, sales managers, trade marketers, category managers, all levels of agency and promotional service company personnel and many more will find the book helpful.

For those on the periphery of the promotional world, or at more senior levels, it is hoped that, as a basic read and occasional reference document, the guide might encourage the adoption of best practice in developing promotions within their organisations.

THE STRUCTURE OF THE HANDBOOK

Structurally, the handbook follows the TQ plan/do/check/act cycle. This is the basic structure of any TQ process.

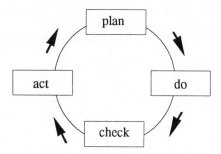

Figure 1.1 TQ cycle

Improvements to creative solutions and the systems of bringing these about will manifest themselves via the check and act processes. Consequently I welcome feedback on the content of this handbook, as only this way can it be effectively improved in the future. The handbook itself is structured as shown in Figure 1.2. Use this structure and the index to help you dip into the appropriate sections as you develop a promotion.

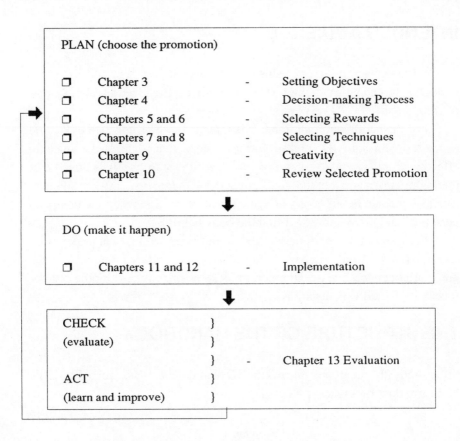

Figure 1.2 Handbook structure

2
Promotion and Total Quality
- Perfect Partners

In this chapter we will address:

- ❏   the difficulty of defining sales promotion;
- ❏   the dynamic environment in which it operates;
- ❏   the concept of TQ (Total Quality) in relation to promotions.

WHAT IS SALES PROMOTION?

Definition

If we go back to basics, promotion first appears in the 'four Ps' of marketing. This is the holistic view that a brand is the sum of its marketing mix: product (function, packaging); price (positioning); place (distribution, location); and promotion. A brand in this context might be a physical product, a service or a whole company. The essential quality is that it is discernible from its competitors by virtue of the elements within the marketing mix. Failure to differentiate and acquire a position in the market to which the special brand values can be ascribed will result in a product that is indistinguishable from others in the marketplace.

All of the 'four Ps' make up the brand personality and all should be in harmony with each other. This grand version of promotion covers everything, including advertising and personal selling and all points in between.

There are a great number of definitions of sales promotion and an even greater number of arguments about it. These principally revolve around whether theme (brand building) support and direct marketing activity are to be included within sales promotion, and whether promotions can be longterm or not.

In my view too much energy is directed at these types of questions. This is energy which could better be used to define the appropriate strategy and tactics required to reach the primary goal of getting the maximum business from potential and existing customers.

However, an indication of what sales promotion is may provide a comfort factor for some. The Institute of Sales Promotion (ISP) definition is:

> **Sales promotion comprises a range of tactical marketing techniques designed within a strategic marketing framework to add value to a product or service in order to achieve specific sales and marketing objectives.**

This is perfectly workable, although my personally preferred definition is:

> **The practice of offering temporary additional value to a brand in order to reach specific marketing objectives.**

Facets of this definition warrant further comment.

❐   *Temporary* - once a promotion becomes longterm in my view it becomes either part of the brand property, eg Miss Pears and Co-op stamps, or part of normal trading terms, eg bulk buying discounts.

❐   *Additional* - this will be in one guise or another:
   ◆ money, eg price, extra value, free sample;
   ◆ goods, eg branded item gift, competition;
   ◆ intangible benefits, eg charity or personality associations.
   This may well involve building brand values but if brand values are the only goal then I would view the activity as a form of advertising.

❐   *Specific marketing objectives* - objectives need to be clearly defined for effective solutions to be found. They may be of a general nature, eg short-term volume gain or very targeted, eg gain trial among women concerned about their health.

The transformation

Another way of defining sales promotion is to look at the process that is occurring, and the inputs and outputs to this as illustrated in Figure 2.1.

Thus we see that the product of a promotion is a satisfied customer need - a vision easily forgotten. I recently asked a friend on the agency side why promotors promote. He said it was frequently not in response to a defined customer need but because the brand manager needed to do 'something' and needed to be seen to be doing it. Promotions are often pushed down the chain of experience as the senior marketers choose the glamour of advertising and leave the slightly soiled world of promotions to the juniors. This is a sorry state of affairs that is bound to result in wasted money and effort. This is something a truly total quality company would never allow since they appreciate the benefits of integrated activity and close working partnerships with, and between, their various suppliers.

Where promotors have clearly identifiable, long-term, major customers these relationship benefits will similarly be realised by encouraging partnership with these customers. For example, there is no point in a manufacturer devising promotions for their consumers if their retail customers find the promotion unacceptable. These principles of partnerships and shared objectives run through all levels of promotional development.

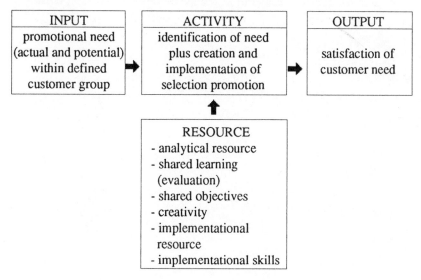

Figure 2.1 The promotional process

The integrated communication package

The array of labels assigned to different techniques is beginning to blur. For example, direct marketing is a very wide-ranging set of techniques which may be a way of purely building brand values, ie effectively a form of advertising, or it may be designed to stimulate sales, ie a form of promotion. Terminology is changing and 'direct promotions' is now a commonly used and appropriate description for many activities. Agencies too are changing, with more becoming 'marketing communications agencies' in order to offer a more flexible and wider range of services to their clients. As more media become available to marketers so this blurring of boundaries will continue.

Likewise, as marketers become more sophisticated, so they are developing comprehensive integrated communication packages that will encompass a range of disciplines (see Figure 2.2).

Despite the offerings of 'one-stop' service shops, many clients will inevitably find themselves working with a number of suppliers providing different services. For the results to work harmoniously and synergistically towards a common goal, close working and sharing of information is essential. Many agencies are too precious and short term, balking at the idea of working with other agencies who might steal a bit of their margin. Similarly, either because they have a poorly structured, total communications strategy or because they naively believe they can get better results by playing agencies off one another, too many clients fail to see the benefits of working closely with a group of long-term quality partners.

THE OLD PERCEPTIONS:

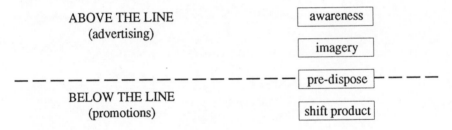

THE NEW REALITY:

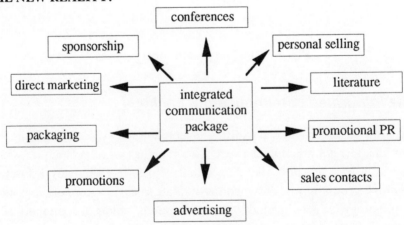

Figure 2.2   Changing communication perceptions

A CHANGING WORLD

The arena in which promotional activity performs is dynamic and ever-changing in response to a host of different environmental influences. These affect consumer attitudes and it is becoming ever more important to understand your customer, or if dealing with an intermediary, your customer's customer as well. Only through this understanding is it possible to plan the types of promotion that will be most effective and then decide on appropriate creative treatments.

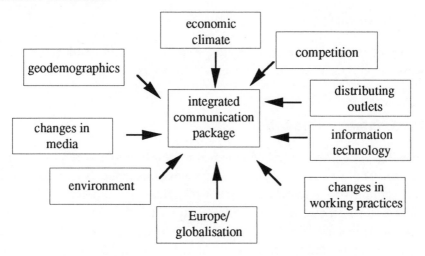

Figure 2.3   The promotional environment

Some of the drivers in this changing world are as follows.

The economic climate

As economies see-saw up and down, so consumers find themselves with more or less money to spend. Recessionary times will drive discounting promotions and those that allow cheap budget stretching, such as joint promotions. In times of plenty the emphasis will be on the added value rather than value for money aspects of the brand.

The European economic commitment/globalisation

In the UK, membership of the community will bring a variety of influences to bear on market performance, outlets for goods, production, and controls over the way in which products may be sold and promoted.

Companies must understand the limitations of Europe - what promotions are and are not legal in different countries, and what are the implications of the various directives before the EC legislature. However, there should be plenty of opportunity for the smaller business as the larger companies take on the larger markets and leave niche markets open to others.

Consumer lifestyles and fashion changes quickly cross national boundaries across the world driven by closer economic links, the global nature of business and corporate alliances, and the increasingly rapid communications systems such as satellite TV.

The retail filter

Most goods are no longer sold on a one-to-one basis, and the retailer intervenes between manufacturer and consumer. Their needs and restrictions must be understood.

More, faster competition

There has been a proliferation in innovative new brands and services within markets. These introductions are more frequent, more quickly introduced and have shorter life-cycles, and many new offerings will fail. Only the most innovative and those that are the fastest to bring products to market will succeed. This requires an ever faster response time for promotions devised to meet competitive threats.

Changing demographics, attitudes and employment

As we approach the end of the 20th century we will see quite marked changes in demographics and lifestyles. The 'greying' of the population is a well-reported phenomenon and we can expect to see more retired people with more leisure time. Whether they will have as much disposable income and whether subsequently wealth will 'cascade down the generations' remains to be seen. Similarly, the two-nation have/have not, employed/unemployed situation awaits the test of time as changes in politics, the economy and working practices rebalance employers' needs. Regardless of the level of employment we can expect to see more and more people working in service industries. Crystal ball gazing is an imprecise science. However, we can be sure that as these changes occur, so the types of promotion that work will also change.

Information technology (IT)

IT continues to surge forward as the cost continues to fall and the applications become more apparent. We are a society with more and more data at our disposal. There are three key facets to IT as far as promotions are concerned: information handling, analysis and communication. Data rich, we need to ensure we are information rich. The winning businesses will be the ones that can analyse and effectively utilise their data.

Media proliferation

In response to, and indeed through, the opportunities presented by the changes above, we are faced with a proliferation of new communication media. Seeing the way through these to identify the big opportunities, the ones relevant to your brand and those which offer the best value for money (with an eye to media cost escalation) is a potential nightmare and a fantastic opportunity.

The environmental factor

While the environment issue waxes and wanes in media and political interest, the underlying importance of the environment to our everyday lives cannot be evaded. How countries, businesses and individuals manage the future of the earth's resources and minimise the environmental impact of the diversity of activities we get up to, will inevitably be of growing importance.

Promotions and marketing in general are, rightly, highly susceptible to criticism. Far too much wasteful and trivial activity has characterised the industry. A responsible attitude is paramount and will become increasingly more important. The use of recyclable and environmentally friendly packaging, promotional advertising and premiums is of major importance.

The quality filter

As more buyers and organisations seek simplicity and closer working with their suppliers so they become more demanding of special treatment and high standards. Many firms are beginning to insist that their short-list of preferred suppliers meet their audited standards or general industry definitions of quality such as BS5750.

There is no room for cheating or irresponsible action in a TQ marketing environment and, indeed, legislation is starting to drum out those who abuse this topic. The TQ promoter will want to seize the opportunity of offering activity that drives the market forward in as sustainable and non-damaging a way as possible.

PRINCIPLES OF TOTAL QUALITY PROMOTIONS

This book cannot hope to offer all the advice and help a company needs to adopt TQ practices. However, this section explores some of the principles of TQ and discusses how the adoption of these and the use of the tools available will result in better promotions.

The unconvinced and uninitiated may ask 'Why Total Quality?' This section will answer this question, demonstrate the enormous cost and productivity benefits possible and hopefully make the reader realise that there is no option as more and more companies move in this direction.

Definition of Total Quality

The *Concise Oxford Dictionary* defines total as:

complete, comprising the whole

and quality as:

degree of excellence.

This is essentially what Total Quality businesses are about. This means ensuring the customer is supplied with an excellent product or service which is thorough and complete, provided by a supplier that considers the customers' needs throughout the full depth and breadth of the organisation.

Total quality thinking and practices started off in Japan after the Second World War. Much of this was initiated by two Americans, W Edwards Deming and Joseph Juran. Japan was keen to rebuild their industry and responded to their philosophy. Important features of this were as follows.

❑   Quality is meeting another's needs. It needs to be pitched to match the customer, since there is no point in supplying a deluxe version when the standard is all that is required, and vice versa. Juran's definition of quality is 'fitness for use', ie meeting customer needs at the level they require.

❑   The key to satisfying customer needs is to improve the processes by which things happen, most customer dissatisfaction being a product of poor processes. This improving of processes increases efficiency and prevents wasteful problems from occuring.

❑   The key to improving processes is to train people and offer hands-on leadership and empowerment to the people doing the job. The fact that Japanese industry dominates so many markets is testimony to the success of this approach.

One of the real benefits of TQ is that there are major cost savings to be made on the way. TQ is all about achieving quality at lower cost. Total Quality Management (TQM) is all about reaching TQ by gaining full commitment from everyone in the business.

The goal of Total Quality companies

We can see from the above that the goal of TQ companies is to meet their customers' needs. If you meet your customers' needs better and more efficiently than the competition, then profits and sales will happen naturally.

This concept is perfectly consonant with the basic marketing principle that a business exists in order to create and retain customers. It is from customers that profits are derived.

Failure to meet customer needs means companies will not be in business long, whereas attention to these needs provides the opportunity of reaping the benefits of a long-term customer base.

The benefits of TQ to promoters

The ability of a company to be top of the customer satisfaction league puts a company in a strong position to expand when the economy is strong and, moreover, helps companies survive when times are hard. For example, UK supermarkets are up at the top end of the customer satisfaction league for retail outlets. This is a part of the reason why they can continue to be profitable even in times of recession.

TQ will benefit the profitability and success of a complete business. This is brought about by an improvement in the effectiveness of individual working processes, including developing and implementing promotions. There will be major ramifications for individuals and their work organisation at all levels within the business. These will affect the promoter, their suppliers and customers alike.

The product of all this effort will be promotions that are far superior to the competition, the establishment of competitive advantage and real rewards to all involved.

Some of the benefits that might be expected are:

❐ errors will reduce - activities will be 'right first time';

❐   the timescale to implement will reduce;

❐   the resource required to implement will decrease;

❐   costs will reduce;

❐   productivity will increase;

❐   improved morale and commitment;

❐   the companies involved will provide an industry benchmark for others to aspire to and will benefit from enhanced image and reputation;

❐   customer/supplier partnerships and stability, allowing long-term investment; and most importantly:

❐   the promotions will satisfy customers' needs and will work.

Promotions are perfectly poised to become paragons of quality. If they do not meet customer requirements they will be costly failures that do not convince the customer to react in the way intended. If they succeed everyone benefits.

Fleshing this out into examples that a promoter or agency can really relate to everyday life, we might see:

❐   promotions coming in on budget;

❐   no more illegal promotions;

❐   no more rush charges for late artwork or amendments;

❐   premiums delivered on time at the right specification;

❐   clear instructions to consumers;

❐   no consumer complaints;

❐   rewards delivered within 28 days;

❐   the opportunity to offer better prices than the competition;

❐   the opportunity to make better margins;

❐   less need to inspect for errors;

❐   a more skilled workforce with a lower staff turnover;

❐   no surprise failures to get listings;

❐   an evaluation history that stops mistakes being repeated;

❐   improved promotion to market time period;

❐   successful promotions;

❐   more customers.

This sounds a very tall order, but improvements in all these areas are perfectly possible through TQ. The potential savings become obvious.

The cost of quality

We have seen some of the benefits. So what of the costs? In fact quality comes free. It is not an effort but a change in thinking and a different way of doing business. The investment of time and resources to start working in a TQ way will be more than recouped by the savings made.

The cost of waste in industry has been estimated at 25-40 per cent of British businesses' time and money. Knowing that so many promotions fail to achieve their objectives, which in themselves are often poorly set, I strongly suspect that the figure is much higher within the promotional process. Reducing costs will allow the release of enormous resources to run more promotions, provide profit for the business or to be invested in other brand support or new markets.

Many of these costs are very well hidden, eg the telephone costs and time spent chasing orders, checking and changing specifictions, amending artwork etc.

There are three facets to the cost of quality:

❑   *prevention* - the cost of making sure things do not go wrong;
❑   *appraisal* - checking and verifying that goods/services are to specification, ie quality control;
❑   *failure* - remedial action to correct problems and the failure to be Right First Time (RFT), the biggest area of saving.

The customer/supplier chain

There is more than one customer on the way to presenting a promotion to its destined target audience. Often the classic customer/supplier order is reversed when the process is examined in detail. The client is a supplier to the agency when presenting the brief. Production is a customer of marketing when marketing presents its plan. The distributor or retail outlet is a supplier for the manufacturer in presenting a medium for selling the manufacturer's wares. When developing a promotion all the links in the chain should be thought through, and each party needs to understand the customer and supplier roles to ensure the needs of each customer are met.

Practical TQ tools and methods

Below is a selection of tools that are particularly useful for promotions.

Process mapping

One of the most useful tools, process maps are valuable at any process level to describe the order and influence on the steps involved in an activity. Process maps can be used to identify the current way things happen and so make visible potential process improvements. They can also be used to record and share agreed ways of doing things. Process mapping involves the analysis of the inputs, outputs and feedback controls to any step in a chain of events. This topic is explored more fully later on in Chapter 11 where their everyday value will become clear.

Networks and timing plans

These are closely aligned to process maps, and define the order and sequence of activities. They are also covered in Chapter 11.

The plan/do/check/act cycle

The basic TQ cycle, this is useful at every process level. Every single process involved in creating and implementing promotions can be described by a PDCA cycle. Understanding and applying this process will help effective implementation and improve future activity.

Customer perception survey

One of the best ways to ascertain your worth, faults and virtues is to ask your customers, be they internal or external to the organisation. If external, you may wish to monitor the competitions' performance too. It may well be that the areas you perceive as weak are not seen as such by your suppliers or they may not be important to them. Key measures will include:

❐   hard, quantifiable measures such as time, price, speed, flexibility, quality;
❐   soft measures such as communication skill and how easy the working relationship is.

Pareto charts

Most people will be familiar with Pareto's law, also known as the 80:20 rule. This should suggest that 80 per cent of failures could be caused by only 20 per cent of the problems. Pareto charts enable a visual representation of this. Repetitive problems are recorded on a histogram or bar chart. The identification of the number of problems by type can then be made. This will allow focus on those problems which are most frequent. It should be noted that comparison to the full cost of those faults or problems may reveal that the most frequent problems may not be the most important or urgent, ie 80 per cent of the costs may come from 20 per cent of the errors. For example, no legal approval may cost a business a lot more than amending copy errors.

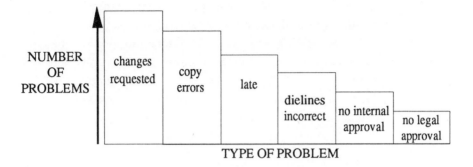

NUMBER OF PROBLEMS

changes requested

copy errors

late

dielines incorrect

no internal approval

no legal approval

TYPE OF PROBLEM

Figure 2.4 Pareto chart of artwork problems

Accreditation

Many companies find that striving for accreditation by the various quality standards, eg the British Standards Institute's BS5750 and the International Standards Organisation's ISO 9000 facilitate their move to Total Quality. Large numbers of manufacturers already have these standards and are beginning to demand that their suppliers have them as a prerequisite to doing business. They see them as an essential part of the guarantee for the supply of consistent quality products to agreed specifications and on time. Growing numbers of service companies, including promotion agencies and handling houses, have and are applying for these standards.

Partnerships

Partnership is a buzzword for the 1990s. Partnerships take many forms, eg fmcg manufacturers are realising this as they work towards category management solutions with the major multiples and as they build stronger bonds with preferred suppliers. Service companies work closely with others to provide a wider service base and promoters see opportunities for synergistic benefits of creating joint activity with other promoters.

Benefits of partnership working of particular worth in the promotions area include:

❏   *shared values* - eg no confusion about the brief and the goals of the promotion;

❏   *understanding of each other's working practices* - eg no selling an idea to the wrong person in an organisation and no disputes over invoices;

❑   *no personal agendas* - eg no time wasting on empire builders or people trying to do dramatic promotions just to be noticed;

❑   *long-term relationships* - eg no agencies charging unreasonable fees and costs, no brand managers stealing agency ideas or running wasteful six-way competitive pitches;

❑   *wide acceptability of results* - the final promotion will be acceptable to the client, the trade outlet/customer and the agency as they will all feel part of the process of bringing it to life;

❑   *lower staff/agency turnover* - happier people equals less staff and agency movement.

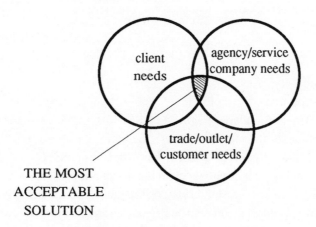

Figure 2.5 Partnership solutions

Partnerships are the basis of trust and understanding, and help the partners understand what is expected of each other. However, partnerships do not negate the role of negotiation. Successful partners will still need to agree deals, but these deals need to be mutually acceptable.

In conclusion, Total Quality is a way of working that will deliver the best results. It is a way of implementing things, not an end itself. The process of running TQ promotions begins first with setting clear objectives for a defined promotional need.

3
Setting Objectives

A frequent assumption is that by the time promotions are addressed, the person entrusted with the brand equity will have a clear idea on the brand strategy. Sadly this is not always so. Indeed, many promotions/communications agencies find themselves in the position of having to define brand strategy before they can get to grips with the promotion. Therefore, this chapter is designed to look at the dynamics driving promotional strategy and the types of objectives that will result. First, let us look at objectives.

PROMOTIONAL GOALS AND OBJECTIVES

Here we look at why promoters promote, the qualities of good objectives and the types of objectives.

Why promoters promote

Promoters promote their products for a wide diversity of reasons. Some of the more common are set out below:

- ❐ to make a name for themselves;
- ❐ because they have the budget;
- ❐ because they want something exciting for the sales force to talk about;
- ❐ because they have identified a specific marketing need that is best addressed promotionally or via an integrated communications strategy of which promotion will be a part.

A fairly cynical list but one that is frequently true. We are primarily interested in the last approach. The rest are largely spurious and while the rest of the book may help them execute the promotion well, the energy will have been wasted. Fortunately, as promoters are becoming more sophisticated, their ability to think their strategy through is improving.

Qualities of objectives

The ultimate goal of all promotions is to sell more of the product or service to the detriment of the competition by maximising sales to existing and potential customers. This may not be an open-ended goal.

There may be some variations linked to a strategy to build sales to a specific level to meet production capacity, or to dominate a particular pricing or service sector.

The *Concise Oxford Dictionary's* definition is:

Objective: the point towards which advance of troops is directed.

This is very appropriate. It demonstrates that this is specifically where we have set out to go to and it is singular. Promotions which have multiple objectives will usually fail to achieve any of them effectively. It may be that fulfilling one objective contributes and can be sympathetic to others but, the more the effort is diluted and ill-directed, the less effective the promotion will be.

The objective of any promotion should be SMART:

S	-	specific
M	-	measurable
A	-	achievable
R	-	relevant
T	-	timed

ie objectives should be simple, clear and action orientated. Adherence to the SMART mnemonic will ensure most of the problems associated with selecting and implementing appropriate activity are removed.

- ❑ *Specific*:
  Focus on the actual task.
- ❑ *Measurable*:
  Everyone will know if the objectives have been achieved and will be able to learn for the future.
- ❑ *Achievable*:
  There is no point in setting unrealistic targets. It will only lead to disappointment from all parties.
- ❑ *Relevant*:
  Objectives need to be the right ones for the brand's problems.
- ❑ *Timed*:
  There can be no question over whether or not the goals are or will be achieved if a deadline is set.

How promotional objectives relate to the classical market model

Trial and loyalty are the two fundamental promotional objectives. These drive volume.

This can be represented by the following equations:

Purchase Volume = Trial x Loyalty

OR:

$$\text{Market Share} = \text{Penetration} \times \frac{\text{Relative Purchase}}{\text{Frequency}} \times \frac{\text{Probability of}}{\text{Repeat Purchase}}$$

In practical terms purchase frequency and repeat vary much less between brand than the number of buyers, ie penetration is the key to a brand's success as big brands have more buyers.

Additionally, dominant brands have a tendency for their buyers to be more loyal. Therefore big brands stay big and small ones remain small.

This means there is a 'double jeopardy' for small brands which will have both a lower level of repeat purchase and smaller user base.

From these we can extrapolate another set of hierarchies for promotional goals. Any of these may become specific objectives for a particular activity, and there is a greater degree of inter-linkage than that shown.

Over-riding each specific objective is visibility. If the promotion and your brand is not visible, then the other objectives cannot be achieved.

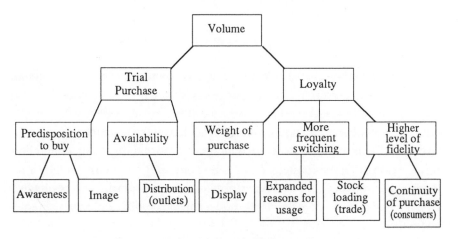

Figure 3.1 Promotional goal hierarchies

The promotional definitions I use are defined below.

Awareness
Definition:

> **Bringing the product and its benefits to the attention of the consumer.**

Not necessarily a call to action. Awareness alone is a poor objective. We are really seeking trial and so awareness is normally more appropriate as a facet of achieving another goal rather than one in its own right.

Trial
Definition:

> **Trial is getting the consumer to use the product for the first time.**

There is a clear relationship between brand share and the penetration of a brand.

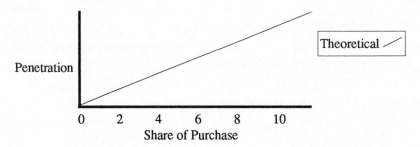

Figure 3.2 Relationship between share and penetration

Re-trial is an inappropriate objective unless consumers have not had enough time to form an opinion. Normally if trialists have not come across to your brand after the first trial you have made one of two errors. Either your product does not appeal or your strategy on how much trial the product required was wrong. Trial is appropriate for new brands or those with a fundamental re-formulation or repositioning. There is no point in trialing either a minor re-launch or a product with inferior performance. Weight of trial will be dictated by degree of difference in the new product and the predisposition of the target audience.

There is one other key piece of learning on trialing - the quicker share. It doesn't do to delay getting your product into the consumer's hands.

Switching
Definition:

> **A consumer choosing one brand in preference to another based on their assessment of the relative added values at the different price points.**

That is, change the added value (eg offer a reward) or the price to incentivise purchase. The customers who come in will tend to be existing customers who have a repertoire of brands.

Image
Definition:

> **Building on the consumer's perception of a brand's value in the same way as advertising, via a promotional device.**

It is difficult to achieve the creation of positive brand imagery through promotions and the marketer has to consider whether money is better spent on media or public relations. However, the creative/descriptive expression of most offers can build some reference to brand values and so support them. Image will affect all elements of the promotional equation. However, it is important to note that it is easier for promotions to have a negative rather than a positive effect on image.

The best promotions deliver more than the consumer expects. Trying to fool the consumer into believing they are getting a fantastic deal only to find a lot of prohibitive small print, shoddy merchandise or long delays will fundamentally damage the consumer's perception of the brand. A quality offering is a must.

Repeat purchase (loyalty)
Definition:

> **The times a consumer chooses a brand, as a percentage of all the occasions they could have chosen it, ie the probability that the consumer will buy a brand on their next shopping trip.**

This is generally about increasing the share of the consumer's portfolio of purchases. Promotions that encourage repeat purchase, ie coming back to buy again next time, is the classic way of building loyalty: encouraging multiple purchase, ie several packs at once, is another - see 'Multiple purchases' below.

Loyalty is invested in consumers not brands. Loyalty has classically been seen as a process of eroding competitor loyals towards brand switching and then on to loyalty to your brand. In fact switchers tend to be switchers and will remain disloyal and likewise if loyals can be moved they will tend to become loyal to the new brand.

Figure 3.3 illustrates this.

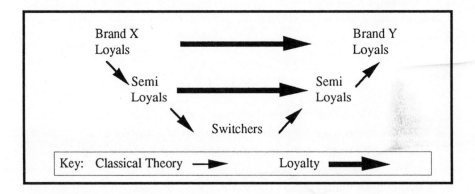

Figure 3.3 Implications for brand growth of the concept of loyalty

Loyalty is difficult to achieve.

This is reinforced by work in 1991 by Professor Andrew Ehrenberg and colleagues Hammond and Goodhardt, *The After-Effects of Large Scale Consumer Promotions* (Centre for Marketing and Communications, London Business School). The conclusions of a study of the after-effects of consumer price promotions on a wide range of established and frequently purchased branded grocery products were:

❏   there is no before or after-effect on sales, ie promotions offer a temporary effect only;

❏   there is no discernible after-effect on consumer loyalty, because the majority of extra buyers in a sales blip have already bought the brand before (80-90 per cent during the last 12 months), ie we are getting brand switches within a portfolio of brands when we promote.

The principle of only loyals coming in on promotions begs the following questions.

❑   Is brand loyalty really 'inertia',ie do people refuse to take up offers because they don't feel it worth the risk?

❑   Do people even notice promotions outside their normal brand portfolio?

❑   Is this true in markets with relatively few promotions?

❑   Is this true for new brands?

❑   Are there other promotions that can be used instead?

Multiple purchases
Definition:

> **Encouraging the consumer to increase the number of packs bought on that shopping trip.**

The consumption of many products, eg snacks, is related to their in-home presence. Multiple purchase can therefore be a strong promotional device. However, in other markets, eg toilet tissues, consumption is constant, regardless of in-home stocks. Snack buyers are just as likely to buy again later, ie this is a good way of freezing out competitors for a short period without affecting subsequent brand share. It is worth noting that as the average weight of purchase does not differ much between large and small brands, encouraging multiple purchase is likely to be proportionately more beneficial for smaller brands.

Display
Definition:

> **Merchandising to provide additional visability in-store.**

This will range from free-standing displays, gondola ends, window displays and shelf barkers to more share of voice within a publication.

Display is all about visibility as is distribution.

Distribution
Definition:

> **Extending the number of outlets stocking a product.**

Distribution does impinge directly on trial, ie distribution gains will give more trial.

Stock loading
Definition:

Forcing stock into a trade above consumer offtake levels.

Stock loading is rarely a worthwhile long-term objective. Stock loading is a manifestation of the 'push' strategy where the manufacturer loads stock into an outlet and relies on the outlet having to promote to push the stock on to the consumer. A 'pull' strategy relies on a more demand-led flow of goods through the outlet with the consumer pulling the stock through.

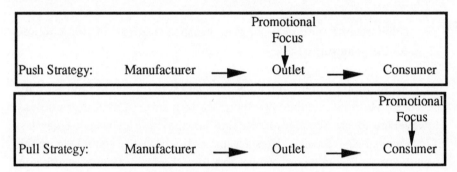

Figure 3.4 Push/pull strategies

Many promotional activities may combine push and pull, ie the trade will need encouragement to ensure they stock enough to meet the consumer demand the manufacturer will be generating. However, a TQ system will involve partnership and good supply chains so push becomes more and more inappropriate.

Interaction
Clearly all the different facets are interlinked: image will impinge on the level of fidelity, visibility will affect switching levels etc. Naturally it would be stupid to offer a loyalty-building promotion if it was not in keeping with the brand image and if distribution was lousy. However, focus on a specific goal will generally offer the best solution to a brand problem and other needs are best addressed through a co-ordinated package of promotions, each directed appropriately. For example on-pack collector schemes will not gain feature or additional distribution. These needs must be addressed separately.

There are three other promotional objectives that are worth mentioning here: they are people-oriented and directed at those within the customer/supplier chain before the end consumer is reached. These may also be required within a total communication package and their orientation is:

❑   *relationship building* - to develop customer/supplier bonds and encourage team/partnership spirit;

❑   *motivational* - to encourage belief and enthusiasm in the product or service. Possibly to enhance focus on a particular topic such as cutting down on waste;

❑   *incentive based* - performance-related activity where rewards are geared to delivery of a specified target.

The above section has illustrated some of the promotional objectives that may be appropriate to a brand's needs. Defining those objectives appropriate to the marketing situation is not an arbitrary issue but will be derived out of a clear vision of the total communication strategy.

PLANNING PROMOTIONAL STRATEGY

There is much debate on strategy versus tactics. In order to have a clear set of promotional goals the full communications strategy needs to be defined.

Strategic hierarchies

Naturally there is a hierarchy of strategies. This is illustrated in Figure 3.5.

Figure 3.5 A hierarchy of strategies

This hierarchy shows how the total communictions strategy for a brand will give mix to the promotional goals (objectives) and subsequently the promotional strategy to meet these goals.

Strategies should be derived through much rigorous analysis of facts. Strategies not developed in this way, where opinion rules, may work occasionally, but the odds for success are much longer than those for failure. There will always be entrepreneurs able to spot an opportunity through gut feel, but the scope for this is very small in today's markets where international players dominate and where competition is so fierce.

Inputs to strategy

Any military leader worth their salt would not ignore the terrain. Likewise, in the happier world of promotions, the promoter cannot ignore the environment in which the activity is to occur. A good understanding of this is intrinsic to the process of defining promotional strategy, as is the check (plan/do/check/act) to make sure your final solution is correct. Long-standing fmcg marketers will know too well the perils of ignoring the powerful retail trade's needs.

The key factors inputting to the promotional strategy will include the following.

❐ *Customer dynamics*:
What is our customer like? What do they want?

❐ *Customer purchase rationale*:
Why does the customer buy our competitors' brands?

❐ *Market positioning*:
Where have we pitched this brand? What is the rest of the market like?

❐ *Postition in product life-cycle*:
Is this a growing, static or declining brand?

❐ *Total communications strategy*:
Does it fit well?

❐ *Category dynamics*:
What are we trying to do with this whole business area?

❐ *Competitive action* :
What is the competition up to?

❐ *Regionality /micro marketing*:
Is a blanket activity appropriate?

❐ *Trade/distribution issues*:
Are there others to consider?

❑   *Production/supply chain issues:*
Are there limitations to what we can do?

Promoting via retailers

A special note is required about this issue.

Pareto's law is much in evidence here with increasing retailer concentration and power, as most fmcg products go through only a few outlets. This changes the rules slightly.

Therefore, while the promotional objectives for a brand must ultimately address the consumer, the trade perspective is key. The strength of the trade means they can force suppliers to direct brand building budgets to help them give added value to their customers' shopping trips, thus increasing their customer base and number of trips - all at the manufacturers' cost.

The majority (but not all) of fmcg brands' consumer promotions are expressed through the trade medium. Therefore, the promotional needs of major individual accounts and classes of trade must be met. Understanding their preferred techniques and systems for progressing promotions is essential.

The trade may expect manufacturers to promote a brand to show commitment to fit in with their marketing strategy. Manufacturers should avoid sacrificing consumer objectives as far as possible and recognise when they are being forced into such a situation.

Conversely, it should also be recognised that many consumer objectives are best met through specific trade-led actions, eg distribution or display drives. Many products are highly susceptable to impulse purchase and repertoire buying. It is essential to command these point-of-sale decisions.

Finally, it must be recognised that the trade's primary promotional vehicle is price promoting in one form or another. The brand manager must adopt a customer focus and promote in the way the trade wants without forgetting the needs of their brands. Forging partnerships and category management is the way to achieve this. Much difficulty in accepting realism is required in what can be achieved through the retail medium. At the end of the day most consumers are only buying 100 or 200 lines from the store's perhaps 10,000+ lines in stock and your promotion is going to be very trivial compared to everything else going on in the store.

This somewhat restrictive pattern of activity applies to any promoter working in an area with a restricted outlet or distributive base. Also worth bearing in mind at this point is the fact that an outlet with such dominance is in the best position to know its customers and a manufacturer's customers.

Manufacturers need to learn to understand their customers within each outlet and retailers need to understand that sharing their knowledge will help manufacturers achieve better promotions (and products) for mutual benefit.

Retailers and service company promotions

Retailers and service companies are effectively brands in their own right and promoting the whole company can in general be treated with the same principles as described throughout the book. Just like a biscuit manufacturer, they are driven by the two key drivers - getting new customers and then keeping them.

Short-term vs long-term promotions

Most promotions are short term in duration and effect. How long short term actually is is arguable. The continued use of a promotion will mean it is likely to become an intrinsic part of the brand proposition or trading terms. Longer-term promotions are most relevant when trying to buy fidelity in mature markets, eg petrol company collector schemes.

The values of a longer-term approach include the following:

☐   *Campaignability:*
A consistent promotional message can be built upon.
☐   *Economy of scale*:
One long-term promotion will cost less than six short ones.
☐   *Commitment:*
A well-determined long-term strategy will mean that the next brand manager will not come along and undo all the good the previous one has done.

Investment strategies and brand life-cycles

The Boston Square

The Boston Consulting Group puts brands into one of four categories: Stars (successful brands); Problem Children (brands in difficulty); Cash Cows (profit generators with limited potential); and Dogs (unprofitable brands with limited potential).

The investment strategy for each of these segementations is illustrated in Figure 3.6.

Understanding your brand's dynamic position on this grid will help you decide on the best investment strategy. It is, of course, essential that honesty prevails, since every brand manager would prefer to see their brand as a potential star even if it is really a dog.

MARKET SHARE

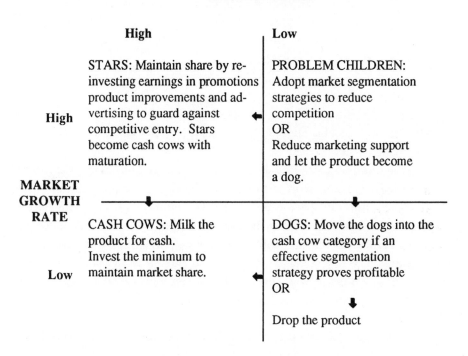

Figure 3.6   The Boston Square

Promotional intention can also be derived from whether brands are growing, stable or declining.

Growth brands
Growth may be from new brands or genuine relaunches, where there are product or advertising improvements.

Promotion here is an investment activity for future profits. Essentially this means trial. Trial is temporary. Repurchase is dependent on the product qualities. Whether the consumer perceives the superior brand values and how well this trial investment is carried out will effect levels of repurchase and therefore the future profitability of the brand.

Investment in launch and relaunch brands is such an important topic and commands such a large slice of promotional spend that it is worth re-iterating a few truisms.

❐   Do not expect too much. Only if you have a real innovation in product performance, or perceived value or image can you expect big share gain.

❐   The first into a market usually gets the biggest share.

❐   Share is related to the degree and speed of penetration.

❐   Promotional spend on a well-tried product which only claims to be 'new' or 'improved', ie it is really the same old line relaunched, is likely to be a waste of money.

Established brands

These are in 'static' markets or market sectors, ie where the consumer sees a repertoire of acceptable alternative brands. It is important to maintain repurchase levels of these brands.

Promotion on these brands is an expense activity to gain a short-term advantage by creating short-term value difference to the competition.

Expenditure on these brands must be tightly controlled and the incremental volume sold should be enough to provide the funding for the activity. A robust investment formula where support is directly linked to sales is essential. The objectives will be to build fidelity to the brand franchise profitability, tempt switchers into the brand and increase consumption.

Declining brands

These are long-established brands with a loyal core. Promotion will not reverse this decline, but will at best slow it down. Only significant product or advertising improvements can reverse the trend.

Promotional spend here is a waste. Support is more likely to encouarge stockloading or loyal consumer buy-forward than new/switched users. Such support is often excessive trade orientation promotion chasing unrealistic volume targets. As a result the brand is further devalued and profits further eroded.

There may be occasional exceptions where money spent on declining brands is worth while, eg to maintain distribution or to boost sales to a level where advertising is viable, but these are few and far between. Restricting support behind declining brands will lead to a longer and more profitable life, providing critical mass is retained and that the trade accept and support the position.

Summary of objectives by brand life-cycle position

Figure 3.7 summarises the key objectives that will be appropriate to brands in different marketing situations and indicates the value of supporting the brand.

Consideration of a portfolio of products in this way will help clarify investment priorities.

LIFE-CYCLE POSITION	PROMOTIONAL INTENTION	TYPE OF PROMOTONAL SPEND
LAUNCH	Awareness Trial Conversion	Investment - long return
GROWING BRAND (or RELAUNCH)	Penetration build Weight of usage Loyalty Tempt competitors' loyals	Investment - shorter return
ESTABLISHED BRAND	Retain loyals Tempt switchers (profitably) Weight of purchase	Cost of doing business
DECLINING BRAND	Only viable options: Retain loyals Bury profitably (or sell)	Potential waste

Figure 3.7   Brand life-cycle effects on promotional intent

Is it worth it?

Pareto's law, also known as the 80:20 rule,infers that you are likely to be spending 80 per cent of your time on small, irrelevant activities that only affect 20 per cent of your business. Conversely, only 20 per cent of your time is spent on the promotions affecting the vital 80 per cent of your business.

It is essential to have a clear vision and ensure the activity is worth while. In fact this is a 'check' from the PDCA cycle. Check your objectives are sound before you progress with choosing the solution to your problem. Too many promoters waste time and money on small-scale, ineffective promotions. All this does is reduce the productivity of the ones that matter, increase the cost of waste, and damage the relationship with the consumer and any intermediaries.

Assuming you have a viable promotional opportunity on your hands, the next step is to decide on an appropriate technique to meet the promotional need.

4

Principles Governing The Decision-Making Process

The previous chapter has given an insight into how to define your promotional goals. Once these have been determined, the next step is to select the promotional strategy to achieve these. I have broken this process down into a series of chapters that cover:

❏ the principles governing the decision-making process;
❏ the rewards the promoter can offer;
❏ the application of individual techniques via the different promotional media available;
❏ what techniques may be appropriate to specific objectives.

In this chapter we look at some of the principles that input to the process of choosing the right promotion:

❏ planning;
❏ creativity;
❏ knowing your customer and the environment;
❏ five promotional drivers;
❏ the dynamics of gaining participation/who responds;
❏ budget setting;
❏ choosing promotions;
❏ promotional law and codes of practice.

PLANNING

At this investigative stage it is easy to underestimate or forget the time needed to implement activities. Time spent now on considering the options will impinge on the time available for the rest of the promotional planning and implementation stages. Time spent planning well should reduce the time needed to implement. However, it is important to have a clear vision of the time available.

This is, therefore, when the PDCA cycle can start to prove its worth. It is important to prepare an outline timing plan even now at this early stage. This way all involved can have a clear understanding of what has to be delivered, by whom and when. The plan will evolve and become more detailed once the technique is selected and the promotion moves into the implementation stage.

The basic TQ practices of timing plans and process mapping are dealt with in detail in Chapter 11. It may well prove beneficial to refer to this section when preparing your initial plan.

Planning is key. Most promotions fail because of poor planning, either in the early stages of defining the task and the solution, or in planning how to implement it. The argument is that by extending the planning time the implementation time can be reduced. The final result is that the whole time required to bring the idea to market is shortened (see Figure 4.1). Planning will continue to become more important as the marketing world continues to become more complex, and is a major focus for this book.

Conventional approach:	plan	implement
TQ approach:	plan	implement

time ➡

Figure 4.1 TQ vs Conventional approaches to planning

CREATIVITY

There are four key areas where creativity is essential for impactful and effective promotions that stand out from the background, and actually create a response. These areas are:

- ❐ technique selection;
- ❐ reward selection;
- ❐ technique application;
- ❐ execution.

As a client I often naively think of creativity just as the execution of a promotion, ie the visualisation, the headline or theme, the copy and maybe the way a response package is put together. My wife, who works for an agency, correctly reminds me that creativity is much more than this. It can be in the selection of a novel or unusual technique, or twisting a standard technique in some clever way, and applying it so that it creates interest and relevance for the target audience.

For example, coupons can be used to gain trial, repeat purchase or multiple purchase. It is the way the offer is structured, visually put together and presented that will dictate both the redemption rate and the consumer's attitude to the brand and offer.

The creativity inherent in the execution is not to be underrated but all links in the chain must be strong for the activity to work to best effect. Executional creativity plus briefing and buying in creative services of all types are dealt with in Chapter 9. This includes a section on brainstorming and creative problem solving. The tools involved will prove highly relevant to technique selection and application.

It is in these key areas of technique selection and application that the science of analysis and understanding meets the art of perceptive creativity. Effective and inspirational promotions demand this blend of fact-based decision making and the creative gift to make an apparently ordinary, unused or seemingly inappropriate technique fit the promotional need.

KNOWING YOUR CUSTOMER AND THE ENVIRONMENT

If you are to choose a promotion that will appeal to your target audience then you need to understand who they are, their habits, preferences and the environment in which your promotion will be presented and used.

It is sobering to realise how few consumers are even aware of the promotion. Of those that are aware, many will not respond. They may not have understood the proposition or may not find it motivating. If they do respond are they the right people and are they responding in the way you want them to? Only by really understanding the consumer and the external limitations as discussed in Chapter 3 can the best technique be derived.

Some of the types of information that may help shape your views on the type of person you are dealing with include:

❐   talking to them;
❐   brand positioning statements;
❐   the advertising;
❐   psychographic and behaviourgraphic profiles;
        (descriptors of the type of people they are, the things they like,

> how they behave and some of their attitudes)
❑   sociodemographic profiles;
❑   purchase patterns;
❑   ad hoc research.

The importance of the medium in which consumers are going to have to respond is also vital. The simple one-to-one communication between manufacturer and customer is blurred by a variety of filters, barriers and distractions. In particular, for fmcg markets, the retailer and/or distributor gets in the way and restricts the promotional techniques available. This is likely to mean that more focus is made on pull strategies where the promoter has to find new ways of making contact with consumers outside the store environment. For example, many promotions now run television commercials supporting promotions to ensure awareness is high, or may run poster campaigns near major outlets.

The level of appeal of different techniques is discussed in more detail later. However, it is interesting to note at this point that promoters do still plan unpopular activities. Research by Harris International Marketing reveals that in 1991 'over two-thirds of managers planned promotions which nearly half of them believe unpopular with the public' and 'about two-thirds of planned unpopular promotions are planned merely because they are convenient or cheap'. However, it must also be noted that many 'unpopular' promotions work well even if the consumer is not excited by them.

One of the other key reasons for promoting via unpopular promotional techniques is that this allows a message about the brand image to be communicated, often quite cheaply. With fmcg products this can therefore potentially act as an image enhancer or piece of advertising at point-of-sale. Whether this achieves its objective is a matter of much conjecture and less research-based fact.

FIVE PROMOTIONAL DRIVERS

Technique selection is also subject to industry trend. At the time of writing, the 'instant win' promotion is all the rage. Pioneered largely by the big canned product manufacturers, Heinz and Pedigree Petfoods, the idea of 'Is there a car in this can?' is immensely stimulating and for the time being has captured the minds of a wide range of promoters from soft drinks and snacks, to batteries and toilet rolls.

This can be used to illustrate five key promotional drivers that will influence the appeal of a promotion. These are detailed below.

New /novel

Promotions that are new and novel will be far more effective than those which run and run. Extra fill packs or special prices have, in many markets, become the sole reason for a purchase decision, ie branding has been devalued. As such they are deathly dull and something like an instant win which, while not building values much, are quite likely to be a trigger to motivate the consumer into a sales purchase.

In time, no doubt, instant win will flag in attractiveness as wear-out sets in and the consumer realises the minimal chance of success. Quite frequently there is a cyclical nature to these trends, eg the big petrol retailers started out with collector schemes such as Green Shield Stamps, went on to a round of competitions led by the classic Shell 'Make Money' and have now ended up back in a new round of collector schemes.

Immediacy

The great thing about opening a canned drink to see if you've won a flight to the USA is its immediacy. You know if you've won then and there. No waiting for a tedious postal draw in six months' time. This promotional facet is always true; you can always expect a much higher participation rate from something that is now rather than later.

There are two other benefits as well. Just how long is a child going to hold on to a bag of Quavers which may or may not have a Nintendo Game Boy waiting inside? It is not suprising that they achieved a significant sales increase. Once the bag is open you have to eat the contents and then it's time for another. Consumption can also be driven by encouraging use-up rather than by opening more packs.

Will Andrex's offer of instant win Peugot 106s on the cardboard tube inside the toilet roll encourage faster use-up? Maybe not, but if the competition is at the bottom of a multi-storey container of biscuits there is a strong incentive to polish off the whole lot quickly.

Barriers to entry

How easy it is to participate is often a good guide to the effectiveness of a technique. The more steps a consumer has to go through to take part in an offer, the less likely it is they will respond. Opening the bag of snacks is instant, you probably will not even have to wait until you get home. If you have to collect the till receipt, peel off a label and fill in a form, or collect six tops, it is not surprising a lower redemption rate will ensue.

Slippage

The redemption rate is not the same as the participation rate. Many of the consumers who start the process of collecting their six packet tops will drop out after only collecting a few tops or will fail to send in before the closing date. This is known as slippage. The level of slippage will be related to the number of proofs of purchase (pops) required and the use-up rate of the product. Naturally an instant win or gift with   purchase is unlikely to suffer much.

Some promoters try to use slippage as a way of controlling redemption, either by making the requirements high or by restricting the number of special packs and the essential tokens on them. This has the advantage of spreading the budget and being able to offer a greater reward. However, it is not very TQ and is likely to leave your consumers mildly dissatisfied with the product. This needs to be thought through carefully.

Appropriateness

The promotion needs to be credible and relevant to the target audience. The Quavers/Game Boy is highly appropriate to the target audience, although it is open to debate as to whether this is more target market overlap rather than true targeting or brand synergy. Overlap, where the promotion is aimed at the same broad band of consumers, is fine, but the promotion is much stronger if brand values are built in too. The reward and/or mechanic should not just meet the aspirations of the target. Ideally it should also complement the brand positioning.

Duracell have introduced a battery strength-testing strip into their blister packs of batteries. This added-value feature of the product has neatly been turned into a promotional vehicle by offering a £1,000 instant win pack where the test strips indicate whether or not a prize has been won when the battery is tested. Not a themed reward but a very good way of offering a promotion that builds on added-value elements of the product.

Matching true values as opposed to just similar positioning is hard to do well and there is often a trade-off between positioning and getting a high response.

THE DYNAMICS OF PARTICIPATION AND RESPONSE

For consumers to respond to a promotional proposition there is a classic sequence of events, more often described in advertising models, which has to occur. This is known by the mnemonic AIDA (attention, interest, desire, action). This mental process may not always dwell for long on individual steps if the decision is an easy one, but the basic sequence is illustrated in an expanded form in Figure 4.2.

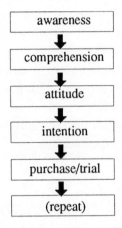

Figure 4.2 Steps to becoming a promotional participant

It can be seen from this that, to be successful, a promotion has to be visible and understood. Once understood it has to be credible and relevant if it is to create the intention to purchase. The discussion below centres on fmcg markets, but the same principles are applicable to any.

Promotions will always appeal to a much wider audience than just the promotional target group. What is so very important is ensuring the offer creates the maximum response in that right target group. Understanding the motivations of these people is essential. For example, if you are running a promotion aimed at a group of teenagers it is essential to know what interests or concerns them. It was reported in *Super Marketing Magazine* that the Leatherhead Food Research Association's Report 'Teenage Eating Habits' reveals that 27 per cent of teenagers claim to be very concerned about the environment and 54 per cent quite concerned. It would be paticularly foolish (apart from irresponsible) to run a promotion aimed at teenagers that offered a premium item made of tropical hardwood from unsustained forests.

In the hard light of day most consumers find most promotions trivial, irrelevant or, worse still, annoying. Research by Harris International Marketing has shown that in 1991, 45 per cent of consumers agreed a lot with the statement 'I prefer no frills'. Only 6 per cent disagreed a lot.

Figure 4.3 illustrates the likely dynamics of promotional respondents. Many are unaware of the activity. Consumers out grocery shopping will often reach past coupons on-shelf in front of the goods, pick the product and just miss the coupon. Of those that are aware many will do nothing: they may well have comprehended, possibly even had an attitude shift and considered the promotion, but their behaviour will remain unaltered. A small proportion will act.

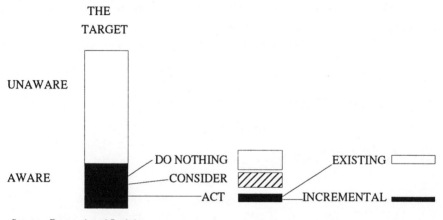

Source: Promotional Insights

Figure 4.3 The bottom-line of promotions

However, the benefits of getting participants is not always as clear cut as the redemption levels achieved. Consumers will come in for a number of reasons. Those that are your existing customers (most) may just be getting a one-off free deal and the money is wasted. Others may simply buy-forward and so future business may be mortgaged away. In some markets, eg snacks and refrigerated items, getting buy-forward is valuable. If it is around the product will get eaten with a net increase in consumption. In others, eg dishwasher powder, buy-forward will make little difference to consumption, although it may have value as a spoiling technique, eg keeping consumers locked into a brand, during a competitor's launch.

Figure 4.4 shows the types of respondents one might typically get to an offer. However, only analysis, evaluation and much consideration will reveal the true dynamics of a promotion. These illustrations show how important this is. Many promotions do work even if the majority do fail to be cost effective.

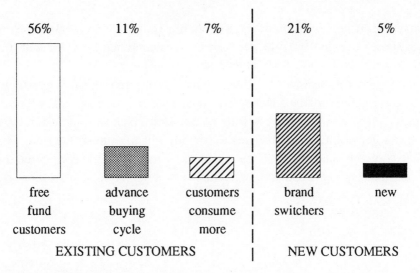

| 56% | 11% | 7% | | 21% | 5% |

free	advance	customers		brand	new
fund	buying	consume		switchers	
customers	cycle	more			

EXISTING CUSTOMERS | NEW CUSTOMERS

Source: Promotional Insights

Figure 4.4 Who buys or responds

BUDGET SETTING

It is appropriate to discuss budget setting at this point since the budget available will influence the scale of activity and the options open to the promoter.

Precise budgets for specific promotions can only be worked out once the concept is well developed. However, before attempting to define the activity a budget will probably need to be set. In many ways it is unfortunate that this is the way most companies operate, but it is a measure of their need for internal budgetary control systems.

We have already seen how promoting at different times in a brand's life-cycle demands different approaches to promotional budget apportionment. New/growth brands will have much higher budget requirements than established brands which will have a fixed percentage of their sales allocated to promotional activity. Declining brands should receive minimal support, often on an ad hoc basis.

From the above we can see that the difficulty comes in setting budgets for the new/growth brands. In practical terms this is often the area likely to receive most of a company's budget and certainly most of the attention.

In my view, the correct way to determine the right budget for a brand is by quantitatively determining the promotional need, eg number of new users, degree of loyalty, number of switchers etc, then allocate a maximum cost per participant. It is then possible to gain creative solutions and match back to the cost per participant and the absolute numbers of participants. This is illustrated in Figure 4.5.

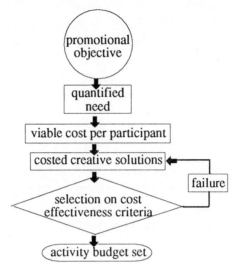

Figure 4.5 Budget setting process

Sadly, this route is rarely used and arbitary budgets are subjectively set on what feels right or what the company sees as its key priorities at that time.

However the budget is derived, it is important to give this area a lot of attention. Promotions are a more complex area than many others in the marketing mix. There are a lot of different cost elements that need to be captured, controlled and monitored.

In general, promotions fall into one of three camps as detailed below.

❐   *Fixed budget promotions*:
      These are where the total cost of the activity can be determined
      in advance. Essentially this is where the number of packs is
      known and the promotional cost per pack is pre-determined, eg
      when a free gift is banded to a pack or a fixed discount is being
      offered on each pack. Occasionally the budget is fixed even if
      the number of packs is not, eg a gift with purchase promotion in
      store.
❐   *Partially fixed budget promotions*:
      These are when most of the costs are known, eg a competition

where the prize is set but there may be small additional handling and judging costs depending on the number responding.

❒   *Variable budget promotions*:
Here a large proportion of the costs are dependent on the number of respondents, eg coupon schemes and sendaway offers. These types of activity require close scrutiny. High redemptions will blow the budget and low ones may mean residual stocks of premium items for sendaways. An important feature of variable cost promotions is risk assessment. It is always worth costing out against minimum and maximum likely redemption levels.

There will be three families of cost:

❒   *creation costs* - the costs to bring a promotional idea into being;
❒   *activity costs* - the costs to make the promotion happen;
❒   *opportunity costs* - the cost of missing out on doing other things because of doing the promotion.

CHOOSING THE RIGHT PROMOTION

It is, of course, impossible for me to tell you how to choose the right promotion. If I could, I would not bother, as I would have made my fortune and be sunning myself on the proverbial tropical shore rather than writing a book on promotions!

However, I can summarise the points raised in the preceding sections to give some indication of the process you should go through in deciding what is best for your brand and marketplace, and I can give an indication of techniques that are sometimes more appropriate to meet different objectives. This process of deciding on the appropriate solution will be governed by a hierarchy of implementational issues which are described in Figure 4.6.

The triumvirate of offer, media and image are interdependent. Only through experience can the best solution be derived from the interplay between these. In many cases the image will dictate the medium and the reward. In others the media route may take primacy over the reward or vice versa. In practical terms this hierarchy is often inverted, as a brainstorming session to generate ideas is likely to predicate any analysis of suitability for the task.

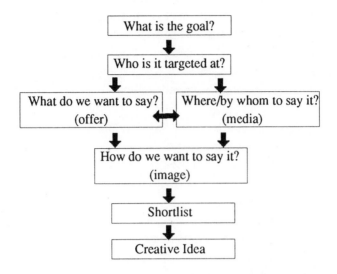

Figure 4.6 Hierarchy of promotion selection

Having looked at the decision-making process it is worth covering the legal and code of conduct checks that protect customers. Any unfamiliar types of promotion referred to will be clarified in Chapters 5 and 6 or the glossary.

PROMOTIONAL LAW AND CODES OF PRACTICE

There are two principle ways in which promotions are controlled, by the law and by the various industry codes of practice.

Obviously the law must be adhered to. The codes are self-regulatory, but they are not just sets of principles. Effective ones have real teeth to police and punish offenders. Codes are an additional set of controls and standards on top of legislation. They should be adhered to in spirit as well as the letter. Finding a way to fudge the issue is not a TQ approach and is not in the interests of the industry at large. In the long run everyone will suffer via consumer backlash and punitive legislation.

Problems of all types occur, from misleading presentation, exaggerated claims, no delivery period, the failure to include full rules and addresses etc. The most frequent problem areas are prize draws and similar competitions, prices and consumer credit problems.

The perpetrators come from all shapes and sizes of company from multi-nationals to local traders. These promoters are failing to complete their 'check', or sadly in a few cases, flagrantly disregarding them and jeopardising every promoter's position. A little background study could so easily remove this type of problem, since most issues are about good practice and are well covered by the various codes. Detailed study or understanding of the pertinent legislation itself is rarely necessary.

The following topics are covered below:

- general standards, codes, laws and their supervision.
- pricing and trading issues.
- competitions and lotteries.
- database management (including data protection).
- mail order.
- telemarketing.
- international promotions.
- specialist trade codes.
- advertorials.
- radio promotions.
- television.

This is not an exhaustive list and neither are the comments appended to the list total or absolute in their coverage of the situation. What they do provide is an introduction to the issues that will come up. I would advise all promoters to take legal advice on every piece of copy, script and visual before implementing a promotion. In complex areas such as price claims, competitions, trade gifts and data protection it is also well worth checking the principles behind the offer and its construction at an early stage.

General standards, laws, codes and their supervision

The main body that supervises the self-regulatory codes for the advertising and promotions industry is the Advertising Standards Authority (ASA). It is the ASA that deals with consumer complaints on promotions. It publishes a monthly report on promotions that fail to meet the code. It makes contact with transgressors for their comments, usually at a high level in the company, so this is an easy way for young brand managers to get themselves noticed quickly in a highly undesirable way. The media often pick up on newsworthy examples, so beware.

The implementation of the codes is by the Committee of Advertising Practice (CAP) and on a day-to-day basis for promotions, by its subcommittee on sales promotion (the Sales Promotion and Direct Response Review Panel). CAP handles promotional complaints from the trade. CAP supervises the following codes which the promoter is most likely to find relevant.

❑   British Code of Advertising Practice (BCAP) (Many promotions are advertised and will therefore need to comply with this.)

❑   The British Code of Sales Promotion Practice (BCSSP, published by CAP and available from the Institute of Sales Promotion (ISP).

❑   The code issued by the Direct Marketing Association UK Limited (DMA (UK)) (This body is an amalgamation of the old British Direct Marketing Association (BDMA) and other direct marketing bodies.)

CAP is a regulatory body. Advice prior to running a promotion is best obtained via the ISP. Other specialist institutes or associations may be able to give advice in specific areas, again the ISP can advise. Services provided by the ISP include:

❑   legal and copy advice;
❑   voice to governments at Westminster and Brussels;
❑   an industry recognised qualification through the ISP Diploma course;
❑   other training events;
❑   low-cost specialist VAT advice;
❑   general advice, contacts and information on promotions;
❑   individual, corporate and consultancy membership;
❑   independent judges and observers;
❑   coupon guidelines;
❑   a regular newsletter on topical issues;
❑   competition registration and judging.

More detail and checklists on some of the issues surrounding different types of promotion will be found in Chapters 11 and 12.

The promoter will carry prime responsibility for all elements of a promotion, although service agencies will share some elements. There is no substitute for the full British Code of Sales Promotion Practice and all promoters should obtain a copy. This document is indispensable.

Pricing and trading issues

It is the job of the local trading standards officer to police these issues.

Trading standards officers work from a large number of departments co-ordinated under the umbrella of the Local Authorities Co-ordinating Body on Trading Standards (LACOTS). Enquiries are normally dealt with by the local department and the interpretation they provide should normally stand good for other areas.

The Office of Fair Trading (OFT) does not have local branches and complaints can be made to the Director-General of Fair Trading. The Control of Misleading Advertisements Regulations 1988 gives support to self-regulation by allowing complaints to be made to the OFT concerning a wide range of misleading advertisements, where advertisements include all forms of promotion but exclude broadcast advertisements. The OFT is concerned more with principles than day-to-day controls which lie with the ASA and local trading standards officers.

There is a vast array of legislation affecting promoters, however they need not panic as most of the issues are covered by adhering to the various codes of practice. A particularly useful publication in the trading environment is the Code of Practice for Traders on Price Indications (often known as 'the Price Code'), which is available from the Consumer Affairs Division of the Department of Trade and Industry.

Seven issues relating to trading deserve specific mention here.

Price claims: problems with price claims is one of the most frequent to arise. The nub of the controls around this area are:

- ☐ do not make misleading offers;
- ☐ make out that a price is less than it in fact is;
- ☐ have hidden extra charges;
- ☐ have hidden restrictions or circumstances of availability;
- ☐ if a comparison or an indication of worth is made then this must be justified in a way that consumers can understand;
- ☐ make sure price claims conforms to approved wording as laid down in legislation.

NB: When comparing your product with a competitor's using their registered trade mark can be an infringement of that mark. This approach should be carefully checked legally.

Extra value claims: again these must be justifiable and conform to the same basic rules as for price claims. Certain products have restrictions on packaging sizes that can be used, eg the Weights and Measures (Miscellaneous Foods) Order 1988 largely prohibits extra value on a wide range of food products.

Trading stamps: where someone, eg a retailer, effectively gives money off by giving a voucher or stamp which can cashed in later, or used to buy or obtain goods or services. To avoid trading stamps being used as disguised price reductions, the Trading Stamps Act 1964 requires that any stamps, vouchers or tokens used in a collector scheme must have a cash value on them (except those printed in newspapers). Persons holding stamps worth over 25p can ask for the cash, so very low values are normally ascribed to such tokens, eg 0.00025p. In theory this could mean that manufacturers offering money off next purchase coupons could be seen as offering trading stamps and a cash value would be necessary for the coupon itself. In practice this is not normally done for this type of promotion.

Dealer loaders gifts and incentives: can result in criminal offences so care is necessary. Permission needs to be sought at a higher level in both giver and recipient's companies, and all gifts of any value are likely to be subject to personal income tax liability for the recipient. Obtain written permissions and receipts.

Anti-competitive pricing: dominant firms trying to squeeze out smaller businesses through unfair pricing and collaborate price fixing are not allowed by either UK or EC law.

Sales away from trade premises: these are protected in two specific ways. The Consumer Credit Act 1974 allows cancellation rights following certain credit and hire agreements signed away from trade premises. The consumer is also protected from pressure selling in unsolicited home visits by the Consumer Protection Regulations 1987 which allow a seven-day cancellation period.

Investments: the promotion of investments is controlled and restricted by the Financial Services Act 1986 plus, under powers derived from that Act, the rules as laid down by the Securities and Investments Board and industry self-regulating bodies.

Competitions and lotteries

The key legislation is the Gaming Act 1968 and the Lotteries and Amusements Act 1976.

Essentially lotteries are illegal, apart from a few specific exceptions which have been legislated for and are subject to specific controls, eg football pools, premium bonds and raffles. A lottery can be described as the distribution of prizes by chance following a contribution by the participants for their chance to participate. Key is the fact that the contribution does not have to be cash, it could be other benefits generated by running the promotion. Contravention of the legislation is serious, may result in unwanted attention from the police and the Director of Public Prosecutions, plus of course high levels of adverse publicity. The Gaming Board for Great Britain has notes for guidance on running lotteries.

'Instant win' and many gamecard promotions such as those run by newspapers get by legally because opportunities for free entry are made available. The TQ promoter might like to consider whether 'free' means totally free or whether they are happy for consumers to pay the cost of a telephone call or postage stamp to get their chance to win.

Competitions are again subject to the Lotteries and Amusements Act. Prohibited competitions are those in which prizes are offered for forecasts of the result of a real event (future or past), or in which success does not depend to a substantial degree on the exercise of skill.

Thus gambling on a future sports event is out, but estimation of results by a panel of judges plus creative solutions such as best names, descriptions, slogans and spot the ball competitions are acceptable. The amount of skill does not have to be that substantial, but it must play a substantial part in determining success. This can result in some rather pathetic tests of skill.

Database management (including data protection)

First and foremost all personal data holders who hold such details on computer have to register themselves under the Data Protection Act 1984 with the Data Protection Registrar. It is not necessary to register if personal data are manually handled or if the data are only about corporate bodies. There are exemptions but most personal data relating to promotions do require registration, eg if a company runs a promotion and asks for information about respondents' shopping habits to build promotional databases to mail further offers, then they must be registered.

The principles behind data protection are:

- ❐   data collection and processing should be fair and lawful;
- ❐   data should be held, disclosed and used lawfully, and only for the registered purposes;
- ❐   data should only be disclosed to the persons described on the register including the subject;
- ❐   data should be adequate, relevant and not excessive to the intended purpose;
- ❐   be accurate and, if necessary, up to date;
- ❐   be suitably secure and protected from loss, unauthorised disclosure or alteration;
- ❐   data should not be held longer than necessary.

The individual has the following rights:

- ❐   to check if data are held;
- ❐   to have access to that data and to amend or delete them;
- ❐   to compensation if damage has resulted from the loss, unauthorised destruction or disclosure of the data and from inaccurate data.

It is a criminal offence to:

- ❐   be unregistered when necessary;
- ❐   act outside the terms of the registration, as a registered data user, or an employee or agent of a registered user.

Registration is cheap and relatively simple. Once the registration application is in, the data user or handler can normally (eg unless recently deregistered) start working immediately as if it has been accepted.

Data users have to reveal:

- ❐   a description of the data they hold;
- ❐   the purposes that the data are being held or used for;
- ❐   the data sources;
- ❐   the disclosures (who the data are to be released to);
- ❐   any transfers (to other countries outside the UK).

The act ensures the UK conforms to the Council of Europe Convention on Data Protection and facilitates cross-boundary data movement and trade.

There are ongoing EC discussions about the whole area of data protection and its use in marketing activities. Marketers are strongly advised to check the latest situation at an early stage with their legal advisers. Possible outcomes of the planned directive include:

❒   a ban on automatic profiling of respondents' details;

❒   a requirement for prior consent for the use of personal data, ie opt in not opt out;

❒   the restriction of transference of personal data to countries where there are lower levels of data protection;

❒   notification of intended further use of personal details at the time of collection or a subsequent communication to seek permission for use.

Consumers are also protected from unwanted direct mail by the Mailing Preference Service (MPS) which helps them to have their names removed or added to lists held and used by MPS members.

The Direct Mail Services Standards Board (DMSSB) monitors direct mail, performs market surveys and identifies companies failing to comply with the law and codes of practice. Offenders are likely to lose postage rebates.

The List and Database Suppliers (LADS) Group works to protect the consumer and build industry standards.

The Direct Mail Information Service (DMIS) provides information on the industry.

The ASA is also available for consumer complainants who have problems with traders failing to respect their interests and wishes in compliance with the Data Protection Act. The CAP Code on List and Database Management is a valuable reference tool. Contradiction of this code can result in the Post Office withholding postage discounts.

All direct marketing activities should adhere to the DMA (UK) Code of Practice.

Mail order

Much of the issues discussed above are relevant here. In addition the mail order industry runs the Mail Order Protection Scheme (MOPS). Run by the Mail Order Committee, this protects consumers responding to mail order advertisements in the national press. The Periodical Publishers Association and the Newspaper Society run similar schemes for magazines and regional press, respectively.

Telemarketing

The specialist body looking after this area is the Independent Committee for the Supervision of Telephone Information Services (ICSTIS).

This body does have some regulatory powers and ICSTIS will charge those in breach of its code for the administrative and legal costs involved in investigating and judging the case. A code of practice is available.

International promotions

Consumer habits and attitudes vary considerably between countries. What is legal in one country is not necessarily legal in another. Figure 4.7 , overleaf, shows a table of what promotions are valid in which European countries. This may, on the face of it, look relatively straightforward if restricting. In fact it is quite complex. While some countries say yes or no to free prize draws, other mechanics have a great number of caveats attached to them in different places. For example Italian and French law allows premium promotions but restricts the value in relation to the price of the product, and in Finland and Norway the premium has to be related to the product in some way.

The list of these country-by-country conditions is almost endless and unless any uniform EC legislation comes along the best route is to seek local promotional and legal expertise. A number of agencies have international offices or alliances and can help in putting international campaigns together.

The European Advertising Standards Alliance (EASA) monitors and directs complaints concerning cross-country promotions and advertising.

On the promotions side, the International Chamber of Commerce (ICC) is responsible for the International Code of Sales Promotion Practice - the British code conforms to the principles of this. The ICC also publishes the International Code of Advertising Practice (ICAP) and has a cross-border complaints mehanism.

The relevance of the EC Distance Selling Directive should be checked when planning future activity that involves contracts being negotiated at a distance between consumers and supplier, eg direct mail, door to door, off the page ads, catalogues and electronic media. It excludes simple advertising.

	UK	Irish Republic	Spain	Germany	France	Denmark	Belgium	Netherlands	Portugal	Italy	Greece	Luxembourg	Austria	Finland	Norway	Sweden	Switzerland
On-pack price reduction	✓	✓	✓	✓	✓	✓	✓	✓	✓	✓	✓	✓	✓	✓	✓	✓	✓
Banded offers	✓	✓	✓	?	?	?	?	✓	✓	✓	✓	X	?	?	?	?	X
In-pack premiums	✓	✓	✓	?	?	?	?	?	✓	✓	✓	X	?	✓	?	?	X
Multiple purchase offers	✓	✓	✓	?	✓	?	?	✓	✓	✓	✓	✓	?	?	?	?	X
Extra product	✓	✓	✓	?	✓	✓	?	?	✓	✓	✓	✓	?	✓	✓	?	?
Free product	✓	✓	✓	✓	✓	✓	✓	✓	✓	✓	✓	✓	✓	✓	✓	✓	✓
Reusable/alternative use pack	✓	✓	✓	✓	✓	✓	✓	✓	✓	✓	✓	✓	?	✓	✓	✓	✓
Free mail ins	✓	✓	✓	X	✓	?	?	✓	✓	✓	✓	?	X	?	?	X	X
With purchase premiums	✓	✓	✓	?	✓	?	?	?	✓	✓	✓	X	?	✓	?	?	X
Cross-product offers	✓	✓	✓	X	✓	?	X	?	✓	✓	✓	X	?	?	?	?	X
Collector devices	✓	✓	✓	X	?	?	?	?	✓	✓	✓	X	X	✓	X	X	X
Competitions	✓	✓	✓	?	?	✓	✓	?	✓	✓	?	?	?	✓	✓	✓	✓
Self-liquidating premiums	✓	✓	✓	✓	✓	✓	✓	?	✓	✓	✓	X	X	✓	X	✓	X
Free draws	✓	✓	✓	X	✓	X	X	X	✓	✓	✓	X	X	✓	X	X	X
Share outs	✓	✓	✓	X	?	X	X	X	✓	?	?	X	X	?	?	X	X
Sweepstake/lottey	?	?	?	?	?	?	?	?	?	?	✓	?	?	✓	X	✓	✓
Money-off vouchers	✓	✓	✓	X	✓	?	✓	✓	✓	✓	✓	?	?	?	X	?	X
Money-off next purchase	✓	✓	✓	X	✓	X	✓	✓	✓	✓	✓	X	X	?	X	X	X
Cash backs	✓	✓	✓	?	✓	✓	✓	✓	✓	X	✓	X	?	?	?	✓	X
In-store demos	✓	✓	✓	✓	✓	✓	✓	✓	✓	✓	✓	✓	✓	✓	✓	✓	✓

✓ Permitted   X not permitted   ? May be permitted

Figure 4.7 Legal promotions by European country

Specialist trade codes

There are many specialist codes including those of the pharmaceuticals, tobacco, animal medicines and mail order industries. BCAP includes special sections on a range of specialised areas.

Advertorials

Most publications set internal limits on the percentage of advertising they will allow. The British Society of Magazine Editors and the Periodical Publishers Association (PPA) are key organisations setting standards in this area. The PPA has issued guidelines which state that 'special advertisement sections' must show the words 'promotion', 'advertisement' or 'advertising' prominently, and the word advertorial is not to be used. Sponsored editorials are editorial items that would be run anyway and do not come under these guidelines.

The need is to get a balanced view on how the public can be best protected from confusion as to whether the item is an advertisement, an editorial endorsement or something completely different. The British Code of Advertising Practice states that advertising should be 'so designed and presented that anyone who looks at it can see, without having to study it closely, that it is an advertisement'. If an advertorial is paid for presumably it is an advertisement.

Radio promotions

The Radio Advertising Bureau is a marketing body representing the independent radio (IR) stations. They can act as an impartial advisory and educative source for advertisers and assist in campaign planning and network initiatives.

The Radio Authority is the government appointed body licensing and regulating the IR industry in accordance with the statutory requirements of the Broadcasting Act 1990. The Radio Authority Code of Advertising Standards and Programme Sponsorship governs radio promotions and anyone running a radio promotion should get a copy of this. Key points covered include:

☐   which programmes can be sponsored, eg news bulletins excluded;

☐   that the licensee has ultimate editorial control of programmes;

☐   that the sponsor's product or service cannot be endorsed within an editorial although sponsors can contribute, eg suggestions and information, to some types of editorial content;

❐   the specified frequency and content of sponsor credits;

❐   prohibited sponsor types.

Promotions run with BBC radio have even greater restrictions.

Television

Special codes to note for television based activity are the Independent Television Committee's (ITC) Code of Advertising Standards and Practice, and the Independent Broadcasters Association (IBA) Code.

Having looked at goal setting and the principles behind promotional selection, we can now move on to look at the rewards the promoter can offer.

5
Rewards - Introduction and Price-Based Techniques

INTRODUCTION

This chapter and the next look at the diversity of reward and incentive techniques available to the promoter. Subsequently we will go on to investigate how they can be applied in the marketplace via the various media options available.

Essentially there are four basic promotional attractants to entice the target consumer to participate:

❑ better price;
❑ free (or nearly free) gifts;
❑ prizes;
❑ emotional benefit (image).

All consumer-oriented promotions exhibit one (or more) of these four expressions.

Naturally there is overlap and promotions would sometimes seem to fit into more than one sub-group. In particular, free is often used to describe a wide range of promotions that sometimes fit more comfortably in one of the other categories, eg extra fill free is really about offering better value for money. Others, such as banded gifts, are certainly providing something free but may also be offering an emotional benefit and better value for money.

It is worth rationalising which types of enticements you believe your target audience will best respond to and the numbers of participants required to make the promotion a success. Thinking this through may well help you structure promotions that better fit the task in hand.

These consumer incentives apply equally well to trade incentives, although for trade customers 'better price' reads 'better price and/or increased profits'. Traders like a good deal but they can also be incentivised by the concept of increased profits. Therefore a strong sales story and a tailored display piece is not much of a reward in its own right, but it does lead to the satisfaction of a promotional need in the end if it drives volume and profit for the trader.

Below you will find a a closer look at some of the main promotional price incentives along with some indication of their strengths and weaknesses, and their appropriateness in different marketing situations. In my view the basic principles will hold good for most markets, and the application of common sense and some considered thought (the best marketing tools there are) will make their relevance to the reader's situation quite clear.

BETTER PRICE

This chapter covers the biggest promotional technique of them all, namely cutting the price. To offer a short-term bargain has always been one of the strongest ways to incentivise a quick purchase decision in the promoter's favour. In practice there is a wide diversity of different value for money offers. Some of these are listed below.

- ☐ *Price off single purchase now*:
  - on regular stock;
  - via special offer pack.
- ☐ *Coupons (money off)*:
  - this purchase;
  - next purchase;
  - this or next purchase;
  - multiple purchase;
  - a series of purchases;
  - vouchers.
- ☐ *Cashback*:
  - money back for single or multiple purchase.
- ☐ *More product free offers*:
  - extra fill (extra value) packs;
  - extra item(s) free.
- ☐ *Multiple purchase price discounts*:
  - banded packs (same product);
  - EPOS (electronic point of sale) type offers.
- ☐ *Trader offers*:
  - invoice discount (price off individual cases);
  - retrospective discounts (eg, overrider payments for hitting agreed annual targets and sell-through allowances);
  - special allowances (eg listing, advertising and display allowances);
  - incentives.

❏   *Credit deals*:
      - financing large purchases;
      - financial purchase incentives.

Price off single purchase now

All these forms of price promotion will have different effects in different markets and marketing situations. In one-off or infrequent purchases such as washing machines, cars or double glazing, price reductions with short time horizons can work well in forcing a purchase decision, whereas discounts off multiple purchases will be appropriate for frequently bought items. For service companies who are all about offering better service levels, a price based offer may be a completely inappropriate promotion. Retailers, on the other hand, offer virtually nothing else but price promotions.

Choosing the level of discount and offer type
In many fmcg markets deciding on the discount level and how to express it presents a continual quandary. However, price is often overrated in terms of an offer and has many undesirable long-term effects.

 Super Marketing Magazine reported on some NOP Omnibus research in August 1992, showing the majority of retail shoppers preferring 'buy two get one free' type offers to all others. Of the sample 40 per cent preferred these compared to 16 per cent for one-off limited price promotions, 15 per cent voted for extra fill and 11 per cent for coupons off this purchase. Which one to go for will depend on what your objectives are at the time and in many cases what the retailer will accept. For example, multiple purchase might be very effective when run just before a competitive relaunch in order to freeze out the competition, but hardly so when attempting to gain trial of a new brand. However if this is the retailer's preferred mechanic and the only way to gain significant in-store feature you are possibly locked into this less than ideal mechanic.

 When setting the offer price does one offer a discount to reach a key price point, eg 99p, or are consumers concerned about the cost for each usage occasion? On packs with diverse fills the latter is hard to work out for most consumers, unless of course they happen to shop in Sainsbury's who thought-fully provide a cost comparison per unit fill on their shelf price tickets, something that could well explain why they are so strong in own brands. In practical terms this price comparison problem is disappearing as European standardisation of pack size becomes the norm. Comparisons will be much easier to make and therefore the key price point will probably become the most important factor. Consumers want an easy life, and the shopping experience to be as simple and hassle free as possible. Spending time comparing every price is going to make a shopping trip far too time consuming. An easily recognisable good deal makes for a quick decision, probably part of the reason why '3 for 2s' and extra fill offers are so preferred at the moment.

How consumers react

There is a sobering reality to be faced when price promoting which is that price promotion on individual items may have some very short-term effect but virtually no long-term one. For this reason the level of discount has to be very carefully monitored to ensure that the promotions are not unprofitable. I would venture that most are loss making. The research by Eherenberg, Hammond and Goodhardt, referred to in Chapter 3, on 25 grocery markets across 4 countries found the following:

❐   for an established brand, sales do not remain high once the promotion is over. The benefit is very short-term and post-promotional sales only show a 1 per cent increase;

❐   buyers coming in because of price promotions had bought the brand before. Eighty per cent of the people buying a price promoted line had bought it in the last year, more if the time period was extended;

❐   price promotions only reach a limited number of those existing customers, typically 10 to 20 per cent.

Whether one implicitly believes the findings verbatim for one's own market is up to the individual, but there are some clear practical indicators here. From this one can see that the value of price cutting is much overrated and in view of the discount levels offered is frequently likely to be an unprofitable volume-buying activity. Steps should be taken to ensure that discounts are small for volume-based sales drives where the objective is to generate profitable business. The extra sales generated should pay for the cost of the discounts.

Manufacturers need to ensure their retail partners understand the limited value of deep price cuts. Overall, value for money in the total shopping bill is clearly a greater attractant than individual deep price cuts. This very strong argument offers enormous reassurance to the consumer: witness the growth of Kwik Save.

Some manufacturers, such as Procter and Gamble, have taken this trimming back of price cuts a step further and introduced 'everyday low pricing' (EDLP) into some markets. Rather than having to offer the consumer infrequent unprofitable discounts that many will not even notice, they have taken the view that it is better to offer an on-going better value for money proposition. Having said all of this, there may well be occasions where unprofitable sales are necessary, eg to block a competitor launch or gain trial of a new brand and additional discounts over EDLP may be forced.

The waste to the manufacturer of over-discounting is also demonstrated in the fact that most shoppers are not aware of the price of individual products.

Neither are they looking for instant big bargains all the time, even if they do respond to them (after all they're not stupid). They are looking for consistent good value and an easy life. Own-label accounts for over a quarter of grocery purchases and this figure is growing, yet the retailer's focus on their own-label lines is to ensure they are good value. Discounts are often used more to get across the message that the whole store is good value, rather than driving individual lines. This is also born out in store choice.

Research has shown convenience as the biggest factor in store choice, even range of products stocked is more important. For example, it was reported in *Super Marketing,* March 1992, that when shopping around using more than one grocery store, better choice was the most important reason for doing this, not price. Research by Harris International Marketing has found that price cuts appeal a lot to 56 per cent of their panel. I do not find this figure high; the surprise is when you look at the converse, because this means 44 per cent are saying that price cuts do not appeal at all or only a little.

Price elasticity

Understanding the price elasticity (share movement related to price change) of a brand will help set appropriate discounts. Market leaders, more expensive brands and brands with very strong emotional benefits tend to be less price sensitive, ie less price elastic, than the market average. If such a brand price promotes, it is unlikely to generate the large volumes necessary to get back the cost of the price discount.

Strongly elastic brands which respond to price cuts are tempting candidates for short-term discounting and in recessionary times it is even more tempting to cut the price. Down trading by consumers is commonplace when times are hard, but it is unlikely that offering price cuts on a product will stop this erosion of the more expensive brands and stimulate profitable brand growth. Better to work towards product innovation in performance or added value through effective positioning.

Controlling prices

Fixing prices is, of course, illegal. However, marketers will wish to pitch their products at different levels in the market. Price promotions can sometimes damage this positioning. One big risk presents itself in price responsive markets where two or three big brands dominate. They can find themselves in a downward spiral of price cutting which will take all the value and profit out of a market. In a recession and/or in a fiercely competitive market it takes strong nerves to resist this. However, it is essential to do so if the business wishes to continue to trade profitably and prevent the market becoming commodity based, with the inevitable result that support budgets will have to be cut and product quality suffer in the long term. Apart from losing money, price cuts open the door for an innovative added-value competitor to come in and steal the market.

Where price cuts are a common feature of a brand's marketing mix, it is important to monitor profitability continuously. We have seen how this can be easily eaten away. The TQ practice of continuous evaluation will help marketers keep a control over the returns they are getting and will give early warning signs of erosion.

The European perspective

There is one further issue to consider when planning price promotion. In a European marketplace the movement of goods will become increasingly easy. With Euro-brands price parity needs to be maintained across the whole of the EC or else there will be plenty of swag merchants ready to shift a few containers across a few borders. The only way to avoid this is by ensuring discounts are kept to a level whereby the cost of transport is prohibitive in comparison. Few retailers are truly European: out of the top 20 only 2 have a significant market share in a second European country. However, European buying networks are being set up. So, while identities will probably be kept separate and joint promotions will be unlikely, some exchange on the types of deals being offered will undoubtedly develop.

Price off a single purchase of regular stock
Advantages:
- ❏   easy and quick to implement;
- ❏   reliable short-term volume generator;
- ❏   widely acceptable to the trade and consumer;
- ❏   costs are predetermined;
- ❏   effective on large or small brands as no economies of scale involved, ie a cost per pack applies and therefore avoids the problems associated with high set-up costs or thresholds to make an activity viable.

Disadvantages:
- competitors can counter quickly;
- can damage brand image in the long term;
- can lead to unprofitable price wars;
- expensive because the full discount is given to every buyer whether it would have affected their purchase decision or not, ie may result in subsidy to loyal users;
- incremental profit rarely covers the cost of promoting;
- trade outlets, in particular retailers, may ask for compensation for the lost margin on the discounted sales, ie maintenance of their normal cash margin not just percentage margin;
- difficult around price increases;
- lack of novelty;
- price elasticity may be encouraged;
- value taken out of the market;
- primarily appeals to bargain hunters and frequent brand switchers, not new buyers.

Price discounts on single packs via special offer packs

The majority of the issues relating to setting the price are equally applicable to the price set via special offer packs. There are also a few further specific points worthy of note.

Advantages:
- highly visible flashes can be employed on-pack;
- trade cannot bunce, ie sell at a higher price than intended , and all the discount is passed on to the consumer;
- costs are fixed.

Disadvantages:
- as above, plus;
- level of discount is fixed and inflexible;
- may not be acceptable to all distributors, retail and wholesale;
- more costly and complex to implement.

Coupons (money off)

A coupon is a note offering a specified discount or saving against the purchase price of a product. It may be subject to certain conditions, eg when and where it can be used. Coupons can be for money off the full price or free product.

Discussion - The Coupon Debating Society

After straight price promotion, couponning is probably the biggest single form of promotion. There are many different uses and users of coupons. The examples and statistics quoted below are generalisms and you should always consider whether your target will respond differently to the norm in the circumstances unique to your promotion.

In terms of controversy, couponning is undoubtedly the biggest issue, with much industry debate on the levels of mis- and malredemption, and the level of discount that should be offered. This debate is continued shortly but first let us look at some of the issues surrounding the reasons why coupons are used and consumers' attitudes to them.

Why coupon?

Coupons can be used by manufacturers, distributors and retailers both strategically and tactically.

Primary strategic uses:

- ❐   to increase repeat purchase, eg via an on-pack coupon;
- ❐   to secure brand penetration, eg via a door drop or press coupon;
- ❐   to encourage cross-product trial, eg via a coupon for one part of a range being carried on another item from the range portfolio;
- ❐   to encourage store loyalty, eg frequent shopper reward programmes.

Tactical uses:

- ❐   to announce new products, eg via retailers' new product booklets;
- ❐   to give a short-term sales boost, eg to reduce high stocks;
- ❐   to provide a sales tool for a sales force;
- ❐   to cushion the effect of a price increase;
- ❐   as a quick counter to competitive activity, eg product launch, new store opening.

Couponning also has advertising benefits:

- ❐   on-pack or on-shelf advertising, ie greater attention is drawn to the product;
- ❐   heightened awareness of the message as a coupon encourages greater attention to an advertisement;

❐   in-home advertising, eg, via a door-to-door leaflet.

The scale of couponning

Couponning is a powerful incentive but has enormous potential for waste. In 1991 over 8 billion coupons were issued in the UK and yet only (only!) 451 million were redeemed, less than 6 per cent of those available. This is trivial compared to the US where 292 billion were distributed and around 14 per cent of grocery purchases were made with a coupon.

Figure 5.1 illustrates how many people use coupons. In fact this research was done in 1989 and the number of coupon users has now increased. Research by Harris International Marketing reveals that coupons appealed a lot to 25 per cent of consumers in 1986 and 35 per cent in 1991. The same research showed 58 per cent of coupon recipients using coupons and 84 per cent of the panel were likely to use them in the future.

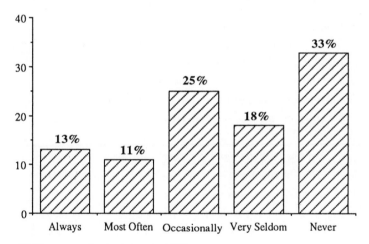

Source: NCH usage and attitudes study 1989

Figure 5.1 Coupon usage

As a rule of thumb I like to think that one-third of people use coupons often, one-third occasionally and one-third not at all. This is very important in understanding how many of your target audience your carefully crafted offer will appeal to. This is low but not as low as many other techniques. What is key is to ensure you motivate the waverers to come in on the offer. This means careful attention to value, presentation and creativity.

Why consumers use coupons

Consumers use coupons for three reasons only:

❐   to get a discount off a product they normally buy;

❏   to overcome the risk inherent in buying a product they do not normally buy;

❏   to get a discount off their total shopping bill regardless of whether or not they have bought the product.

Users' attitudes to coupons vary greatly and these are illustrated in Figure 5.2.

Research by the Added Value Company in 1991 revealed the following figures for attitudes to coupon use among coupon users:

❏   encourage me to try new products   40%
❏   encourage me to buy brands I have used in the past 34%
❏   make me buy things I do not buy regularly   22%
❏   make me switch brands   14%

Why some consumers do not use coupons

The UK consumer is not attuned to regular coupon usage in the same way as their US counterparts. Essentially consumers find coupons rather trivial and most coupon non-users cannot be bothered or are not interested, consider them a hassle or just forget to take them along on their shopping trip. Some of the reasons why coupons are not used are revealed in Figure 5.2.

❏	can't be bothered/not interested/it's a hassle	61%
❏	forget to take them with me	17%
❏	too busy/in too much of a hurry	9%
❏	do not use a particular product	8%
❏	not enough off/not worth the saving	5%
❏	never receive them	3%
❏	prefer lower prices	3%
❏	always throw away the packaging	3%
❏	do not feel the need to use them	3%
❏	embarrassing/feel mean using them	2%
❏	shops do not like them	1%

Source: NCH usage and attitudes study 1989

Figure 5.2 Reasons for non coupon users not using coupons

The Added Value Company research shows that light coupon users account for 33 per cent of users but only 7 per cent of coupons. Clearly, for really effective activity the promoter will need to understand how to motivate these light users into participating in that specific promotion. This is particularly relevant when misredemption is taken into account. There will always be a fixed pool of misredeemers and anything that grows the number of true re-deemers will spread the cost of misredemption more widely, thus making the activity more cost effective.

For this reason mass couponning designed to increase volume through brand switching within a portfolio of purchases is likely to perform more effectively on brands that:

❏ are big;
❏ have good distribution;
❏ have strong penetration.

For smaller brands with less sales potential the misredeemers may well swamp any true redeemers and make the whole activity uneconomical. Coupon promotions on such brands need to be more carefully targeted.

How frequently are they used?

Coupon redemption is primarily on the main shopping trip, since they are primarily redeemed through the grocery multiples who take about 86 per cent of all coupons (source: ISP/Added Value Company). Consumers do not always do main grocery shops every week but may spread them out over a longer period. The most common redemption frequency is monthly. Usage frequency is illustrated below in Figure 5.3.

❏	weekly or more often	9%
❏	every two weeks	12%
❏	every month	36%
❏	every three months	23%
❏	longer than three months	20%

Source: NCH 1989

Figure 5.3 Frequency of coupon usage

How many at a time?

Most coupons are redeemed in dribs and drabs. NCH (Nielsen Clearning House) reports that the average UK user redeems 1.7 coupons per shopping trip. Only 1 per cent of shoppers redeem ten or more at a time.

How do consumers like to receive coupons?

The essential message is 'easily'. Therefore door drops and on-packs come out on top. However, usage is also determined by the way coupons can most effectively be delivered by manufacturers, and the scope and scale of the media available. Figure 5.4 illustrates.

❐	delivered through the letterbox	48% (23%)
❐	cut from newspapers	3% (6%)
❐	cut from magazines	3% (3%)
❐	on- or in-pack	26% (37%)
❐	in-store handouts	5% (28%)
❐	no preference/others	15% (3%)

Source: NCH 1989 usage and attitudes study (and 1992 redemptions)

Figure 5.4 Preferred delivery methods (vs redemptions 1992)

Who redeems?

So who are these coupon users? They are predominantly female (88 per cent), fairly close to the national IPA social grade breaks, but with an older profile. This is detailed in Figure 5.5. Much as stereotyping is an unpleasant thing to do it does look like couponning is a 'female' type occupation. It is worth bearing this in mind when considering the creative treatment used.

		coupon users %	national population %
Class	A/B	15	18
	C1	24	24
	C2	25	27
	DE	36	31
Sex	Male	12	49
	Female	88	51
Age	25-34	17	23
	35-44	15	20
	45-54	17	17
	55-64	19	15
	65+	31	23

Source: Added Value Company

Figure 5.5 Profile of all coupon users

According to NCH the MOSAIC geodemographics profile of coupon users is similar to the national population.

What value to offer?

Coupons can work well in drawing attention to new products and encouraging trial as well as bolstering brand loyalty. However, the former is likely to be a harder task. This means offering a higher incentive for brand switching and trial than loyalty.

For loyalty 7 to 15 per cent discount off the regular price is probably adequate and on-pack coupons offering money off next purchase can be given very low values. For switching and trial 12-25 per cent may be called for. Figure 5.6 illustrates how increased coupon value gives diminishing returns, even free product vouchers only encourage switching three-quarters of the time.

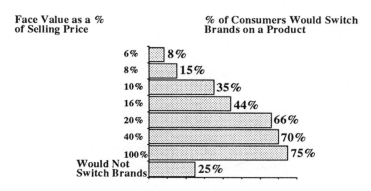

Source: NCH, 1989

Figure 5.6 Coupon value vs brand switching behaviour

Coupon abuse

There are two forms of coupon abuse, mal- and misredemption.

> *Malredemption* - this is the fraudulent acquisition and cashing of coupons. This is small scale and only accounts for about 1 per cent of coupon abuse and with thoughtful implementation it can be negligible. In the US it is the major form where retailers merrily spend time clipping and cashing in coupons from free-standing inserts (books of coupons). Malredemption can occur via a number of ways, but key ones to watch out for are:

❏   the retailer clipping press coupons;
❏   retailers peeling off on-pack coupons;
❏   printers cashing in run-ons or proofs;
❏   the box of coupons falling off the delivery lorry;
❏   distributors siphoning off a few boxes;
❏   self printing;
❏   photocopying (growing with the introduction of quality colour photocopiers).

Misredemption - this is where the consumer uses the coupon but not against the product specified on the coupon. This is the big cause for concern in the UK. Many elements of the retail (and wholesale) trade turn a blind eye to misredemption and some actively encourage it. This 'endorsement' of coupon abuse is the key factor responsible for its growth. A key to efficient large scale couponning is to bring in as many additional true redeemers as possible to lessen the negative effect of the misredeemers.

The misredemption level will vary by:

❏   the coupon value, since higher levels tempt in more genuine users;
❏   the media where the coupon is presented;
❏   retailers where the coupon is likely to/can be redeemed;
❏   creativity, eg the strength of branding;
❏   brand distribution, eg brands with small distribution will suffer more from misredemption;
❏   the brand franchise, big, strong brands with good penetration will suffer less.

Recent research used by the ISP for its 1992 Coupon Review provides some useful insights into the level of misredemption. This revealed that the majority of users used coupons correctly, only 28 per cent of coupon users having misredeemed coupons at some time. These misredeemers were not split socio-demographically from other coupon users; it was an attitudinal difference. This means it is not straightforward to target away from coupon abusers.

Misredeemers were found to be heavier coupon users, accounting for 53 per cent of all coupons redeemed. However, they claimed that only half the coupons they used were actually misredeemed giving an average misredemption level for all coupons of 27 per cent. This is illustrated in Figure 5.7.

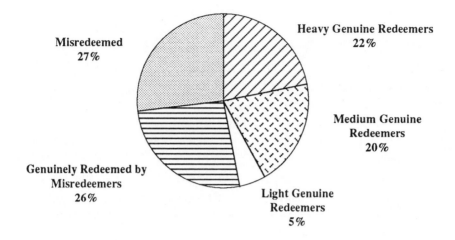

Source: Added Value Company 1991

Figure 5.7 Misredemption as a proportion of redemptions

The existence of misredemption does not mean that coupons should not be used. Some are secure, eg some accounts such as Tesco undertake not to misredeem Tesco specific coupons. A number of outlets take this approach. The problem lies in generally available and usable coupons such as in the press, door drops and free standing inserts (FSIs), where many retailers will happily accept these coupons provided they stock the product, whether or not that item is bought. Even here couponning can still be viable but misredemption must be costed in. The cost per new user model in Chapter 9 allows this sort of problem to be taken account of when costing out proposed promotions.

It is worth knowing who is taking your misredeemed money as this helps to provide an indication of the profitability of a particular outlet to your business. The work done by the Added Value Company showed the multiple grocery retailers, in particular Tesco and Sainsbury, as being by far the biggest recipients of correctly and misredeemed coupons. As coupon retailers' policies and practices are amended and manufacturer coupon applications evolve so this picture will no doubt change.

The retailer perspective
The UK retailer hates coupons because they are a hassle but loves coupons because they are extra money in the till at the expense of the manufacturers. This is true even for the correct use of coupons since consumers will have a fixed housekeeping budget that they can spend, and coupons expand this and effectively allow them to spend more money.

On this basis if the retailer is not funding then why should they worry about what the coupon is redeemed against if it increases the size of the shopping basket passing the till? In fact this attitude is in danger of backfiring as manufacturers withdraw coupon based promotional support for brands and retailers lose a valuable promotional device.

Coupons are a preferred technique in some outlets for announcing new products in store and often door-to-door. They are also used as a substitute for EPOS promotions where this facility is not available. This can be expected to drop off as more more retailers introduce bar code scanning. In due course, the scanning of coupons themselves will be commonplace, providing the potential for greater security if purchase verification is built in and for greater creativity.

Advantages and disadvantages by coupon offer type
Commonly used coupon types include:

- money off this purchase;
- money off next purchase;
- money off this or next purchase;
- multiple purchase;
- those valid off a series of purchases;
- cross purchase;
- alternative choice;
- validated coupons.

Money off this purchase (MOTP) - this means the coupon is available for use here and now, when you buy this pack.
Advantages:
- flexible tool, can address volume, loyalty, switching within a portfolio and trial;
- instant;
- high take up on the offer.

Disadvantages:
- misredemption, eg if removed from the pack;
- malredemption (as above);
- distanced from the purchase decision unless on-pack or displayed at point of sale;
- a hassle for the retailer and slows their checkout.

Money off next purchase (MONP) - this means the coupon is available for use on the next shopping visit. The coupon may be offered in-store, eg on-pack, by a demonstrator, or it may be delivered to the consumer outside the store environment.

Advantages:

- ❏   if on-pack provides an incentive to loyals to purchase initially as well as subsequently with the coupon, the classic loyalty builder;
- ❏   cost can be split over the two purchases.

Disadvantages:

- ❏   delayed use, therefore sales effect not pronounced;
- ❏   lower redemption rate than MOTP;
- ❏   minimal trade interest;
- ❏   may not be used for the correct product on the return visit.

This or next purchase - this is a combination of the above two offers and depending when used is likely to have similar advantages and disadvantages. Typically used for on-pack promotions to encourage there and then purchase, it can be used on the subsequent visit if unused the first time. A consumer may not have realised it was for immediate use at the time of purchase.

Advantages:

- ❏   may drive more volume than just money off next purchase;
- ❏   will not disappoint as MONP coupons might.

Disadvantages:

- ❏   may be removed from the pack and mis- or malredeemed.

Multiple purchase - coupon valid only when several packs are bought. These may be the same item or a combination of brands. They may be incorporated into carrier bags at point-of sale (multi-bags), where the bag is filled with the requisite number of items and the coupon detached from a push out part of the handle.

Advantages:

- ❏   can drive continued loyalty through bulk purchase;
- ❏   can freeze out the competition;
- ❏   high value offer can attract but the costs split over several purchases;
- ❏   can drive range/portfolio purchase.

Disadvantages:

- ❏   appeals to a limited audience, loyals who are coupon users and who are prepared to bulk buy;

❏   high value coupon equals high risk of coupon abuse;

❏   retailers may not understand or redeem correctly.

A series of purchases - a series of coupons issued often with sequential usage dates. They may be phased carefully to ensure that purchase number two cannot be made until purchase number one has been used up and so on. Great care is needed to ensure the validity dates' phasing matches usage and re-purchase timescales.

Advantages:

❏   can time-date to spread the purchases out and avoid misredemption;

❏   high level expenditure not demanded on one occasion.

Disadvantages:

❏   high drop-out rate if not targeted at strong prospects;

❏   mis- and malredemption risk if all can be redeemed at the same point in time.

Cross-purchase - coupons carried on one product valid for another product.

Advantages:

❏   cheap and potentially well-targeted distribution;

❏   provides an offer for carrier brand;

❏   can share budget with the other party.

Disadvantages:

❏   often a slow redemption rate;

❏   sales effect minimal on both brands;

❏   cross-purchase profile rarely matches as well as expected;

❏   no trade appeal;

❏   purchaser of carrier brand may get several coupons;

❏   requirement for the same distribution.

Alternative choice and validated coupons - here the coupon is put together in a special way. For alternative choice coupons, depending on how the recipient cuts the coupon out or opens it out, it can be used for one of a choice of brands or values. Sometimes coupons can be validated for different offers by sticking promotional tokens on to a portion of the coupon.

Advantages:

❏   versatile, a choice of offers can be made.

Disadvantages:

❏   consumers get confused by what can be a creative mess;

❏   consumers may try to cheat by attempting to redeem each portion

of coupon separately;
❏　　may be difficult to use in-store;
❏　　may not conform to coupon layout guidelines;
❏　　rely on checkout operators to police.

Gift vouchers - gift vouchers are sometimes offered as a reward, although they tend to be used more for longer-term collector and incentive schemes than quick to to enter sendaways or gifts with purchase. However, they are not really 'better price' unless related back to the parent brand.
Advantages:
❏　　'shopping vouchers' - effectively cash to go back into the store;
❏　　stimulates further purchase;
❏　　can cost less than cash by buying at a discount or offering your own vouchers;
❏　　careful voucher choice can target or theme the offer.
Disadvantages:
❏　　may not appeal to everyone;
❏　　outlets accepting may have limited distribution;
❏　　less attractive at low face values.

Cashbacks

These are promotions where the customer is offered money back for single or multiple purchases.

Discussion - *paying the purchaser to buy*
Traditionally cashbacks have been used in fmcg markets to generate loyalty through collector schemes, but this is waning in popularity. Refunds are frequently offered against single purchase. The try me free variety offers a no risk entry into the brand and as such is discussed in more detail in Chapter 6.

In high ticket items significant and motivating cashbacks can be employed. This can be linked to a further offer or used to build a database for subsequent dialogue with the consumer, eg Whirlpool home appliances recently offered up to £50 cashback against washing machines and other white goods, and used the application form as an opportunity for purchasers to buy into their ten year parts guarantee. In my view they missed a trick by not stating the cost of this extended warranty on the leaflet, but the idea of using one offer to push others is in there.
Advantages:
❏　　simple and cheap to administer;
❏　　no sourcing problems (no risk of out of stocks);

- ❏ universal appeal, therefore higher redemption rates possible;
- ❏ can scale the offer to build longer-term loyalty by offering bigger refunds for greater numbers of purchases, eg £1 for three pack tops, £3 for six;
- ❏ can drive for rapid response/sales boost by offering greater rewards for applying quickly;
- ❏ can be run on- or off-pack.
- ❏ on single purchase offers a good trialing mechanic.

Disadvantages:

- ❏ expensive compared to a premium offer, £1 can buy an item of greater perceived value;
- ❏ boring and offers no brand value enhancement;
- ❏ on fmcg items the level of discount that can be given if the offer is to remain profitable is not motivating;
- ❏ can easily be countered by the competition with the same or stronger reward level;
- ❏ high purchase frequency required for multiple purchase offers;
- ❏ redemption levels uncertain;
- ❏ mostly appeals to loyals only.

More product free offers

Discussion - giving your product away

More product free is probably the third most widely used technique in fmcg markets. This offer is not restricted to fmcg only, it is present in a wide range of different markets in all sorts of varieties, eg as extended memberships or subscriptions and as extra service elements bolted on to the basic package in service based businesses.

Extra fill packs, also known as extra value (EV) packs, are very common special packs that provide a strong value for money offer to the consumer. Extra fill might mean 10 per cent free on a washing-up liquid bottle or can of beer. In both cases the claim could be the same, eg 220 ml for the price of 200 ml, but the effect is dramatically different.

In both cases it seems like a good deal to the consumer, but the manufacturer needs to understand the effect on the market. In the case of the bigger beer can, the purchaser will simply benefit from a larger drink which may not in any way affect the total number of cans drunk. However, as far as the washing-up liquid is concerned, the extra fill will simply provide more wash-ups to the bottle and result in a decrease in units sold. Consequently, the value of the market will shrink.

Where the product is not in single use units like the beer can or, say, packets of crisps, extra value should be approached with great caution and only the minimum extra free offered. Where possible the slippery slope to discounting and commodity pricing should be avoided.

In addition to the more in a pack proposition extra value often features in multi-pack selling units, eg beer again where one free can might be offered on a four-pack, or on toilet roll where again a free roll might be on offer. This offering of part of the normal retail unit free of charge is still the slippery slope, the extra can or roll will not increase consumption and may erode market values.

Extra fill free packs
Advantages:

- ❏   cheap to offer, the product cost is less than the perceived cost to the consumer and certainly less than an equivalent price cut;
- ❏   can help trading up by accustoming consumers to using larger sizes;
- ❏   loved by some trade outlets.

Disadvantages:

- ❏   loathed by some trade outlets, some of whom may demand margin compensation for the equivalent number of lost sales;
- ❏   the extra fill represents possible factory costs and unacceptable complexity;
- ❏   direct product profitability (DPP) issues with the trade regarding merchandising, warehousing and transport if pack and shipper configurations alter;
- ❏   everybody gets it whether they want it or not, ie loyals are subsidised;
- ❏   can devalue the market by decreasing paid for consumption;
- ❏   can shift the market towards being commodity based where the presence of EV becomes the main element in the purchase decision;
- ❏   losing its ability to drive volume;
- ❏   some retailers, eg discounters may insist on its availability.

Extra items (free)
Where part of a multi-pack is given away free, apart from the DPP issues, essentially the same advantages and disadvantages apply as above. Extra items free can be a consumer offer, or a trade offer, eg free pack in a bulk outer, or free stock when a set number of cases are bought.

Multiple purchase price discounts

Discussion - a fair deal for some

I like this sort of offer, it sounds like a sensible thing to do, 'If you buy more of my product I'll give you a good price', what could be fairer than that?

Originally this was the classic offer to encourage consumers to buy more of a product at one go. Twin-packs and multi-packs available at a discounted retail price became a common way to boost consumption and consumer loyalty to a particular brand. This type of promotional pack eventually stopped being a promotion and became a regular line, eg soap and snacks multi-packs. Later, incentivising multiple purchase became a common form of sendaway offer, where for proof(s) of purchase the consumer would be offered a free product or voucher off a subsequent purchase. Now, this promotional approach is being increasingly used by retailers as scanning technology has developed to allow the discounts to be given instantly at the check-out.

Used wisely this can offer the consumer realistic rewards in return for a greater purchase commitment on their part. Cleverly, the offer has been extended beyond a discount for buying a number of the same products. Devices such as Safeway's 'Link and Save', where the consumer has to buy complementary products instead, offers far-reaching opportunities to the resourceful promoter, eg to drive penetration of a smaller brand by offering a discount when linked to a more frequently bought item.

The same principles on discount levels apply as discussed for price off a single purchase. The temptation, particularly for retailers, with this type of promotional reward and the simple application system is to continually up the ante. The pressure is there to give stronger and stronger discounts. 'Three for two' offers abound and the the consumer is understandably delighted. The NOP Omnibus study mentioned above shows these as the most popular of promotions, more than twice as popular as the next most popular reward, which is straight price cuts. This is understandable since most single pack price discounts never reach the one-third off level. The ludicrous end point is 'buy one get one free', also known as a BOGOF, and so it should. Three for twos are rarely going to make money and unless a product has exceptional margins BOGOFs will never be profitable.

When multi-buy EPOS promotions are in the promotional plan, measuring profitability shifts (for retailer and manufacturer) is essential.

Banded packs (same product)
Advantages:
- ❏ highly visible on shelf;
- ❏ locks the consumer in;
- ❏ no novelty, easily copied;
- ❏ only appeals to existing users.

Disadvantages:
- ❏ price point may be too high;
- ❏ special packing costs;
- ❏ subsidises loyals;
- ❏ trade may delist regular size while multi-packs are on sale resulting in possible loss of franchise if some consumers not prepared to buy the multi-pack;
- ❏ trade may not list, eg for DPP issues.

EPOS type offers
Advantages:
- ❏ wide appeal;
- ❏ simple for the consumer to understand the offer and to participate;
- ❏ cheap to set up;
- ❏ quick to set up;
- ❏ versatile;
- ❏ no hidden costs.

Disadvantages:
- ❏ easy to offer too much discount;
- ❏ easy to counter;
- ❏ boring;
- ❏ subsidises loyals;
- ❏ focus is on price not added value.

Trader offers

These are 'push' based offers designed to encourage the trade or their employees to push your products out to the consumer or the next step in the chain, eg from a wholesaler to an independent retailer. Always monitor performance and pay only if the agreement is fulfilled.

The multiples, wholesalers and independent retailers are driven by the same basic business principles as manufacturers. They need to see a healthy return on capital employed to ensure they remain in business, grow their product categories according to their plans, and keep any shareholders happy and their employees in work. It is the mix of goods they sell and the profitability of them that will be the foundation of their success. Consequently, they are always going to be interested in rewards that offer them better value for money, ie enhanced profitability.

Although many of the rewards mentioned above and below are applicable to promoting with the trade, there are also special categories of price reward that deserve a specific mention with businesses rather than consumers in mind.

The types of price based rewards offered to businesses will depend on the type of business that they are, ie the rewards that a multiple chain buyer will find appealing will not necessarily be the same as those that will appeal to a sole trader. The TQ process of understanding the linkages in the customer/supplier chain are essential here to devise appropriate incentives.

Typical price-based rewards include the following.

❑ *Invoice discount:*
  price off individual cases provided by a reduced invoice charge over the standard price list. It is very widely used both as a simple special price offer and as a method of paying for a range of possible offers, eg bulk purchase, rapid/cash payment, guaranteed future orders, buying a specific mix of products.

❑ *Retrospective payments:*
  eg over-rider payments for hitting agreed annual turnover targets and sell-through allowances.

❑ *Stock discounts:*
  payment given in the form of free stock.

❑ *Tiered pricing scales:*
  discounts and allowances for specified purchase levels.

❑ *One-off allowances:*
  eg for display, listings and advertising.

❑ *Credit deals:*
  see below.

In general, trade offers have similar advantages and disadvantages.
Advantages:
  ❑ quick to turn on;
  ❑ simple.
Disadvantages:
  ❑ benefit may not be passed on to the consumer;

❐ easily countered;

❐ risk of becoming part of the normal trading terms.

Credit deals

Financing large purchases/financial purchase incentive
Better value for money can be presented by making payment easy. This is particularly relevant to big, one-off purchases such as cars or major items for the house, but is also applicable to many business-to-business promotions. Types of offer include:

❐ buy now pay later, ie credit period;

❐ 0 per cent finance, ie interest free loans to buy goods;

❐ low interest rates, ie cheap loans to buy the goods.

Advantages:

❐ cheaper for the promoter as they can usually buy money or arrange deals with a finance house more cheaply than the consumer can;

❐ can bring in customers who have disposable income but no savings for a cash purchase;

❐ compares favourably to credit and interest rates;

❐ customers may not wish to take out loans secured against their homes.

Disadvantages:

❐ complex to administrate;

❐ more difficult/costly to obtain the finance for unsecured loans;

❐ customers may 'disappear' with the goods if they are portable;

❐ non-portable goods, eg carpets not easily reclaimed if payments not kept up.

Having covered price based rewards, we can now look at other ways of adding value to the promotional proposition.

6

Rewards - Better Value Without Discounting

This chapter covers the following rewards which are less price oriented:

- ❏ free (or nearly free) gifts;
- ❏ prizes;
- ❏ emotional benefit (image).

It has the same basic format as the previous chapter.

FREE (OR NEARLY FREE) GIFTS

To be offered something free is one of the more pleasant things that can happen. In promotional terms this usually means one of two things: either a free product so we can try it to see if we like it; or a free gift if we buy a specific item.

I have included the words 'or nearly free' because rewards often include some costs, be it product to qualify for a free offer or a postage contribution. Naturally we quickly get into the 'there's no such thing as a free lunch' argument but most consumers are happy enough to appreciate the straight-forward nature of a free offer.

For the sake of tidiness, the reward of a free product conditional on purchase of the same product, eg extra value or banded packs, has been viewed as better value for money. The essential rewards that fall into the free category follow.

- ❏ *Free product:*
  - sampling;
  - banded as a gift.
- ❏ *Free item:*
  - gift with purchase (on- or off-pack);
  - sendaways (including nearly free items);
  - container offers.
- ❏ *Collector schemes.*

Free product

Discussion - giving your product away

Unless it is part of creating a better value for money package, giving product away is all about getting trial. In this light we can see that giving people free product is much more than offering an interesting reward as part of another promotion, it is providing an opportunity to drive your brand forward. Indeed it may well be the beginning and the end of the whole activity.

Giving product away might mean a real sample to use or eat in fmcg markets. In others it might be all about free trial of a service for a limited period. For example, we have just been converted to pulse dialling by BT and have happily taken up their free offer on a call waiting advice service, and thousands of people will have taken up *Reader's Digest* and *Which?* offers of free home trials.

Free trial might be even more short-term, such as test driving a car or having a free camcorder try-out for a day.

Sampling can involve full-size product or sample sizes. Full-size product is expensive to give away but clearly is highly impactful. For some products a full-size sample is the only way to try it, eg a can of Murphy's draught Irish stout via a roadshow with the *Newcastle Evening Chronicle*. For others just a trial sachet or a scent strip is enough to indicate whether the product is of interest. Sampling is becoming one of the most popular ways of gaining product trial: to give some idea of scale approximately 300 million samples were dropped door-to-door in the UK in 1991. Add to this all the samples given away in the press, via in-store tastings, goody bag hand-outs etc and the scale of activity becomes clear.

We have discussed the value of product trialing with particular reference to fmcg markets in the chapter on objective setting. To recap on the main learning from this and to summarise other key points about trial:

- ❑ good penetration is the key to a big brand share;
- ❑ getting early trial of a new product will boost its share;
- ❑ there is no point in sampling inferior brands;
- ❑ resampling is rarely effective;
- ❑ the environment in which a product is received will affect the way in which it is perceived.

Independent research from RSGB Omnibus commissioned by door drop agency Circular Distributors reveals that 79 per cent of housewives gave product sampling as the main reason for purchasing a brand new product on the market and 71 per cent as the main reason for brand switching to a new product. This is illustrated in Figures 6.1 and 6.2 which show sampling to be way ahead of coupons and TV advertising.

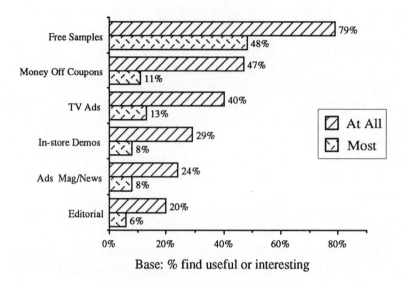

Base: % find useful or interesting

(Source RSGB/The Human Factor/Circular Distributors)

Figure 6.1   Media influence on housewives buying new product/variety

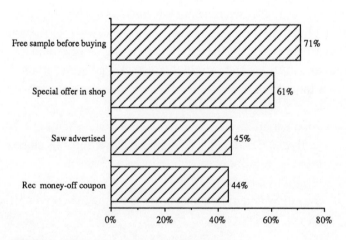

(Source: RSGB/The Human Factor/Circular Distributors)

Figure 6.2   Reasons for housewives switching to another brand

Attitudinally sampling is highly regarded by consumers as an open thing to do, done by big, well-known companies. Perhaps most significant of all, as shown in Figure 6.3, here 94 per cent of the respondents agreed with the statement 'samples give you a better idea of the product than ads'.

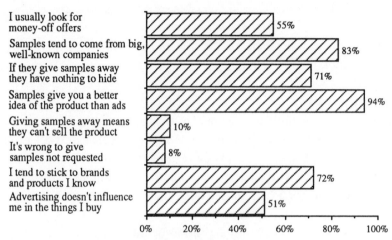

(Source: RSGB/The Human Factor/Circular Distributors)

Figure 6.3 Belief in sampling (housewives)

We have seen how consumer sampling is important and appreciated, it is not looked on as junk mail or the equivalent. In the same way trade sampling is of value. If you have a new product with demonstrable attributes why not ensure your distribution is assured by making the decision-makers aware of just how how good it is? This may mean simply a sample for the buyer to try or it could mean something more strategic such as a mailing to all independent retailers or agents. Whatever the distribution medium someone is going to place the order and a product is likely to have more impact than yet another trade press ad or printed mailer.

Sampling
Free distribution of product or trial usage.
Advantages:
- true values appreciated by consumer;
- high levels of product trial;
- positive consumer reaction versus other techniques;
- easy for the consumer to participate;
- may help secure trade distribution;
- may help secure display if in-store;
- can drive rapid purchase and build brand share quickly.

Disadvantages:

- ❏   expensive;
- ❏   possible long production lead times;
- ❏   can be wasteful if targeting not viable, in which case it is not usually suitable for niche brands;
- ❏   product must have appreciable superior benefits in use or is just an expensive awareness exercise;
- ❏   conversion levels usually low unless combined with other motivations to purchase, eg display.

Free product as a gift

This is where a free sample of one brand is given away as a gift with a carrier brand. This may be by banding the products together as in an on-pack offer or a magazine cover mount, or it could quite easily be included inside a carton or simply given away with a purchase. It may also be a delayed offer where consumers send off for a free sample or voucher for a free sample.

Advantages:

- ❏   provides an offer on the carrier brand;
- ❏   can target using appropriate carriers;
- ❏   cheap, no distribution costs and carrier can share the packaging or other costs;
- ❏   high visibility;
- ❏   may get extra shelf space;
- ❏   if a sendaway only interested consumers likely to apply;
- ❏   unique and novel offer.

Disadvantages:

- ❏   potential transport, warehousing and merchandising difficulties and costs;
- ❏   limited retailer acceptability;
- ❏   samples wasted if consumer makes several purchases of carrier brand or if product has poor user match;
- ❏   sample may be pilfered or removed and sold separately.

Try me free

There are two types of try me free:

- ❏   completely free;
- ❏   on approval.

The first is when the pack pronounces that the consumer can try it free of charge. The usual technique is to ask the consumer to send in for a full cash refund of the purchase price. The consumer generally has to keep the till receipt and send it in, usually with a proof of purchase, although this is not always asked for now that most grocery till receipts are fully itemised. This is a bold statement about the product proclaiming its worth. It is such a good product that you can try it without risk and is therefore highly appropriate at the launch of a fmcg brand.

The other type of try me free is the 'on approval' offer where the product or service can be tried at low risk. The usual arrangement is that you try the product and if you do not like it you can return or cancel. The catch is that you often have to return goods at your own expense and if you miss the cancellation date you are stuck with a bill. This is a perfectly valid proposition providing all the rules are clear to the applicant. Having been caught myself I recommend a hint for the reader - put a note in your diary for two weeks before the cancellation date straight away. I am sure I have just saved you at least the cost of this book many times over.

Completely free
Advantages:
- ❏ strong trial motivater as risk to consumer removed;
- ❏ high slippage, many people will not apply.

Disadvantages:
- ❏ collecting till receipts is a hassle;
- ❏ will attract pure bargain hunters who will not buy your brand again;
- ❏ costly, high redemption rate and fulfilment costs.

On approval
Advantages:
- ❏ allows consumers to make up their minds on complex or expensive propositions;
- ❏ shows there is nothing to hide;
- ❏ draws in applicants who would have declined otherwise.

Disadvantages:
- ❏ freeloaders may apply for the free period only;
- ❏ returns may be damaged;
- ❏ consumers may be annoyed by expensive return costs or missing the return-by date, thus jeopardising any long-term relationship.

Free item

Discussion

A free item excludes the same product given away with a purchase or purchases. Here the consumer is rewarded with a special gift, known as a premium, for buying the brand. A present is always nice to get and like a sample will have few negative connotations provided the consumer gets what they have been promised. The main consumer dislike of this type of offer is purely the general dislike of promotions per se or the hassle factor of any collector or sendaway element.

There are five basic types of free premium offer:

- ❏   free in-pack;
- ❏   free on-pack;
- ❏   free with purchase but detached from the pack;
- ❏   free on application;
- ❏   free container premium.

There is also one 'nearly free' premium offer. This is the self-liquidating promotion (SLP), where typically the consumer collects proofs of purchase (POPs) to qualify for an attractive premium at a discounted price. Often the more POPs the cheaper the cost and in some cases it is eventually free. The idea is that the promoter recoups all the costs involved from the respondents. In practice this is unusual and I would classify this type of promotion as an image-based reward and it reappears below.

Sendaways are low redeemers compared to coupons: recent research by Harris International Marketing showed only 28 per cent of consumers liked free mail-ins a lot. For free giveaways the figure was 38 per cent and 43 per cent for container premiums. SLPs are the least interesting at 18 per cent.

Promotional Insight's report Promotion '92 advises that the big fmcg players are, cereals, bakery products such as biscuits, and drink. The childrens' cereal manufacturers are constantly striving for innovative, visible, free gifts, eg holograms on the front of Frosties, to attract youngsters' attention and create 'pester power' to make mum buy. Premium offers are powerful tools that I suspect stick in children's memories. I can certainly remember my Weetabix Ten-in-one-Scope.

Premiums are booming. A multitude of industries have taken them up, for example, a survey by Market Movements indicates over half of financial direct mail uses premium offers. Mail order and publications are big users too.

Gift with purchase (in-, on- or off-pack)

This type of offer is expensive to run and is generally designed to bring in new users where a greater investment per participant can be afforded.

Gift with purchase offers (GWPs), may be presented in-, on- or off-pack. On-pack gifts are offered much less at the time of writing. This is particularly true in the retail trade if a change in pack size is likely as this causes DPP problems in the warehousing, delivery and merchandising chain. All rules are there to be broken of course, and a strong reward such as a free mug given away with a 300 ml jar of Nescafe and packaged up nicely in an open cardboard box was enough of an incentive for my local supermarket to change its shelf plans.

Off-pack gifts where the reward is presented at the same time as the purchase but not physically associated with it have been the domain of the department store and petrol forecourt where the administration can be more easily handled. However, it is widening its presence in response to the general trend of the promotional industry towards instant gratification. It is important to ensure that gifts in-store do not clash with trade interests, eg some retailers will not accept gifts that they already sell as they view it as a lost purchase.

Advantages:

- ❏ if very good, it is very good;
- ❏ high visibility;
- ❏ free is a strong claim;
- ❏ perceived value can be up to three or four times the actual cost;
- ❏ novel and unique, eg the Nescafe mug was branded, so nobody could copy this offer;
- ❏ a strong gift will tempt even new users;
- ❏ may gain display space, especially if off-pack, as extra point-of-sale material will be needed to announce the offer;
- ❏ instant;
- ❏ high incremental sales;
- ❏ good choice of gift can make a statement about the brand's qualities.

Disadvantages:

- ❏ if very bad, it is very bad;
- ❏ expensive, as there are a lot of gifts to be bought and contract packers and special packaging needs to be employed for in/on-pack;
- ❏ listings difficulties, trade particularly reluctant for on- and off-pack offers;
- ❏ in/on-pack may cause packaging difficulties, eg instability, safety precautions;

❒ gifts may be wasted on consumers who do not want them, especially if in/on-pack;

❒ difficult to find items that appeal to all users;

❒ logistics difficulties if off-pack, eg number required, delivery co-ordination, merchandising, special packaging;

❒ risk of pilferage;

❒ wastage through multiple purchase unless gift is cheap and incremental sales are profitable;

❒ sourcing resource required.

Sendaways

Here we are essentially talking about the Free Mail-in (FMI).

These types of offer currently appear less common than in the 1970s and early 1980s when they were all the rage.

Advantages:

❒ can afford to offer a stronger premium as budget is carried over more packs and not everyone will take up the offer;

❒ free is a strong claim;

❒ perceived value can be up to three or four times the actual cost;

❒ can be novel and unique, also a good choice of gift can make a statement about the brand's qualities;

❒ can drive loyalty, eg lock in portfolio buyers;

❒ strong offers with low POPs may encourage immediate multiple purchase and so drive volume;

❒ reward may stay around for some time reminding the consumer of the product;

❒ can repeat the promotion offering sets of premiums to collect.

Disadvantages:

❒ not instant;

❒ expensive, special print on pack, premiums, handling, packing and postage likely to be payable;

❒ the budget is open ended depending on the redemption level;

❒ redemption difficult to predict;

❒ handling arrangements need to be set up;

❒ trade generally unmoved by these offers which frequently offer low sales uplift;

❒ unlikely to gain feature in-store;

❒ mostly appeals to existing users;

❒ gifts may be wasted on consumers who would have bought anyway;

- ❑ difficult to find items that appeal to all users;
- ❑ wastage through multiple purchase unless gift is cheap and incremental sales are profitable;
- ❑ sourcing resource required;
- ❑ POPs have to be carefully judged to ensure incremental purchase without being off-putting;
- ❑ poor fulfilment can damage the brand's franchise.

Container premiums

Like all good ideas this one is very simple. The container that the product comes in is the premium and provides added value to the brand. The classic is coffee being sold in a storage jar, but many types of reusable containers are possible. I suppose even a conference document holder is some sort of container premium.

Certainly capable of generating trial, if it is also collectable like the storage jar, a container premium can drive loyalty.

Advantages:
- ❑ strong appeal;
- ❑ highly visible;
- ❑ instant;
- ❑ unique;
- ❑ can up the pack fill and charge more;
- ❑ can be collectable;
- ❑ long-lasting reminder of the brand when in use.

Disadvantages:
- ❑ factory complexity;
- ❑ trade and consumer acceptability needs to be reviewed carefully;
- ❑ long lead times to implement, effectively, a new pack;
- ❑ expensive;
- ❑ everyone gets it whether they want it or not.

Collector schemes

Presents awarded through collection schemes are slightly different to on-pack sendaways and the like. These are long-running promotions demanding a high level of purchases to collect enough points or tokens to qualify for a reward.

One of the most remembered is the Green Shield Stamp. More contemporary is the petrol retailer's collector schemes, be they stamps or points on magnetic swipe cards. These promotions are strategic activities designed to build loyalty where consumers are fickle but make frequent purchases. If maintained for a long period they will become part of the brand property, eg Co-op Stamps.

They can also be built upon tactically via special extra promotions such as double points weeks to drive short-term volume or counter competitive action.

Advantages:

- ❐ long term;
- ❐ can build loyalty;
- ❐ can offer a wide range of rewards;
- ❐ can identify a loyal customer base.

Disadvantages:

- ❐ not easy to opt out once committed;
- ❐ delayed;
- ❐ not exciting;
- ❐ may become part of the brand property;
- ❐ high spend required to qualify for rewards.

Free money

Cashbacks and try me frees have been discussed above. There is one other sort of free money. This the cash share-out. Here everyone who applies with the correct POPs (or with the right competition answer) gets a share in the prize fund.

Advantages:

- ❐ fixed prize fund;
- ❐ simple administration;
- ❐ sounds like a big offer.

Disadvantages:

- ❐ low redemption rates;
- ❐ no added value, cash says less about a brand than a relevant premium offer.

Getting a share of a cash lump sum is related to the next section on prizes.

PRIZES

There are three families of prize promotion:

- ❐ *competitions*;
- ❐ *lotteries*;
- ❐ *games*.

For the sake of clarity it is worth defining these straight away.

Competitions (also known as contests)
The allocation of prizes is based upon the judgement of merit and not by chance or gratuitous distribution. Success must depend to a substantial degree on the exercise of mental and/or physical skill and/or judgement. Purchase of a product as a condition of entry is allowed.

Lotteries (also known as sweepstakes and raffles)
Entry tickets are sold and the prizes allocated purely on chance. The organiser or agent is restricted in what they can ask as regards contribution in order to enter. This is tightly controlled by law and consequently is a less common promotional tool. Most are small activities run by charities and voluntary organisations. Registration with the local council is required. Instant win promotions may appear similar to lotteries, but they avoid this by offering a free entry route.

Games (including free draws and game card promotions)
The allocation of prizes without the use of skill or judgement. In many games there is a participative element as the entrant plays the game, to see if they have won. No money and no purchase can be demanded of the participant.

Legality and ethics
Prize promotions are dangerous waters. They are complex legally and should always be checked thoroughly by experts to avoid prosecution and costly mistakes. There is also a long trail of embarrassing episodes where too many winning game cards have been printed or someone has cracked the competition code and bought container loads of competition packs to claim their prizes. The British Code of Sales Promotion Practice offers good basic guidance on what is acceptable but specific legal input should also be sought.

It is important not only to adhere to the law but also to act in the spirit of it. TQ promotions will not seek to con their customers. This area is also full of suspect players who damage the promotions industry. In my view the time-share operators who write telling you that you have won a car or a TV set or a holiday in Spain, subject to all sorts of strange conditions, are a scourge. Likewise, those who offer prizes over the phone when consumers call premium rate phone lines. This last type I would not call a promotion at all, since they rarely promote a product and in my view are often a relatively cynical way of profiteering out of the weakness of others.

Expectations

Prize based promotions demanding an entry tend to get the lowest response rates of just about any sort of promotion. Many competitions are designed in a way that puts the casual entrant off and leaves it to the professional entrants perusing their copy of *Competitors Journal* for the latest offerings. The art of good competition design is to make entry easy and attractive without getting too many winners.

In fact because of the low entry rate the odds on winning most send-in competitions are much higher than one might expect. I have seen many competitions offering prizes worth several thousands of pounds yet only attracting a few hundred entries.

Despite this, competitions are continually run by all sorts of businesses. The reason for this is sometimes stupidity and sometimes the acceptance that it can provide a message that says something about the image of the carrier brand at quite reasonable cost and without the complexity or uncertainty of a send-away offer, and occasionally because they actually work in that market.

Having damned competitions it must be said that sometimes they work tremendously well. If they are easy enough to get into, if the consumer feels they have a chance of winning or the prize is big, exciting or hyped enough to capture their interest then the promoter has a winner of their own on their hands.

Contests, free draws and lotteries ask the consumer for a one-off involvement and then usually a long wait for their prize if they are so lucky. Games such as those run by many newspapers are more involving, as they may require participation every day with, for example, the chance of a daily win or collecting up for a monthly big prize pot via a scratch-card or card and stickers. Even more motivating (for me anyway), is the instant win promotion. These sail close to the wind in legal terms but get away with being acceptable on-pack providing they offer a no purchase necessary alternative method of entry. To me they remain honest fun so long as consumers do not get them out of perspective and start buying products to win prizes rather than because they have a use for that product.

What prizes?

The glamour and lure of a monster prize will attract far more interest than a vast array of tiny prizes. The chance to win a million pounds and change your whole life just has to appeal to someone trapped in nine-to-five job they hate. The prize structure should always be kept simple and a whole raft of prizes (1st, 2nd, 10th etc) should be avoided as they are both cumbersome to communicate and ineffective.

If a big prize just cannot be offered then there a couple of other worthwhile options. First, one can offer something that is highly relevant to the promotional target audience and so has much more intrinsic appeal. Secondly, one can escalate the offer by offering a chance to win something even bigger, eg the prize could be a pools entry or some Premium Bonds. This latter approach needs care as a big flash to win £2 million can look rather thin when the consumer realises all they get is a pools entry. Remember, prizes are not always won or claimed and this can have an effect on promotional costs.

The established view of the order of appeal for prizes is as follows.

❒ First: money.
❒ Second: houses.
❒ Third: cars.
❒ Fourth: holidays.
❒ Fifth: anything else.

Competitions

There are a range of different competition mechanics one might adopt. These include:

❒ *questions* - eg on general or often product knowledge;
❒ *slogans* - eg the best rhyme, riddle or statement on a topic;
❒ *rankings* - eg rank a list of attributes against specified criteria;
❒ *creatives* - eg write a story or draw a picture;
❒ *estimates* - eg the distance the ship sailed going from X to Y;
❒ *detective work* - eg clues to where the pirate buried the treasure;
❒ *spot the difference* - eg the differences between two pictures;
❒ *X marks the spot* - eg spot the ball;
❒ *mystery objects* - eg identify the close-up shot of an everyday object.

All competitions that have definitive answers will need an effective tiebreak, one that is not too tricky to enter to be off putting or difficult to judge, but which will require skill and judgement. Creatives and spot the ball types rarely need a tiebreak.

Advantages:
❒ virtually fixed costs;
❒ can (occasionally) be used as a lever for display;
❒ can also add trade offer in independents;
❒ versatile prize structure;

❏   big or wacky prizes can generate excitement;

❏   can be set up quickly;

❏   often cheap;

❏   minimal sourcing problems.

Disadvantages:

❏   not usually immediate;

❏   low consumer participation/interest;

❏   low sales effect;

❏   minimal trade interest.

Lotteries

Advantages:

❏   useful small-scale fund raiser.

Disadvantages:

❏   great legal care required;

❏   complex administration.

Games

These will include mechanics like these.

❏   *Free draws*:
    the first out of the hat wins;

❏   *Matching games*:
    - match the number or picture on your game card to
      the one in the store, newspaper etc;
    - issue lots of game pieces and match two halves;
    - issue lots of pieces and collect the set.

❏   *Instant win*:
    eg scratch off or peel and reveal games.

Advantages:

❏   greater participation than competitions;

❏   versatile, can be instant or delayed win, or both;

❏   can boost sales if captures consumers' imaginations;

❏   game/scratch-card can retain loyalty.

Disadvantages:

❏   cannot ask for proof of purchase;

❏   needs to be large scale to get high levels of awareness and
    interest;

❏   many fall into obscurity;

❏   game/scratch-cards require frequent purchases;

□   game/scratch-cards of limited application, eg more appropriate for retailers and newspapers;

□   game/scratch-cards complex to design and print.

Share-outs

Here a cash lump sum is put up for sharing out between all qualifying applicants. The share-out is usually a send in and everyone can share in the pool if they provide a proof of purchase, or by competition where only those with the right answer share the prize money.

Advantages:

□   simple offer;

□   easy to handle;

□   fixed prize fund.

Disadvantages:

□   a lot of winners can mean high administration costs;

□   possoble credibility gap;

□   relatively low redemption rate.

EMOTIONAL BENEFITS (IMAGE)

Ideally all promotions should get across something of the brand image in their execution, even if it is only in the creativity.

In some cases the main thrust of a promotion is to heighten awareness of the brand values, and build the image of the brand in the eyes of the consumer and potential consumer.

This reward is often seen as a tenuous one that comes in for a lot of criticism, primarily because of the difficulty of measurement. However, there is no doubt that promotions can develop a brand personality much as advertising can. Indeed, various forms of media exposure are intrinsic to the execution of this type of promotion.

Key routes include:

□   *sponsorship/link ups:*
  - events;
  - charity;
  - character merchandising;
  - personality promotions;

□   *self-liquidating promotions;*

□   *money back guarantees and challenges;*

❏   *trade relations, staff incentives and corporate hospitality*;
❏   *service*.

Sponsorships and link-ups

The principles working behind sponsorships and link-ups are threefold.

❏   The transference of the personality and qualities associated with the selected partner to the sponsor brand.
❏   The gaining of media coverage.
❏   The endorsement of a product by a personality or organisation.

Any combination of these might be involved in a promotion, but such associations are often platforms on which other, more conventional, promotions are run.

Originally sponsorship was all about responsibility, payment of a scholarship or school prize, or payments to help a sports team afford to buy equipment and travel to matches. Endorsement is slightly different in that payment is made to an individual or organisation in exchange for its name being linked to the product and endorsing its quality.

The distinction between sponsorship and endorsement is becoming blurred. Sponsorship has escalated in terms of providing sponsors with media coverage and image enhancement. Naturally the cost of sponsorship has escalated accordingly, and now sponsorship payments exceed the costs the sports team needs or the cost of running a concert, and sponsorship and endorsement have virtually become undistinguishable.

Events

These tend to be sports or music. The primary appeal of this as a promotional technique to provide an image to present to the consumer frequently in conjunction with some other promotion and reward.

The classic big event sponsorship is the Olympics. Manufacturers will pay vast amounts to become the official sponsors, thus getting product visibility on TV coverage, a media claim and presence at the venue. Coca-Cola repeatedly paid $33m to be the official soft drink at the Barcelona Olympics and sponsorship. A whole host of other brands have also paid large sums, eg Mars, Kodak, Philips and Seiko Sponsorship are responsible for a large portion of the income from the Olympics, almost as much as from the TV rights.

Sports sponsorship generally is big money and provides a unique opportunity for those companies that cannot advertise, eg cigarette companies.

This attachment of a handle is a good way to get mentions if you have a big organisation which is not well known or has a normally undifferentiated proposition, eg in financial services. It affords a high level of awareness.

Long-term events are more robust to sponsor than individual ones since they may not prove popular or they may have organisational problems and your one chance has been blown.

Charity

Associations with charities can demonstrate the caring nature of the sponsor. A frequent link-up is to offer a fixed donation for every proof of purchase collected. This can work tremendously well if it captures the imagination of support groups who go out and sell the promotion for you.

The charity will be selected to suit the brand need. Retailers will show they care by linking with children's charities, particularly appealing to the family shopper. Manufacturers will link with environmental charities to show they care about waste, pollution and environmental matters in general.

Charities are frequently used in conjunction with other rewards. The charity may be to add tone of voice to another main promotional thrust, for example a coupon as a reward for the consumer and for every one used the charity gets a payment. Anneka's (Rice) Andrex Appeal door dropped leaflets with coupons on them and for every coupon used 5p was donated to Guide Dogs for the Blind; needless to say the guide dog featured was a labrador with puppies. In another promotion Bovril was seeking trial and helped volunteers sell warming cups of Bovril at Lions Club Bonfire nights. Bovril got trial and the Lions £25,000.

It's not all down to the local groups though, as bigger charities are staffed by marketing professionals keen to tap this vein. The World Wide Fund for Nature has linked with a vast array of companies from Cadbury's to NatWest and Ariel. Such organisations see corporate link-ups as a key funding resource.

Character merchandising

Here the image borrowed may even be fictional. It certainly will have even stronger character images associated, apart from major sports persons or music stars who may themselves be the subject of character merchandising.

The value of these strong images with specific qualities is that while they are hot property they can provide a real boost to an otherwise mundane promotion. If Batman is in with the kids right now then a model Batmobile in the cereal packet is going to work a lot harder than a model of a production sports car.

Personalities

This is essentially the same as the link-ups above, but there are two inherent big risks. First, should the personality fall into disgrace your money has been wasted and, worse, your brand may be tarnished. Secondly, if your personality is uncooperative or says stupid things you have again wasted your money and potentially damaged your brand.

Having said that, there is much to be gained from the association with the success of a winner.

Exploitation of sponsorship and link-ups

To make these types of association work well requires more than passive participation. Exploitation requires adequate resource and time to understand how best to crank the whole thing up with the consumer and also those closer to home. Link-ups provide good opportunities to develop public relations with clients, trade, suppliers and employees.

Advantages:

- ❐ makes the mundane interesting;
- ❐ adds the qualities of the associated organisation/event/person;
- ❐ can generate high levels of motivation/participation;
- ❐ associated body may provide organisational or human resources;
- ❐ can work with limited budgets;
- ❐ can provide cheap/difficult to obtain media coverage;
- ❐ great hype potential.

Disadvantages:

- ❐ most associations are longer term;
- ❐ sales benefit low unless enhancing another incentive;
- ❐ hard to drop once locked in;
- ❐ can be protracted to implement;
- ❐ demands big resources to maximise effects;
- ❐ may be expensive hidden costs, eg on the PR side;
- ❐ reliance on individual personalities or events is risky;
- ❐ at events, the consumer may not notice the sponsor in the shadow of the main activity;
- ❐ may distract from real brand values.

Self-liquidating promotions (SLPs)

These provide an opportunity to say something about the brand qualities at relatively little cost. Redemptions will be low but the objective is to get an image-based message across. SLPs that work well will be distinctive and have a cachet that can be associated with the brand.

The idea (if not the practice) is that SLPs should pay their own way. They can even yield a profit but normally the promoter would be seeking to offer the consumer the best possible value. The main exception is catalogues, eg where branded clothes and other merchandise are offered for sale. Such activities can be long lived and profit centres in their own right. They need a strong brand to support them and it is debatable as to whether they are true promotions.

Advantages:

❐ brand statement can be made;
❐ potentially low-cost activity;

Disadvantages:

❐ minimal sales effect;
❐ no trade interest;
❐ low participation;
❐ difficulties of premium stock control.

Money back guarantees/challenges

These are a brave statement that the product is worth the money. Any quibbles and the consumer gets their money back. Many comestibles, especially snacks, carry this message as part of the standard pack, it is part of the brand proposition. Others may make special attention of the claim. This can be particularly effective when announcing a new product and is rather like the 'try me free' in removing some of the risk for the consumer, but it is not offering money back as a matter of course.

One trick is to provide a money back claim form on the reverse of a coupon off the next purchase. Then make the claim 'Xp off your next purchase or your money back'.

Trade relations, staff incentives and corporate hospitality

The incentivisation of individuals is an important form of promotion, and many of the rewards and techniques described in this book are applicable. The psychology and practice of this form of promotion is an enormous field which is better covered in other works.

Cash, vouchers, premium items, meals and travel are all popular rewards to staff for achieving such goals as production, sales and distribution targets. One value of non-cash awards is that they are less likely to be looked on as part of salary and so it is less of a problem if not awarded at a later date.

Motivating business contacts is slightly more complex as care has to be taken to avoid bribery. More acceptable types of motivation are along the lines of being taken along to a sponsored event, providing training sessions, teambuilding activities or product information seminars for buyers and distributors. These can certainly be carried out in pleasant surroundings with suitable hospitality laid on.

Service

Providing service benefits to customers can give real benefits. These are not necessarily true promotions in their own right, but service enhancements are often linked into promotional activity. This is particularly so for the distributive and retail side where such additional service might include:

- ❐ shelf/space planning;
- ❐ merchandising support;
- ❐ special display fixtures;
- ❐ market information;
- ❐ information for their customers. .

Product or service support schemes

Here added value is given to the brand proposition by offering additional services or support, eg an extended guarantee, free insurance or after sales service.

Advantages:
- ❐ the perceived value is higher than the cost to provide;
- ❐ can buy low-cost bulk insurance and similar services;
- ❐ can generate leads for further product sales or renewals of the services provided.

Disadvantages:
- ❐ may have complex administration;
- ❐ may require third party involvement.

There is a wide choice of different media and applications by which all these rewards can be offered to the target audience. The next section provides a critique of the value of these different communication methods.

7
Media and Applications

There are four broad media classifications for communicating a promotion:

- one-to-one contact;
- mass media;
- point-of-purchase;
- communication to known consumer types.

Most of the rewards discussed above can be offered through all these various media options. Selecting the right one is part of the fundamental creative and analytical process of designing truly effective promotions.

Obviously there is overlap, eg one-to-one contact and point-of-purchase promotions will be working together in a shop where the salesperson is dealing directly with the consumer at the point of purchase. However, it is convenient to break the communication process into these four categories in order to describe the possible routes with clarity. We can then go on to look at some application principles in greater depths in Chapter 8.

ONE-TO-ONE CONTACT

If you have a tangible product, one you can demonstrate or even talk about effectively, then getting out to meet your potential customers face-to-face can be highly productive.

The types of media this may incorporate include:

- roadshows;
- exhibitions;
- demonstrators and tastings;
- personal direct selling;
- personal recommendation.

Roadshows

Roadshows are a great vehicle for physically getting out to the people. The scale of activity can vary . It may be that all that is required is a simple and quickly set up glorified trestle-table type of affair to sample a new drink or snack. This type of activity is common in high traffic areas such as station concourses which may have to be set up and cleared away each day. Others may try to build coverage and excitement using a highly mobile stage. Other roadshows may involve much more expensive and highly complex high-tech devices such as video-walls which often require plenty of set-up time, and semi-permanent sites with power and other facilities, meaning they are likely to stay in one place for several days.

Advantages:

❒	high visibility in the location;

❒	can link with local media/personalities to build the event;

❒	can combine with other promotions to build attendance;

❒	can offer physical trial or strong image and product story;

❒	good selective sampling vehicle.

Disadvantages:

❒	sets can be costly so small events often disproportionately expensive;

❒	staffing and transport costs high;

❒	can be difficult to find good venues;

❒	insurance can be high;

❒	effectiveness will depend on interested and motivated staff;

❒	the event may overpower the brand;

❒	only limited coverage possible;

❒	the best venues may have long leadtimes for booking space.

Exhibitions

These are good shop windows for business-to-business in particular. There are also many wider opportunities to target the consumer, via general or special interest shows.

Attendees will be looking to buy, specifically looking for new ideas or having a general look round. Exhibitors will be looking to sell and to announce their services. There will be a lot of competition and those who are demonstrating a product, or presenting something new or innovative will be able to attract the greatest interest.

There are also other ways to attract an audience, for example running a free draw will work but may not invite the right audience. Free giveaways are often used to lure customers, and the more intriguing and relevant ones will work best. Something that is fun, novel or attractive and that will help customers do their job better may well pull in more of the right sort of people, providing it is sufficiently publicised.

Ensure the exhibition has good publicity, number and quality of attendees.

Demonstrators and tastings

These will obviously be an inherent part of roadshows and exhibitions, but also have relevance in any environment where the consumer is likely to be found. In particular this is a highly appropriate route to use in the food and drink industry where in-shop tastings are a common example we have all come across. Other products can also benefit, for example demonstrating the benefits of a new cosmetic product or DIY tool.

Advantages:

- ❐ good for trial of new product;
- ❐ offers direct customer contact;
- ❐ offers the opportunity for customer feedback.

Disadvantages:

- ❐ variable staff quality, motivation and commitment;
- ❐ high cost;
- ❐ limited number of demonstrations can be made;
- ❐ site location limitations.

This touches very closely on the next topic.

Personal direct selling

This is the classic face-to-face selling. The consumer is sold to on a more or less one-to -one basis. It is a standard form of selling for many businesses, eg the car showroom, Avon cosmetics, Tupperware parties, insurance sales-persons and the department store perfumery counter. As such it is a medium for a range of promotional activity to help boost sales performance.

Where direct selling is standard practice it is hard to call it a sales promotion technique. One would normally look at the promotion as some-thing extra and special the salesperson offers within the normal sales inter-view. However, in a market not typified by direct selling it could become a promotional technique in its own right.

Personal recommendation

This is the ultimate way of promoting products. Give the customer something so good they feel they have to tell their friends about it. How can you resist something your friend lays their credibility on the line for?

Not really a way of promoting, this is the end result of a truly TQ product proposition, and of course it's free.

MASS COMMUNICATION

This is the big league, and is the route for many mass market products. They need to be big or have a big potential as the costs for high coverage will be prohibitive to the small players.

Typical media are:

- ☐   door drops;
- ☐   press promotions;
- ☐   radio;
- ☐   television;
- ☐   cinema and video;
- ☐   public relations activities;
- ☐   third-party links (including sponsorship).

Door drops

Unaddressed mail accounts for about one-third of all items coming through the letterbox. About half of this third is free newspapers, the rest being essentially a mixture of samples, brochures, leaflets and coupons. This material is present in large quantities and it is like most promotions, fairly trivial stuff. However, it can work and there is a lot of information available to help ascertain the appropriateness for the marketing situation in hand.

Door-to-door coverage is about 95 per cent of households, although most activity is more restricted than this. Of the 22.2 million homes in the country national drops rarely go over 17 million and 10 million or less is common. This is partly driven by budget and partly by the opportunities available to target door drops. Many drops are very small, just a few thousand round local retailers or a tightly contained catchment area for a local business.

Types of door drop
There are five main types of door-to-door distribution.

- ☐   *Shareplan* - the item is delivered with up to approximately five non-competing items against a set schedule of dates. Distribution takes about three weeks to complete. This is one of the cheapest and most commonly used forms of distribution.
- ☐   *Solus*- the item is delivered on its own at a timing to suit the client. It is slightly quicker to complete the drop and benefits from being more likely to be the only thing on the mat. The cost is likely to be about 2.5 times a shared drop.

❐   *Free newspapers* - here the item, normally a leaflet or brochure, is delivered with the local free newspaper. There is a wide coverage and some targeting is possible. Ensure the items are dropped as intended and that the items accompany the paper and are not tucked inside. The real advantage to this system is speed of delivery, normally within three days.

❐   *Personal calls* - this is where the distributor actually knocks on the door to deliver the goods personally. This is very expensive, maybe 10 or 15 times a shareplan cost, depending on the item to be dropped. There is limited penetration with around 60 per cent of households being out at the time of call. Knock and drops are slow to implement and will normally need to be rolled out gradually. They are mainly used for:
   - large samples that won't go through a letterbox;
   - samples needing special safety precautions or which are perishable and cannot be left.
   - obtaining customer response data, eg a signature for receipt, competitive usage data (which may be used to determine whether or not a sample is left). It should be noted that distributors are not research staff so any questioning or screen ing has to be simply devised for effective implementation.

❐   *Household delivery service* - this is offered by the Post Office. It can be more expensive than, say, a shareplan but it does offer the kudos of coming with the mail and has virtually 100 per cent coverage.

Door dropping information and offers

Door drops are an established medium for presenting consumers with brochures, product information, advertising and offers. Leaflet usage and attitude research commissioned by Circular Distributors showed that about half (48 per cent) of adults receiving leaflets or coupons claim to keep and read at least some of the leaflets they receive, with about 13 per cent reading most of what they receive. Figure 7.1 indicates the consumer's response to items delivered via this medium.

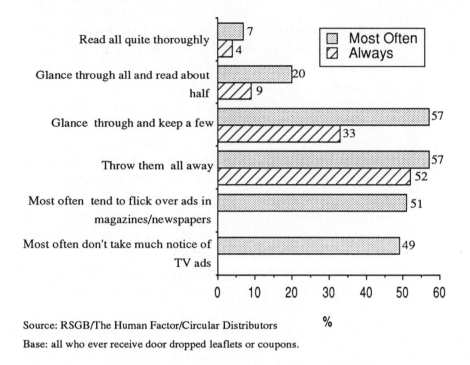

Source: RSGB/The Human Factor/Circular Distributors
Base: all who ever receive door dropped leaflets or coupons.

Figure 7.1   Response to door dropped leaflets

The same research shows that all or half of leaflets are read by 27 per cent of respondents, whereas for mailshots the figure was only 6 per cent. On the down side nearly 60 per cent claimed to throw all leaflets and mailshots away. While many items are discarded, interesting ones will generate a response. The research shows that among all recipients of leaflets 39 per cent have gone on to make an enquiry related to the communication, 47 per cent have been prompted to purchase and 37 per cent have tried something new.

The first step in dealing with a door dropped item is the sort process and, after this there are various options that present themselves:

- ❐   throwing out;
- ❐   setting aside for later or for other members of the family;
- ❐   looking at there and then;
- ❐   keeping for later use/reference.

Those good enough to get past this sort tend to be kept around for several day: 72 per cent of the sample retained the leaflets they kept for a few days or longer. Recall appears to vary between 50 and 80+ per cent.

Figure 7.2 illustrates the general usefulness of items coming through the letterbox. Pack recognition plus the simplicity of the message seem to be the most important aspects of whether a door drop leaflet will work. If the consumer can quickly understand whether the promotion is relevant to them then they will respond accordingly. If it is clear that they are going to be rewarded for participation and what they have to do is easy then that's fine. If it is complex, if they have to struggle to see the deal, or claims are ridiculous or a confusing challenge then the door drop will be wasted.

Score (out of 10) of all receivers saying 'find useful':

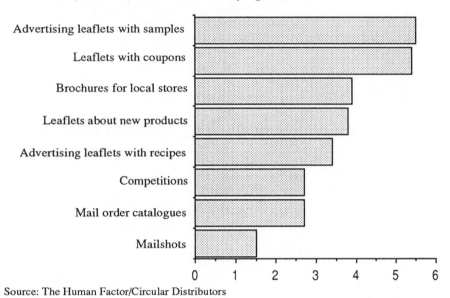

Source: The Human Factor/Circular Distributors

Figure 7.2   Usefulness of items through the letterbox

Door dropping samples
Sampling is highly appropriate to the door drop medium, in part because it is such a simple message. Research shows that more than two-thirds of respondents claimed to have bought a product outside their normal repertoire as a result of receiving a door dropped sample. Figure 7.3 shows the usage of door dropped samples, with 72 per cent of housewives using samples often and 75 per cent of these samples being used within a week or two.

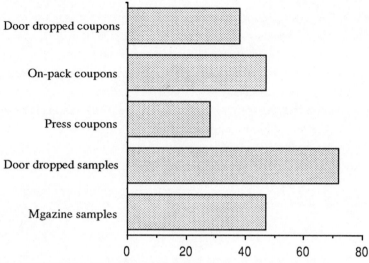

Source: RSGB/ The Human Factor/Circular Distributors

Figure 7.3 Usage of promotional items 'often'

One of the characteristics of door dropping is the high wastage. For cheap leaflets this is not important but for expensive samples this is not the case. It is possible to improve the efficiency of a drop either by targeting based on the types of property you wish to hit or even more effectively, if expensively, via the knock and drop system. There is a trade-off which needs to be calculated to ascertain the best option.

Press promotions

The press has always been a popular promotional medium. There are different families of press exposure:

- national newspapers;
- women's press;
- specialist interest magazines;
- local newspapers.

Each of these will have its value as a promotional medium.

National newspapers are classically the domain of the retailer with special deal announcements and the direct sales company selling off the page. Although relatively cheap they have quality limitations and the readership needs to be carefully scrutinised. One major advantage they have is a short lead time which allows for swift action to counter competitive activity. The quality papers tend to have colour supplements and these present an entirely different medium, to all intents and purposes similar to women's magazines.

The advantage of women's magazines is the flexibility to choose appropriate titles that will appeal to the target audience and it can be well worth tailoring the promotional message to appeal to the particular type of reader.

Many brands run theme advertising in the women's press and this presents an opportunity to piggy-back an offer. There has been research to show that advertisements with response devices on them are noticed more than straight theme ads. These offers might be full-blown incentives to purchase or just a simple toll-free phone number to find out more information. Redemptions tend to be lower than on-pack, point-of-sale or door-to-door, but well-constructed press activity can also perform a theme role.

Local newspapers are ideal tactical tools for local store activity. Their use for national brands is less common, unless linked to some local activity.

In addition to using press purely as an advertising medium for promotions, it can be used in barter deals where media space is provided cheaply or even free in exchange for a special offer for the publication readers. For example, a travel company may offer an exclusive competition or 'kids go free' offer to a publication in exchange for a strong on-the-page presence of the company's logo and perhaps a telephone number for a brochure. The cost of this will be cheaper to the holiday company and the magazine than if they were buying outright, and the consumer gets a good offer into the bargain.

The press is also home to the advertorial. Here paid for space is used in editorial style to talk up a product and its benefits in depth. The theory is that the consumer reads it more like an article and dwells on the subject matter for longer than a simple ad. This is a strong method of gaining implied product endorsement by the publication. Taking an example quoted in *Marketing Week* (16 October 1992) shows the pulling power. A miniature liqueur bottle offered to *Woman's Realm* readers pulled in nearly five times as many replies to the advertorial as the advertisement. However, the value of true editorial is far greater still and generated approximately 100 times the response of the ad!

Radio

Radio can be used to support a promotional programme in two main ways. The first is as a media option to announce or advertise a promotion. This may be geographically targeted, eg the special offers at your local furniture warehouse store this weekend, or as part of a national campaign. In the latter case it may be supporting other advertising. Radio is particularly good at reaching medium, light and non-TV viewers who tend to be heavier radio listeners. The second option is to be more than an advertisement and to provide a real promotional medium by providing the listener with all they need to respond to the offer.

Most radio promotions are on independent radio (IR). IR reach is quite high, with around 60 per cent of men and women tuning in each week. IR programming is split between AM and FM, with the FM networks generally targeting the 15-30 age group and the AM (Gold) stations targeting the older (35-54) listeners.

Radio promotions may be fully paid up ads where the promoter buys air-time and asks the consumer to respond, eg to call a toll-free telephone number to find out more about a product or to take up a special deal.

Other promotions can be co-operative activities with the radio station. These are typically barter arrangements whereby the radio stations are offered some special benefit, eg prizes in exchange for air-time (ads, pre-recorded trailers and DJ mentions). The radio stations may demand some purchase of advertising space as well, but the rate is likely to be negotiable depending on the whole package. The stronger the offer to the radio station the better the deal that can be struck and the more the DJs are likely to be motivated.

Quite often this type of activity is combined with an extra element to bring them to life, eg a door drop or roadshow. This offers a vehicle to tell the consumers about the competition, eg to listen out for 'trigger' records and may give the chance of added exposure through live radio broadcasts from the roadshow. The radio station will be looking for promotions that build loyalty or drag new listeners in and this should be considered when structuring the proposal. With all this activity going on the softer elements of branding may be lost. Therefore this approach is better for brands where mentions are more important than descriptions.

This co-operative approach has some notable advantages and disadvantages.

Advantages:

❏   personal endorsement from the radio station/DJs;
❏   potential for good value for money air-time;
❏   high level of brand name mentions.

Disadvantages:

❏   radio stations may give more weight to the offer rather than the brand in DJ mentions;
❏   DJ mentions may not get branding across;
❏   complex to negotiate/administer, specialist agency input required.

Television

Television may be used in most of the same ways as radio, with announcement of promotions, direct response and programme sponsorship. Bearing in mind the different scale and regionality structures the issues are basically similar.

Also available are product placement opportunities. Here the products are provided as props to be featured on screen. Payment by the companies seeking exposure is not allowed and neither is any influencing of the content or scheduling of programmes. Free supply of products, thus cutting down production costs, is allowed so long as, according to the Independent Television Commission (ITC), they are not there with 'undue prominence'. EC directives also ban paid for product placement. Despite the restrictions product placement is growing and the products given exposure may range from new cars to bottles of beer.

Cinema and video

Apart from product placement opportunities, sampling and sponsorship deals, cinema and video offer other forms of link-ups. Films are often looking to help fund costs and to gain additional publicity once launched. If a brand is offering extended awareness of the film via say an on-pack offer, then reciprocal deals may be possible, eg tickets, advertising and case advertising on videos.

Public relations

Public relations (PR) exists at many levels, eg consumer based, the distributive trade, the community and employees. Public relations are essentially all the non-paid communications between a brand or organisation and these audiences. Present at all times whether they are managed or not, a positive approach will obviously yield a better image and response.

PR has its own role to play in the marketing mix and it can also play a good supporting role when running promotions, eg:

- ❐ information to interested parties;
- ❐ favourable publicity via opinion formers;
- ❐ extended communication beyond that which is sometimes possible (or allowed) via advertising;
- ❐ influence on the external environment, such as government offices;
- ❐ a spokesperson for the brand or organisation;
- ❐ a media or trade contact;

- ❏   internal liaison;
- ❏   expanded coverage where media support budgets are restricted;
- ❏   a contact point for emergency or crisis management when a promotion goes wrong for unexpected reasons;
- ❏   local media coverage for an activity, such as via local press and radio.

Third-party links

There are a wide number of avenues that offer third-party opportunities and several have been covered above. Others can range from the simple cross promotion where brands with similar profiles carry reciprocal offers on-pack to the blockbusters run by the big retailers and travel companies. This special type of promotion has become more and more important as companies seek more cost-effective ways of promoting, and see sharing the cost with another party both as an opportunity to cut or share costs and as an opportunity to target particular consumer profiles.

This area may be a mass communication or it might be tightly targeted. It might be at or away from the point of purchase. Because it is so important a promotional technique it has its own section, 'Joint promotions', below.

POINT-OF-PURCHASE PROMOTIONS

Point-of-purchase or point-of-sale promotions have great value in markets where impulse purchases are easily gained, eg the supermarket. This medium not only provides a route into reward based promotions, but also offers the opportunity to run information linked activities which inform the consumer about their considered purchase and help them make their decision.

Topics under this media umbrella include:

- ❏   using the product as the communication vehicle;
- ❏   retail promotions;
- ❏   tailormades and account specifics;
- ❏   outlet led/preferred activity;
- ❏   demonstrators and tastings.

Using the product as the communication vehicle

In many ways this subject has been covered in Chapter 6. An on- or in-pack promotion can be designed to meet the classic objectives of trial and loyalty. However, they have some significant shortcomings:

❐ they will not attract new users who do not come into contact with the product/outlet;

❐ announcing the offer may involve expensive pack changes or point-of-sale material;

❐ there may be very restricted space for making the promotional announcement;

❐ they may be seen only by those looking at the product on the shelf;

❐ for manufacturers not all outlets may accept the promotional pack;

❐ there are likely to be long leadtimes so offers may no longer be relevant or pitched at the right strength for the market once implemented.

Despite this they can be very impactful and provide particularly strong purchase incentives at the point of sale. Additionally, they can be a genuine talking point for retailers and distributors who see these offers as being presented to their customers unlike off-pack out-of-store promotions which are diffuse and less likely to affect their distribution and merchandising plans.

Retail promotions

Broadly speaking, retailers are running promotions to achieve five tasks:

❐ stealing share from competitive retailers;

❐ building customer loyalty;

❐ building the shopping basket size;

❐ encouraging purchase/wider use of different parts of the store;

❐ building category volume and profit.

Manufacturers should bear this in mind when deciding if they should be promoting through the retailer. If they can help the retailer achieve one of these at the same time as driving their own business they may well get greater retailer support.

Retailers will use a variety of approaches to announce offers, and direct and encourage the consumer to the store and to participate in:

❑   *in-store activity* - eg price, GWPs, tailormade leaflets and coupons;

❑   *press promotions* - usually announcement of special prices or local store marketing, sometimes coupons;

❑   *door drops* - usually coupons, often associated with new store openings, countering competitive activity and usually directing consumers to a particular store;

❑   *posters*;

❑   *local radio* - eg to announce and remind that a promotion is happening in store, possibly linked to some urgency, eg only this weekend 25 per cent off everything at your local DIY store;

❑   *TV* - eg for blockbuster offers, again often with a sense of urgency;

❑   *direct mail* - to known shoppers and those within the catchment area of specific stores;

❑   *information technology based techniques.*

In-store activity primarily revolves around price. This may be a straight price-cut on the shelf price or coupons on the shelf. EPOS promotions are now well established in many grocery multiples and allow instant price discounting of single and multiple purchases. They also allow special discounts or even free packs when certain combinations of product are bought. This is a good way to build cross-usage or introduce a new product to users of an existing one.

Occasionally one of the big retailers will run a store-wide promotion geared to attracting loyalty or building the basket size. Sainsbury linked up with British Airways to offer discounted flights. The location reached was dependent on the cash value of receipts saved, presumably encouraging consumer loyalty to the store and may well have been an enticement to buy more to reach the offer thresholds. Boots have run a promotion with British Rail more than once. Here, presumably, Boots wanted to drive up the basket size so only a single purchase above a certain threshold qualified the consumer for a two for the price of one train ticket offer.

The manufacturer can and should use these retailer devices to promote to the consumer, but always with an eye to the cost and returns gained from such activity. Retailers have a nasty habit of playing manufacturers off against each other and also using manufacturer's promotional money to their own ends. Manufacturers should be aware as to whether their investment is being passed on to the consumer. Retailers likewise need to have their shoppers top of mind and be aware of whether they are promoting against competitors or to their consumer.

Tailormades and account specifics

This does not refer to price promotions and multi-buys of one guise or another. Here we are referring to the more creative activity.

Retailers tend to prefer to think of special promotions that manufacturers run in their stores as tailormades rather than account specifics. It makes them feel more special, and it sounds like the promotion is being run just for them and not one of a series of similar activities in a number of outlets.

Many retailers will have specific preferences for what they like to see offered and most of the multiples have restrictions on the size, format and layout that can be used.

In reality the classic leaflet led account specific promotion is generally a waste of time with very low consumer participation and extremely low effect on sales. Some retailers use them as a profit centre by virtue of the charges for participation. Most retailers have come to recognise the low value of this type of tailormades, and do not encourage such complex and usually unrewarding activity. Coupled with the restrictions on what can be said and done they are generally best left alone. The better ones are those that offer an instant reward, next easy-entry sendaways and lastly competitions.

Outlet led/preferred activities

Retailers now tend to lean more towards generic activity which manufacturers can buy into: new product booklets, in-store coupons, special price offers, gifts with purchase and all sorts of EPOS promotions such as multi-purchase offers. Occasionally they will also run major multi-brand events, which can work well although the cost of entry can be high.

Performance will vary and generally only big brands will be able to get the increases in sale necessary to pay for participation. However, participation is often a cost of doing business with the account.

My view of these techniques, run through the in-store medium, is set out below. You must make your own judgements based on evaluation, the responsiveness of your brand to promotion and an assessment of all the ancillary issues such as getting your product listed or maintaining distribution.

❑   *New product booklets* - more valuable to secure listings than to get sales movement.

❑   *In-store coupons* - some limited effect, they are not used up by every customer so they can be cheaper than price cutting. However the discount funded by the promoter is usually off retail not the cost price of the product, ie an expensive discount.

❏   *Special price offers* - good consumer motivater, cheaper than coupons as funded at cost not retail. Some compensation for loss of trade margin at the higher price may be asked for.

❏   *Gifts with purchase* - potentially good sales uplift and potential for trial providing you can get a mutually agreeable and affordable gift and get over the administrative hurdles.

❏   *EPOS promotions* - comments as above for price discounts of single packs. Off multiple purchase they can provide a good sales boost, but at an expensive cost, they are unlikely to prove profitable in the short term. Cross-product EPOS promotions where two different products have to be bought to qualify for the discount can be good for driving product trial, and as far as the retailer is concerned, shopping in different parts of the store.

❏   *Major multi-brand events* - the value will depend on the overall proposition, individual brands will risk being lost in the overall event but can benefit if the deal is right.

❏   *Information leaflets at point of sale* - useful to highlight new products or those with a special story to tell. Unlikely to give big volume increases but can be a useful part of a strategy to build penetration long-term. Can usefully be combined with a coupon offer.

When promoting with retailers, sharing of retail sales data is to be encouraged if the best offers are to be developed. This information will also be necessary if accurate payment for price discounted sales is to be made. Like any organisation, retailers are not always perfect in implementing activities, and it is prudent to check the placement of coupons and leaflets and any display feature that is agreed to ensure that which has been promised is delivered and is working satisfactorily.

Demonstrators and tastings

See under 'one-to-one contact' above.

COMMUNICATING TO KNOWN CONSUMER TYPES

Direct marketing and direct promotions

It is not really necessary to draw a line and say that this promotion is part of direct marketing or this one is a direct promotion. Drayton Bird in *'Common Sense Direct Marketing'* defines direct marketing as:

> **any activity which creates and profitably exploits a direct relationship between you and the prospect.**

I have not yet come across a definition of direct promotion, but my stab at it would be:

> **any promotional activity which works through direct contact with the current or potential customer.**

These terminologies are very broad based, 'direct' is the difficult word to get to grips with, it simply means straight to, ie no intermediaries. Direct promotions in the widest sense can be run via virtually all communication media as door drops, press promotions and face-to-face selling, as well as all the high technology and direct mail approaches. Figure 7.4 illustrates.

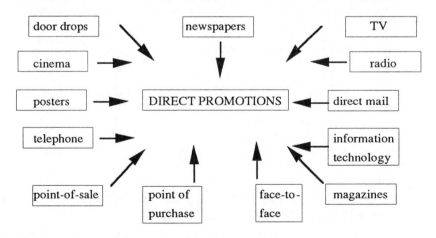

Figure 7.4 Direct promotional media

What is being focused on here is the ways for the promoter to identify and access specific types of known customers and potential customers, that will prove cost-effective compared to mass communication methods.

Identifying customer types

Communicating to known consumer types is a mixed bag of applications whereby the consumer, customer or prospect is communicated with in a more directed way. Mass media and point of purchase/sale promotions cannot be targeted very finely, despite the broad-stroke selectivity of deciding which neighbourhoods to do a door drop in (see 'Targeting' in Chapter 8) or selecting more suitable publications and promotional partners. These communication methods allow no identification of individuals or tight groups. Even though face-to-face or one-to-one, selling may allow the customer to be chosen, without leads, little will be known about the prospect and there is minimal potential for presenting an offer specially tailored to the individual's needs and interests.

The aim of this type of promotion is to isolate individuals or groups who can be sold to in a special rather than generic way. This may be a one-off promotion or, more typically, there may be potential for continued dialogue, ie relationship marketing. These promotions have the potential to be true TQ activities designed to meet precise customer needs. As customers become more individual in outlook, more demanding in their needs and are faced by more market-place options tempting them to become more fickle, so the need develops to treat them more specially, as valued individuals.

Prospects can be accessed in one of three ways:

❐   buy in a list or target group to approach;
❐   build your own list or target group;
❐   encourage customers to self-select.

Adopting direct marketing as a primary way of doing business or communicating with your product users requires a change in focus for many businesses from a product based outlook to a customer based outlook. It relies heavily on the building and manipulation of databases.

The essence of what direct marketing and promotion is setting out to achieve is embodied in the loyalty ladder. The goal is constantly to push people up the ladder. This is illustrated in Figure 7.5.

| Advocates - customers who recommend and sell your product for you. |
| Loyals - customers who always buy your goods. |
| Occasionals - customers who sometimes buy your product. |
| Prospects - customers who don't buy your product but might in the future. |

Figure 7.5 The loyalty ladder

The attractions of this type of promotion are :

❑   direct manufacturer contact with customers, gets around the retailer barrier;

❑   customers can be offered help to understand and select from the plethora of propositions they are constantly presented with;

❑   you can ask customers what they want;

❑   customers can be offered what they ask for;

❑   you can learn from your customers' responses;

❑   responses are measurable;

❑   the message can be constantly refined;

❑   testing of promotions, ideas and products is made easy;

❑   it is secret and the competition will not know everything you are up to;

❑   allows identification of the most responsive prospects or those with the biggest business potential;

❑   allows the marketing budget to be directed at these;

❑   is a counter to increasing media fragmentation of the conventional advertising media;

❑   the necessary technology is becoming cheaper and easier to use;

❑   you can record your customers' responses and preferences to be

able to deal with them as individuals and learn general principles;
- ❏ you can cross sell other products;
- ❏ many customers prefer buying direct because it is:
  - quicker and convenient with no visits to the store or salespersons' chat;
  - perceived as cheaper;
  - private;
  - more informative than a salesperson or shop;
  - safe, money back guarantees are the norm.

The risks are:

- ❏ the 'junk mail' image;
- ❏ some people prefer privacy;
- ❏ data protection issues;
- ❏ high set-up costs;

Market applications

One of the difficulties in making direct marketing work in fmcg is the difficulty of making the commitment to drop other forms of advertising and promotion. Trying to make a go of it when the budget is split into too many parts, none of which perform to the optimum, is a common mistake. Instant profits are not likely, and the relationship has to be learned and worked upon. Unless the promotion is a one-hit wonder to drive penetration or a single sale, direct marketing is normally a long-term commitment. Directional approaches that allow communication to known consumer types include:

- ❏ direct mail;
- ❏ direct response TV, radio and press;
- ❏ clubs, societies and organisations;
- ❏ telemarketing;
- ❏ local store marketing;
- ❏ other IT led promotions;

The responses we might hope to achieve are:

- ❏ a direct sale;
- ❏ an indirect sale;

❐   product or service trial;
❐   requests for information, quotes or demonstrations;
❐   attendance to a show, shop or event;
❐   enhancement of product image;
❐   the establishment of a longer-term relationship.

Direct mail

Commonly confused with direct marketing of which it is but a part, direct mail is still big business. It accounted for 10.6 per cent of advertising expenditure in 1991 and the spend in 1992 was £945 million (source: DMIS). The split was approximately two-thirds production and one-third postage.

Consumer direct mail

Consumer mailings account for approximately two-thirds of all direct mail expenditure. When the consumer gets it, 80 per cent is opened, 63 per cent is opened and read, and 29 per cent is passed on to someone else (source: DMIS Trends Survey 1992).

Direct mail is highly prevalent in charities and service industries such as entertainment, travel, financial markets, retail via catalogue shopping, telephone shopping and in high ticket items such as cars. Noteworthy is the fact that 7.7 per cent of mailings are by retailers and 5.8 per cent by manufacturers (source: Royal Mail).

It is less prevalent in fmcg markets which, in order to recoup the high investment per customer, requires products that have:

❐   high unit price;
❐   high frequency of purchase;
❐   high margin;
❐   a propensity towards high loyalty;
❐   high appeal to a definable target group.

Individual fmcg purchases are unlikely to pay back and the lifetime value of a customer needs to be the measure against which costs are judged. However, if we can deliver a relevant message to someone we know is likely to be interested in the product, we can afford to incentivise them heavily and cut out a lot of waste.

The key to making direct mail work is to make it wanted or appreciated.

Humans love their pets and a number of petfood manufacturers have built up databases of pet owners. If Pedigree petfoods sends a birthday card out to a cat they are bound to endear themselves as a manufacturer who is trying to show they care about pussy as an individual. Nestle's brand Friskies has used a database established via a door drop sampling exercise into a mailing list for *Tails*, 'the pet owners magazine from Friskies petfood'. They have used this to establish a relationship with the consumer. This has a head start on becoming cost effective versus other media since the penetration of petfood is low. Mass media would involve a lot of wastage putting up the cost per consumer. This targeting aspect is important. Another example is nappy manufacturers who have been highly active in this area and the maintenance of a continued relationship with mums must have helped the market share of Pampers. However, the case for fmcg direct mail is far from proven, but with big players like Nestle coming in via petfood and also their Buitoni pasta products, the interest is warming up.

Business direct mail

Business communications account for about one-third of all direct mail. The big users are suppliers of business services, business goods and office equipment, insurance, accommodation, travel and conferences.

The average manager receives 14 items of direct mail per week at work. When it is received most is opened (91 per cent) and a lot is redirected to a colleague (28 per cent). The biggest single action is to bin it, often without even opening it as the recipient can see what it is from the outside and knows it is of little value or recognises it is a duplicate. Poor targeting of business direct mail is one of the main reasons for it being discarded. About 10 per cent is filed or responded to (source: DMIS Business Attitudes to Direct Mail 1991).

Response rates and costs of direct mail

Traditionally, a 2 per cent response figure has been a benchmark for direct mail. In fact the variation can be enormous from zero to high double figures and the indications are that average responses are higher than 2 per cent. A survey carried out by *Precision Marketing* in conjunction with the Direct Mail Information Service (DMIS)found the average campaign response was 7.28 per cent and the average from all responses was 5.09 per cent,

The cost of creating and mailing a direct mail package is high, and the survey found them varying from around 40p to £10 costs with an average of around £1, while the DMIS average is about 43p. The survey's cost per response had an astronomic £59.27 average. Having said that, £60 is not a lot to invest in selling an expensive item like a boat and many responses will cost far less. Response rates and cost efficiency can be boosted by many factors, for example:

❏   mailing known responders;
❏   mailing existing users rather than cold lists;
❏   improved targeting;
❏   incentivising responses, eg with prizes and offers;
❏   having easy response devices, eg freephone and freepost.

Direct response

Direct response is all about getting the consumer to self-select and actively respond to you directly after seeing your promotional message. The likely responses being sought are:

❏   a direct sale;
❏   a quote;
❏   a trial offer;
❏   a request for a demonstration or more product information;
❏   stockist details.

All of these might be supplemented with some sort of additional promotion to encourage response.
    The medium might be:

❏   in the press;
❏   on television;
❏   on the radio;
❏   on posters.

This area is typified by the ad in the colour supplement for the mail order rowing machine (mine is rusting in the garage), or the new car with a number for a brochure or test drive. Radio and TV are becoming more common, usually offering toll-free numbers to ask about services such as car insurance or mobile telephones. New ground is being broken all the time and this is a growth area; direct response television (DRTV) in particular is growing. One innovative ad I saw recently offered a toll-free number to call to get your free sample of dog food. Direct response can be phenomenally successful, examples I saw reported in *Marketing* (3 December 1991) include two insertions by the Scarborough Building Society pulling in £6.96 million, full page ads from Rover offering a prize car as an incentive attracting 120,000 showroom visitors and a questionnaire on headache problems in a *Sunday Express* 'health book' got Glaxo 110,000 names for a database.

Clubs societies and organisations

Where you have an established base of people with a common interest there are clearly opportunities to market to them with a fair degree of confidence that an appealing offer can be put together. Regular communication should be able to maintain their interest and fidelity to your brand, or so the theory goes. In reality long-running clubs relating to consumer goods are rarely successful. The ones that do best are where collectables are established or when there is a strong personality involved such as with fan clubs; brands rarely have this degree of interest. The types of clubs that are viable tend to be selling media eg for books or recordings.

One area of heavy promotional activity is that aimed at children. Here there are large numbers of clubs, such as *The Sunday Times* Funday Times Club, the Woolworth Kids Club, and the Heinz baby club. Kids tend to enjoy belonging to something and obviously receiving post is a novelty at a young age. Promoting to kids provides the opportunity of pester power where the kids nag their poor parents to buy particular toys and goods.

Setting up a club is a long-term commitment. It may be easy to set something up but you need to be prepared to carry through. Otherwise how do you sign off without damaging the relationship with some of your customers, undoubtedly the best ones? It is wise to consider carefully whether to avoid regular communications, eg monthly magazines and making future promises. Kids are often promoted to via schools under the guise of educational aids which are much welcomed by under-funded schools. I remember my information pack on cocoa beans and chocolate from Cadbury's, which left a lasting impact.

Telemarketing

Telemarketing will either be inbound or outbound, run in-house or by specialist agencies. Despite often getting, occasionally justifiable, bad press, this type of marketing is on the increase and standards are rising as the industry rallies to ensure there are codes of practice.

A survey performed by telemarketing company Adlink and reported on in *Marketing* (19 December 1992) among the top 200 advertisers showed 63 per cent had used telemarketing and four out of five intended to do so in the future. Indeed, three-quarters saw it as a permanent part of their marketing strategy.

Inbound

Inbound calls generally stem from the type of direct response promotions outlined above.

A list of key promotional uses for inbound calls is:

- the supply of brochures and information packs;
- the supply of on-line information;
- customer care;
- order taking;
- staking claims or registering for a promotion;
- lead generation for follow-up communication by mail or personal call;
- competitions.

Outbound

This is the domain of selling and information gathering.

The types of calls that may be made are:

- order taking (telesales);
- lead generation;
- making appointments;
- list building;
- market research and surveys;
- customer care;
- updating records (list cleaning);
- as a follow up to other activities, eg mail shots.

Linking to direct mail

Outbound calls in particular are often linked to direct mail campaigns.

Sometimes it is appropriate that the telephone call precedes the mail package, eg to confirm the correct person or address for a mailing, or to confirm who the decision maker is in an organisation. At other times a telephone call will follow the mail package, eg to ensure the information has been received and understood, and to elicit the level of interest and hopefully an order.

Charges

There are a number of charging systems, which are explored in more detail in Chapters 11 and 12. The three principle formats are toll-free, local call and premium call rates.

Toll-free calls are where the consumer does not pay for the call. Examples of where these are especially useful include:

❑   *for customer generation* - eg First Direct have used toll-free numbers extensively in their recruitment drive for banking customers;

❑   *urgent help-lines* - specially where the caller may not be at home or have money available for a call, eg Norwich Union's insurance helpline; and Auto glass windscreen repairs;

❑   *the establishment of customer care programmes* - these are valuable where there are long-term relationships. Large numbers of fmcg manufacturers in a truly TQ move are now putting toll-free numbers on their products to encourage consumers to call in with any enquiries they have.

In promotional terms, toll-free numbers are most typically used where more budget per item is available, eg in driving market penetration, sales and sales leads, but clearly service enhancement and customer care are important in building customer loyalty. They have the advantage that more space on ads and promotional literature can be directed to the message rather than spent on a response coupon, although sometimes it is worth offering alternative response methods.

Local call rates are less often used promotionally. Here the charges are made at local rates no matter where the call is made from. This is particularly appropriate for on-going relationships where the customer accepts that there will be costs associated with the service, recognises it has value to them and is therefore worth paying for. For example, once First Direct has established its user base the day-to-day telephone banking service is at local call rates. Premium call rates are the most commonly associated with promotions, not always favourably. Charges are subject to a premium and are generally used as a cash generator. This might be for a competition where the call funds the prizes. I believe the consumer is beginning to see through this practice and this form of activity seems to be dropping away. In other instances high value information might be on offer.

Advantages and disadvantages of telemarketing

Advantages:

❑   cheaper than a personal call;

❑   customers can respond when they want to;

❏   the operator response can be adjusted according to consumer needs;

❏   messages can be got out quickly, eg if responding to a competitive threat;

❏   responses can be received quickly after the call stimulus as there are no forms to fill in;

❏   easy for the consumer, telephones are generally closer to hand than postboxes and calls easier to make than filling in forms;

❏   easy and quick to expand the geographic operational boundaries, eg national from a regional or national to international.

Disadvantages:

❏   sometimes has a negative image;

❏   some people don't like using the telephone;

❏   some consumers see calls to their home as an invasion of privacy;

❏   cost to the caller can be higher than the post;

❏   inbound peaks following direct response messages eg on TV can result in peaks that cannot be handled economically, ie some customer loss will occur;

❏   telephone numbers can be difficult to remember or inconvenient to jot down.

Local store marketing

With the advent of technology has come a much greater ability to analyse an individual outlet's sales patterns and the typologies of the customers shopping there. The shoppers who visit a Tesco in Bournemouth with a high retirement population will not the same as one in an inner London catchment area. Stores need to be able to tailor the products stocked, their merchandising and their promotions to suit these different audiences.

A big superstore might carry 15-20,000 lines, but most shoppers probably only buy a hundred or so with any regularity. The ability to focus on individuals can provide for great efficiency in promotional spend, however it is very complex to work with and IT will be the way to facilitate this in the long term.

8

Application Principles Explored

After we have looked at the four media families, we can now look at the following list of promotional application principles which qualify the way in which the rewards and media options can be combined.

- ❐ *Trial gaining* - the how and what of getting products tried.
- ❐ *Targeting* - the above media can all have varying degrees of targeting, and the principles of this are discussed here.
- ❐ *Technology*- the impact of information technology (IT) on promotional communications.
- ❐ *Joint activity*- the opportunities afforded by working in part-nership with another product or organisation are sufficiently different to require a special mention.
- ❐ *Redemptions*- some of the influences, including proofs of purchase, on redemption levels on offer types.
- ❐ *Buy-outs*- this is a method of fixing budget commitments.
- ❐ *Promotion types to match objectives*- which promotions will satisfy the promotional need.

TRIAL GAINING

There are essentially three ways of getting people to try your product. Give it to them free (remove the risk), incentivise them to buy it or give it enough kudos to ensure that people want to go out and buy it.

The number of ways of expressing these inducements and of getting the message across are legion. Figure 8.1 illustrates some examples of the possible combinations.

Issues concerning trial gaining include:

- ❐ the cost per worthwhile trialist (see model in Chapter 10);
- ❐ any additional benefit of the selected technique, eg media benefit to existing users, distribution gains etc;
- ❐ wastage, what doesn't get to the target;

- ❏ consumer motivation;
- ❏ environment it is tried in;
- ❏ further calls to action;
- ❏ consonance with brand image;
- ❏ quantity needed to convince;
- ❏ timing, eg versus launch or advertising;
- ❏ distribution and availability of product.

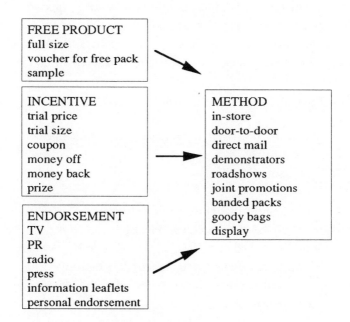

Figure 8.1 The what and how of trial gaining

And also for trial sizes:

- ❏ value for money versus normal product;
- ❏ reason for purchase, eg travel rather than trial;
- ❏ expense of set-up costs;
- ❏ whether product benefits are clear;
- ❏ if distribution is guaranteed.

TARGETING

No matter how powerful the promotional message it will not be effective for you if the right people do not see it or if the wrong people respond. Because of this, targeting your promotional message can offer significantly enhanced promotional efficiency. Targeting is a highly TQ oriented approach allowing companies to get really close to and understand their customers.

Targeting can be achieved by buying lists or building your own database. The data on it may be used directly or other data sources applied to profile list members. Once profiled you can take specific action according to their different descriptions. You can develop your own systems, but typically promoters will, at least in part, overlay commercial classification systems to profile their databases.

The primary uses and applications of targeting for promoters are:

- ❐ locating prospective promotional respondents;
- ❐ door drops;
- ❐ direct mail;
- ❐ telemarketing;
- ❐ promotions linked to specific stores;
- ❐ decisions on media locations, eg poster sites;
- ❐ profiling customer lists, eg buyers, non-buyers. Often using a profile of known responders or non-responders, databases are checked against these profiles to choose likely or avoid unlikely candidates on a new list;
- ❐ finding promotional partners, eg matching for joint promotions;
- ❐ finding suitable rewards by understanding the consumer's interests;
- ❐ evaluation, eg the profile of promotional respondents.

There are three key issues driving targeting.

- ❐ *Accuracy* - most targeting is not 100 per cent accurate, as even databases are subject to inaccuracies. Targeting systems are limited geographically and also because classifications are not always based on known data but on modelled data. To cost out the efficiency gains versus the cost of targeting it is important to have an idea of the degree of accuracy. All other things being equal, the degree of accuracy will dictate the response rate.

❑ *Understanding your target* - to ascertain the degree of accuracy you will need a benchmark of who your target market is. In reality this is often hard to define precisely and you will have to accept that you are buying a tendency towards an improved focus of activity. It will be through the evaluation of response rates that the true level of efficiency improvements will begin to emerge.

❑ *Cost* - targeting is costly but if effective will cut waste and generate efficiency. Unsurprisingly the cost usually goes up as the degree of targeting goes up. The promoter has to trade one against the other to decide the optimum route.

The inter-relationship between these three factors is illustrated in Figure 8.2.

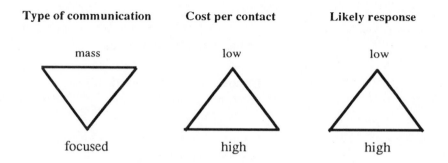

Type of communication   **Cost per contact**   **Likely response**

mass   low   low

focused   high   high

Figure 8.2 The dynamics of targeting

The geographic building blocks of targeting

To target consumers we need to identify where they are. The main two building blocks of targeting systems are census and postal geography.

Census geography

A lot of the information used in targeting systems uses the basic data available from the government's national Census of Population as a foundation. On this is overlaid a vast range of other data from all the various sources that each targeting system will have bought or built up.

Not all information in the census is made available commercially, but a wide range of information on housing type, household composition, occupation and various socioeconomic indicators is accessible.

Census information is available using a specific geography to define groups of people. The census building blocks are enumeration districts (EDs), each containing about 160-200 households. This is the smallest level for which census information is publicly available. There are approximately 130,000 such EDs. The EDs are aggregated up into wards, then local authorities, then counties. The information is held by the Office of Population Censuses and Surveys (OPCS). In Scotland the data structure is slightly different and the information held by the General Register Office (GRO).

Postal geography

Unfortunately most applications of the databased information have to be related to postal geography for implementation, eg mailings, door drops. Postal geography is based on postcodes, and the boundaries and size of each postcode or group of postcodes will not match up exactly with census geography. The structure of a postcode number AB12 3CD is as follows:

Outward code:	AB	Identifies to 120 postcode areas, each with around 192,000 households.
	AB12	Identifies to 2,900 districts, with an average of 7,930 households each.
Inward code:	AB12 3	Identifies to 9,000 sectors, with an average of 2,550 households each.
	AB12 3CD	Identifies to 1.6 million units, eg groups of around 15 houses or large users with their own dedicated postcode.

Because the two systems do not match perfectly, much work has to be done by the targeting companies to get as good a match as possible. The quality of, say, a geodemographic targeting system may depend on the quality of this matching. Since postcodes change, constant updating of records is important.

Base data for targeting

In addition to knowing where the consumer is, we need to know facts about them. Data sources include:

- ❐ census data;
- ❐ survey data, eg questionnaires;
- ❐ market research data;

❐ financial data, eg county court judgments;
❐ owned databases;
❐ any other databases.

Different sets of geographic and base data are combined in many different ways by the various targeting companies.

The data are also available at different levels of detail. Many of the targeting systems can be used for the same types of end purpose. You need to consider what is suitable for the task in hand, whether the data are robust enough and whether they represent good value. If you are running a door drop which operates at the postcode sector level, it is unlikely that you will go down to a very fine level of detail when targeting. If a mailing is planned then a greater degree of analysis will be required to identify prospects. Geographically, postcode sectors are likely to be too big and variable an area to justify a mailing at this level.

Types of targeting

There are four main families of targeting.

❐ *Geographic* - where the target is physically located.
❐ *Socioeconomic* - social and economic status of the target.
❐ *Geodemographic* - classification of people based on where they live.
❐ *Questionnaire based lifestyle/behaviourgraphic* - based on what people do or say they do.

These can be used in isolation or combined. There are ready-made systems which utilise more than one type or you can buy into more than one compatible system and overlay them.

These targeting types are are looked at in more detail below. There are many commercial systems available and a few of the more widely used ones are touched upon below to illustrate the principles of how these systems are structured. There are many others and your direct promotional marketing specialist can advise.

Geographic targeting

This is the basic location of individuals (or businesses). It requires locational information about those individuals and a map to apply it to. Geographic targeting, or the use of geographic information systems (GIS), is based on highly sophisticated computerised mapping. The types of bases that might be used for this are:

❐   county;
❐   sales area;
❐   TV region;
❐   independent commercial radio region;
❐   major urban areas;
❐   retail catchment area;
❐   postcode geography;
❐   your own described boundaries.

One of the major uses of geographic targeting is door dropping around nominated retailers and individual stores. This can be done geographically by simply drawing a circle around the store, but more accurate are such calculations as drive time. This will take into account such influences as motorway connections and so the mapping also needs to detail infrastructure information.
Data sources include:

❐   your own data;
❐   Address-point (grid references for individual postal addresses) from Ordnance Survey;
❐   basic mapping systems from all the major geodemographic companies;
❐   Central Postcode Directory (CPD) from the Post Office gives map references for postcodes;
❐   various business reference sources, eg:
    - GOAD PLANS (retail outlet information) from Chas E Goad Ltd
    - Retail Locations (retail outlet information)
    - IGD (grocery outlet information)
    - Dun and Bradstreet (business information)
    - Connections in Business (business information) from BT's *Yellow Pages*.

Socioeconomic targeting

A very broad based classification with many limitations, eg it has a poor measure of disposable income and attitudes.
There are various socioeconomic grading systems, as follows.

IPA social grade:

A	Upper middle class	Higher managerial, administrative or professional.
B	Middle class	Intermediate managerial, administrative or professional.
C1	Lower middle class	Supervisory or clerical, junior managerial, administration or professional.
C2	Skilled working class	Skilled manual workers.
D	Working class	Semi-skilled and unskilled manual workers.
E	Those at lowest level of subsistence	State pensioners or widows and widowers (no other earner), casual or lowest grade workers.

Census definitions of socioeconomic groups:

SEG 1   employers and managers in central and local government, industry, commerce etc - large establishments;

SEG 2   employers and managers in industry, commerce etc - small establishments;

SEG 3   professional workers - self-employed;

SEG 4   professional workers - employees;

SEG 5   intermediate non-manual workers
5.1 ancillary workers and artists
5.2 foremen and supervisors, non-manual;

SEG 6   junior non-manual workers;

SEG 7   personal service workers;

SEG 8   foremen and supervisors, manual;

SEG 9   skilled manual workers;

SEG 10   semi-skilled manual workers;

SEG 11   unskilled manual workers;

SEG 12   own account workers (other than professional);

SEG 13   farmers - employers and managers;

SEG 14   farmers - own account;

SEG 15   agricultural workers;
SEG 16   members of the armed forces;
SEG 17   inadequately described or non-stated occupations.

Retired and permanently sick are classified according to their previous occupation.

Geodemographic systems

These are based on the principle 'you are where you live'. The theory is that by classifying the housing type you can identify similar groups of people with similar values. Different systems will choose different data from the census and other sources, and combine it in different ways to come up with their own classification systems. They will choose data sources that discriminate well for the end use.

The classifications will often be at more than one level, ie there may be a large number of groups defined using clusters of people with similar attributes. Then these clusters may be aggregated up into just a few sub-sets. The different levels of discrimination will be useful for different applications dependent on the degree of targeting that is appropriate. This is illustrated below for ACORN Lifestyles. Other systems have similar multi-level structures.

The basic building blocks are based on census data. Consequently there is a need to update as new census data leads to significant changes.

Using the example of the door drop around a store, provided a suitable system was used, you could match the characteristics of people within the catchment area and drop to those areas with a higher proportion of people having the same profile as your brand's target market.

The application of research data can enrich the strength of the match to your target. Different research data can be matched to a number different targeting systems but not necessarily all. The suppliers of the service can advise. You may wish to take this into account when deciding on which targeting approach to adopt.

Such research options includes:

❑   the Target Group Index (TGI);
❑   AGB Superpanel;
❑   Nielsen Homescan;
❑   BARB for TV audience measure;
❑   NRS for newspaper and magazine readership;
❑   FRS for the financial services market.

Some of the more commonly used geodemographic systems are as follows.

ACORN
This is a 'Classification of Residential Neighbourhoods' available from CACI. This uses 40 key census variables, eg age, sex, housing type, socio-economic status, household characteristics etc, to classify people at the ED level into 38 neighbourhood types which can be aggregated up into 11 neighbourhood groups. Consumers' postcodes are used as the location device and these are allocated to the nearest ED.

ACORN Lifestyles
A newer option from CACI. It uses the electoral role, ACORN information plus MONICA (a model that predicts people's ages from their given names) to provide 6 neighbourhood types, 24 lifestyle groups and 81 lifestyle types.

The six neighbourhood types are:

Rural areas and villages	Suburbia
Council areas	Metropolitan and cosmopolitan city
Traditional urban households	Homesharers

These are then subdivided, eg the neighbourhood type 'traditional urban households' contains 4 lifestyle groups containing 12 lifestyle types:

Group: LS Younger urban singles
Type: - LS61 men
             - LS62 women

Group: LT Older urban singles
Type: - LT63 men
             - LT64 women

Group: LU Younger traditional urban couples and families
Type: - LU65 youngest couples
              - LU66 youngest couples with elderly person
              - LU67 maturing couples
              - LU68 maturing families

Group: LV Older traditional urban couples and families
Type: - LV69 established couples
               - LV70 established families with older children
               - LV71 retired couples
               - LV72 retired families

PiN

'Pinpoint identified neighbourhoods' from Pinpoint uses 104 key census variables to produce classifications at the 12, 25 and 60 level. The correlation of EDs and postcodes has been argued to be more accurate than some other systems, improving the efficiency of the targeting.

FiNPiN

Also from Pinpoint, FiNPiN is used for financial services and 58 census variables are used. The database is clustered into 40 demographic groups and then aggregated up into 10 and 4 levels on a financial base.

GEOPIN 2

This links PiN and FiNPiN with such information as Target Group Index (TGI) data, and AA roadmap information.

MOSAIC

Available from CCN, in addition to census data, for example it has county court judgments and other credit worthiness information. It segments the population into 58 neighbourhood types within 10 groupings.

Questionnaire based lifestyle/behaviourgraphic systems

Questionnaire based databases are limited in size by the number of responses. However, sometimes the database is expanded by linking in the list to the electoral role and other sources such as the big geodemographic databases. Questionnaire respondents can then be profiled against these lists and a bigger database modelled according to similar characteristics as defined by the geodemographic database.

Taking the door drop example a stage further, if you have the data you could in theory also choose to drop to areas where you actually know which shop consumers normally use and which brands they buy.

The Lifestyle Selector

NDL offer this system. It has largely been built up using over nine million questionnaires built into warranty cards for brown and white goods. There are over 140 demographic and lifestyle discriminators in the system ,and it can be used at various levels for door-to-door, direct mail and similar applications.

The Facts of Living Survey

This is a multi-media distributed questionnaire by ICD. This contains information on such things as household composition, type of housing, occupation, home appliances, financial interests, leisure interests etc.

The National Shoppers Survey (NSS)

This database of over three million households from CMT is based on a multi-media distributed questionnaire, usually incentivised by the promise of coupons. It contains lifestyle details as well as specific branded information about shopping habits, often paid for by sponsoring manufacturers. It has spawned a number of other products from the CMT stable.

Behaviourbank

This allows access to the CMT database to select consumers by demographics, lifestyles and various other special selections.

PERSONA

Using over 100 lifestyle and demographic criteria, PERSONA from CMT has described 20 distinct types of behaviourgraphically distinct consumer:

Cultural Travellers	Crisps and Videos	Young Affluentials
Golf Clubs and Volvos	Bon Viveurs	Tradition and Charity
Achievers	Trinkets and Treasures	New Techers
Safe and Sensible	Health and Humanities	Craftsmen and Home-
Carry on Camping	Wildlife Trustees	makers
Fads and Fashions	Home and Gardent	Field and Stream
Survivors	Retired Villagers	Pubs, Pool and Bingo

PERSONA Geotargeting

Here CCN has linked the PERSONA information to the MOSAIC neighbourhood classification system, plus other geographical options to provide a life-style input to geodemographic systems.

INFORMATION TECHNOLOGY LED PROMOTIONS

Smart cards and other plastic cards

Plastic cards can carry a wide range of technology based messaging systems and may be used for a variety of promotional purposes. The size of credit cards they are highly tactile and have retentive value. Devices are needed to extract the information from the card (readers) and to add information (writers).

The types of card available are listed below.

- ☐ *Printed cards* - ordinary plastic cards printed with a promotional message, eg a discount card.

- ☐ *Bar code cards* - cards with a printed bar code carrying data such as a unique membership number. This might qualify the holder or selected holders to special discounts or offers.

- ☐ *Magnetic strip cards* - like cashpoint cards, they carry encoded information in a magnetic strip on the back of the card. This can then be passed through a reader/writer device and messages read, added or taken away. This is still a fairly cheap device with cards costing only a few pence, readers tens of pounds and writers a few hundred pounds.This is the type of system the petrol companies have used for points collector cards, eg the Argos/Mobil Premier Points system. The memory is low level, maybe only a couple of hundred characters, but if required the back-up intelligence in the reader/writer can be quite sophisticated.

- ☐ *Laser cards* - here a laser melts pits into a reflective surface. The pits are digitally encoded and read back by laser, rather like a CD. A lot of data can be put on a card, maybe 2 megabytes. The cards will cost in excess of £1 and the reader/writers will be more expensive than for magnetic strip cards. Once encoded the data cannot be changed, but more data can be added.

- ☐ *Optical cards* - these are like BT Phonecards, where the data are destroyed as they are read. A large memory capacity is possible and they are useful for a wide variety of credit type facilities.

- ☐ *Integrated chip (IC) card* - these contain a silicon chip and are available in two sorts. The simpler is the cheaper memory-only chip, which can contain many thousands of characters but it is likely to be used for a single application, eg French telephone cards. The other is the true 'smart card'. This contains a memory and a microprocessor.

- ☐ *Smart cards* - these will cost a few pounds each but they have large memory capacity, a variety of functions and data can be loaded, unloaded and read. The reader/writers are relatively low cost. Interaction could be by inserting into a physical port, eg at a special point in a supermarket or even read at a distance via electronic signals. There are four main uses:
  - service, eg medical records, membership records etc;
  - security, eg as a pass;

- financial, eg as an electronic purse holding credits which can be purchased and topped up;
- retail, which is the big area for the promoter.

These cards offer enormous potential for promotions because of their adaptability and the depth of information they can hold, for example details of products purchased and how often. This will allow very specific targeting of offers.

Multi-media

In-store radio and television has been used for some time with mixed results. These media can be annoying or irrelevant and even the promotional videotaped demonstration can be a bit of a turn off as the consumer cannot interact or adjust the sequence of the message or find out more information.

One advance on this is based on interactive video systems that allow all types of information and transactions to occur at the press of a few buttons or even by touchscreens. Written information can be provided and even moving pictures can be shown from hard disc or CD sources.

This approach is a step on the way to shopless shopping. No longer is a fully merchandised retail environment required. The shopper accesses an in-store video screen console which provides information to help them select their goods. This can potentially extend product choice while minimising stockholding at individual outlets. Such systems could allow shoppers to make their purchases from the screen via a swipe of the credit card or print off a list for the sales team to deal with personally. Apart from reducing the demands on sales assistants, such systems will be accurate, ie not reliant on the salesperson's memory, and will be capable of announcing all sorts of promotional offers related to the shoppers' areas of interest.

Systems of this type are being developed mainly for retail application, but in due course may well have 'desk-to-desk' applications in business-to-business promotions.

ESEL

Electronic shelf-edge labelling (ESEL) is likely to be one of the next major steps in the progress of technology based cost savings in the supermarket environment. Hard wired or remote controlled labels will be able to have their prices checked and updated instantly. This will ensure accuracy and, most important from a promotion stand-point, flexibility. With suitable announcements, the retailer will be able to make special offers happen and ensure the shopper knows about it in seconds.

Electronic screens on shopping trolleys

Here small video screens are carried on the handles of shopping trolleys, as the shopper passes trigger points in store, offers and messages are flashed up on screen.

Interactive TV

Beyond direct response to television advertisements, and conveniently languishing at home, lies interactive TV. Here the participant will actually communicate to the promoter via the TV itself, probably by a touchscreen or keypad. This may be to place an order (home shopping) to be delivered or collected later, request information or actively participate in some activity.

Intelligent packaging

An example of intelligent packaging includes a system where tiny microchips are incorporated into goods at manufacture. As a security device these electronic tags could be deactivated at the checkout, but otherwise would raise an alarm. Such a device is translatable to promotions, eg with products carrying special promotional messages or proofs of purchase locked up inside the microchips.

JOINT PROMOTIONS

Types of joint promotion

A summary of the main types available includes:

- ❏ outright sponsorship (covered under image based rewards, above);
- ❏ press/radio barter deals/TV programme sponsorship (covered above);
- ❏ product placement (covered above);
- ❏ cinema and video link-ups (see above);
- ❏ use of other organisations' and businesses' facilities;
- ❏ promotions advertised via other products or services.

The last two are the most classic sorts of joint promotion and are where some of the biggest opportunities lie.

This is where partnership or affinity marketing can flourish. The principle is simple and creates added value for the promoters participating by sharing the creation and implementation costs. By combining forces the partners can often make offers that would be unaffordable to them individually and help each other achieve mutual objectives.

Most of the usual rewards can be offered in this way. Providing a free sample to the customers of another business may provide the opportunity for both targeting and cheap sample distribution. The recipient business may be happy to distribute the samples free as they are getting an added value promotion at a knock-down price.

Others may wish to run the same offer across a range of products, thus increasing the scale of the promotion, sharing the set-up costs and offering extended opportunities for proofs of purchase. This is the classic 'multi-brand' which has tended to fade away as companies realise the complexities and timing problems in implementation, and the difficulties inherent in trying to drive more than one set of product purchases.

Free and part-funded joint promotions

One of the most popular approaches is to offer a reward of high perceived value that in reality is virtually free for all parties. This is typified in the travel and accommodation industries. Getting bums on empty seats is a good way to build awareness and usage of a travel medium: after all if the train/plane/boat or bus is going anyway the additional cost of extra passengers is minimal. As far as accommodation is concerned these promotions have the potential to pay for themselves, eg a number of agencies offer free accommodation with the caveat that you must eat in the hotel. The small cost of filling the empty room needs to be offset by the incremental business derived from the meals.

In some cases it may be possible to offer a reward and end up with a free promotion! We can illustrate how this might work in a fictitious promotion between Sam's shoe stores and the National Omnibus Co-operative (NOC). Sam's wants to sell its walking shoes and the NOC wants to boost awareness and customers taking their bus trips to the mountains which are currently only part full. Therefore the deal is hatched that with every pair of Sam's walking shoes they are offering a buy one get one free bus ride to the mountains with the NOC. The sums, as worked out in Figure 8.3, show how the promotional reward is free-funded, leaving Sam's and NOC simply to work out how to split the costs of getting the promotion out to the consumer. Obviously careful research has to be carried out to ensure there are not too many freeloaders. However get the balance right, and what appears to be a massive scale promotion to the consumer can cost very little.

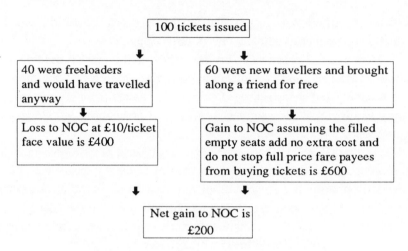

Figure 8.3 How joint promotions can self-fund

Issues relating to joint promotions

There are certain things to match up when proposing a joint activity.

❑   *Brand image* - the images of all parties must be sympathetic to one another.

❑   *Target market* - the customer base should have similar profiles.

❑   *Size match* - brands should have similar stature or else you run the risk of one being lost within the other.

❑   *Quality/quantity trade-off* - you may be able to trade-off the size of the opportunity against the quality of the target audience match.

❑   *Distribution match* - for fmcg brands in a retail environment, normally the distribution of the carrier brand should not exceed that of the carried brand. Otherwise consumers may not be able to find the carried brand when they wish to make a later purchase. However, in some cases seeking partners with wider distribution may provide opportunities to extend distribution. If the partner is a retail outlet or service then all consumers seeing the offer need to have access to the outlet/service or alternative arrangements offered. Equal distribution is usually best.

A cautionary note

It is particularly important to ensure consumers are not disappointed when running holiday, flight and other service types of promotion.

Unavailability of rooms or flights etc, difficulty or restrictions in making bookings are all going to count against the promotion and make the consumer question the value of the offer. This is quite likely to result in negative associations with the brand, especially if the promotion has been part of the factor influencing a high value purchase or an extended period of loyalty.

Truly effective promotions of this type must be capable of delivering their promises. Due attention should be paid to the danger and poor quality approach of making the budget work by relying on large drop-out rates from consumers who find the deal too complex. Likewise, if you are placing your trust in a supplier who has calculated their costs based on a risk calculation of the number of applicants, you could end up with a bust supplier who cannot deliver your promise. Bailing them out will be expensive.

Advantages and disadvantages

The advantages and disadvantages of joint promotions can be summarised as follows.

Advantages:
- ❑   set-up, publicity and administration costs can be shared;
- ❑   more than one partner creates greater visibility;
- ❑   bigger scale allows economies to be made in buying etc;
- ❑   partners can build on each other's franchise and potentially extend their user base;
- ❑   rewards may be available free/cheaply;
- ❑   risk can be shared between the partners.

Disadvantages:
- ❑   poor matches may be detrimental to the image of one party;
- ❑   complex to implement and administer;
- ❑   time-consuming to set up and long lead times often required,
- ❑   legal contract necessary to protect the interests of both parties.

Joint promotions tend to have either long or short lead times. The latter are particularly difficult to set up as most organisations plan their budget commitments some way ahead. In these situations an off-the-peg joint promotion may be the answer, eg offers from the leisure and travel industry.

REDEMPTION LEVELS (INCLUDING COUPONS)

This old chestnut is the hardest nut of all to crack. To make a fact based decision relies on the TQ check. Only by evaluation and recording what happens is it possible to make a sensible prediction against future activity.

Issues that will affect the number of redemptions are included in the checklist.

Checklist of redemption influences

☐ *simplicity and clarity of understanding of the offer;*
☐ *ease of participation, ie barriers to entry;*
☐ *creativity, ie originality and presentation of the offer;*
☐ *publicity and awareness of the offer;*
☐ *strength of offer;*
☐ *strength of brand;*
☐ *relevance to those exposed to the offer;*
☐ *availability (distribution) of the offer;*
☐ *competitive activity;*
☐ *relevance of the offer to the brand and its marketing needs;*
☐ *support from the trade and sales team;*
☐ *the number of entry opportunities;*
☐ *the number of proofs of purchase required.*

Information sources

There is nothing to beat experience, so if you do not have it on record within your organisation you will have to go out and find it. There are two routes to do this.

First the promotion can be tested. Qualitative research to determine the most suitable or check the gross negatives in a short-list of promotional ideas is well established. Quantitative research to predict consumer reaction is more difficult because people do not always do as they say they will and because their reaction in the real world may be tempered by all sorts of topical issues such as the economy, current affairs and the environment in which it is presented. The best way to get a real measure is to run a test market, either geographical or as a short run. This will provide reasonably robust data, but it takes time to run, review and roll-out and is likely only to be considered for the biggest of promotions.

The second source of information is buying in experience. This will include other, more experienced, promoters, established agencies, and handling houses. They will be wrong but probably more right than you. However, be sure the experience is really there and beware the over-optimistic agency telling you how wonderful their promotion is and how high the redemptions will be. That is unless you are happy to end up with a warehouse full of promotional stock.

Number of proofs of purchase required

Getting the number required right is usually a product of experience. In very broad terms, the essential dynamics are that high levels of POPs will give low redemptions primarily from highly disposed customers, ie loyals, and conversely a low POP requirement will give high redemptions, from no/low loyalty applicants. This is illustrated in Figure 8.4.

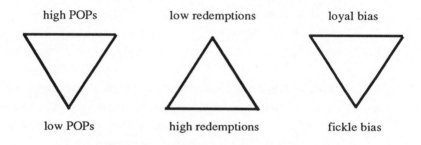

Figure 8.4 The effect of proof of purchase level

Redemption truisms

Because every market, brand and offer is different it is impossible to be precise about redemption rates for most offers, but here are some general observations. While they will not be robust for all situations, they are worth considering or disproving before you set off down a particular route:

- ❏ competitions and SLPs redeem at similar levels and at about one-fifth or one-sixth the rate of free sendaways;
- ❏ offers requiring only one proof of purchase will redeem three or four times, as well as offers requiring multiple POPs;
- ❏ cross promotions within brand ranges redeem higher than those between brands;
- ❏ cross promotions do not redeem as high as promotions on one brand and rarely as high as you think they will;

❐   hardly anyone asks for their money back on a money-back guarantee;

❐   on-packs redeem more strongly than door drops (three or four times as strong for instant redemption, more for send aways);

❐   door drops redeem more strongly than press promotions (two or three times as strongly);

❐   asking for postage on a FMI will not affect the redemption rate a great deal, so long as it is easy for the consumer to send it in;

❐   starter tokens can encourage people to begin collecting;

❐   outlet specific offers redeem lower than national offers (usually);

❐   outlet specific offers run outside the store environment will redeem much lower than those inside the store (1:20 ratio);

❐   less than 80 per cent of people who have asked for a free product voucher will redeem it;

❐   promotions directed at promotionally responsive people get higher redemption rates, eg bouncebacks (offer included within the redemption pack of other offers), offers sent to known promotional responders;

❐   competitions with complex tie-breakers get low redemption rates;

❐   free draws redeem several times more highly than competitions;

❐   the most attractive competition prizes are first cash, then houses, cars, holidays, others. Exceptions will be prizes that have a specific appeal and relevance for the product user;

❐   promotions appealing to altruism, eg charity offers redeem poorly unless there is something in it for the consumer as well;

❐   coupons have been subject to more research and discussion than any other offer (some detailed findings follow);

❐   expect a small rush of late entrants to a competition at the end of a promotion.

Coupons

According to a survey by NOP/Omnibus (*Supermarketing* 11 September 1992) coupon users most frequently get their coupons from product packaging (43 per cent), then door drop leaflets (29 per cent), next press (18 per cent) and finally in-store (8 per cent). The redemption rates follow a different pattern, see Figure 8.5.

Medium	Industry Average *	Range
In-store	27%	2-80%
In/on-pack	25%	10-60%
Free standing inserts	12%	8-15%
Door-to-door	11%	4-24%
Magazines	2.8%	0.5-8%
National press	1.9%	0.25-8%
Direct mail	Depends on targeting	

*Source: NCH

Figure 8.5 Coupon redemption rates by media

Comments on coupon redemption by media

☐   *In-store* - close to the point of purchase these coupons can achieve high redemption levels and draw attention to a brand. They are therefore useful in driving penetration as well as short-term volume gains. The redemption rate does not depend only on the number of coupons available and often these vastly outnumber the possible sales. It is best to cross check the estimate against sales expectations. Position in-store and availability of demonstrator support will also influence redemption levels. Consumers will sometimes see the coupon, register the offer and take the product but forget to use the coupon. Most stores offer guarantees of no mis- or malredemption but it may sometimes be prudent to try to agree maximum redemption levels or proof of product sales versus coupons redeemed.

☐   *In/on-pack* - the money off next purchase coupon on-pack is the classic loyalty builder. If the coupon is off this purchase it can drive penetration and if off another product it can encourage cross usage. Redemptions are high and will be affected by how easy it is to get at and use the coupon. Money off this purchase will redeem higher (1.5-2 times) than money off next purchase. Remarkably, not all money off this purchase coupons are used, as consumers probably do not realise it is an instant offer until they get home. For this reason it is probably best to make it clear that the consumer can also use it for their next purchase too, in order to ensure you retain satisfied customers.

☐   *Free standing inserts (FSIs)* - these books of coupons are typically distributed door-to-door or inserted in newspapers and can be presented in a classy format. In my view these coupons appeal most strongly to the bargain hunter and the misredeemer and as such work best on big brands to drive switching among portfolio buyers.

☐   *Door drops* - here I include coupons on leaflets not in FSIs, even though these are often dropped door-to-door. The rate depends very much on coupon value, visual creativity, and the penetration and availability of the brand in question. This is a good medium for increasing brand penetration.

☐   *Magazines* - redemption depends on the match of the reader to the brand and magazines do offer some targeting scope in this way. While less cost effective and slower to mount than door drops, press coupons do offer opportunities to include coupons in effective press ads. Ads with coupons can get more attention from the consumer.

☐   *National press (newspapers)* - these can be quick and cheap to set up and tend to be a tactical tool to gain short-term volume from switchers and portfolio buyers, eg if sales are down or a competitor is relaunching. Due to high misredemption they are best run on high penetration brands. It is more an offer-led medium than an image-linked one. Retailers (and occasionally man-manufacturers) may run pages of coupons, normally paid for by the manufacturer. These redeem higher than single coupons.

☐   *Direct mail* - this is an expensive way to distribute coupons but can be very effective if the database is well targeted. Coupons can be personalised and redeemers tracked by individual. Personalisation is likely to reduce misredemption. Depending on the target audience, the coupon may drive trial or repeat purchase, switching may be viable but costs may prohibit addressing this objective.

Speed of coupon redemption

Coupons tend to get used up quite quickly, within a month. Newspaper and door drops and FSIs redeem particularly quickly, as the coupons are put out in a short period, and they are used and gone. Most of the coupons will be in the first or second month and the promotion effectively finished after five or six months. Magazines are similar but monthlies may take a little longer with significant redemptions running on to months five and six. On-packs will probably peak three to six months after launch and run on for a year or so.

Checklist of influences on coupon redemption

☐   *absolute value* - coupons under 15p will have significantly re-
       duced redemption levels but increasing the level too high will
       show diminishing returns;
☐   *relative value* - compared to the purchase price;
☐   *distribution medium* - see above;
☐   *design*;
☐   *ease of access*;
☐   *penetration of product*;
☐   *purchase cycle of product*;
☐   *competitive activity*;
☐   *economic climate*;
☐   *length of validity of the coupon*;
☐   *whether for immediate or delayed use*;
☐   *the receptiveness of the participant.*

BUY OUTS AND FIXED FEE PROMOTIONS

Buy-outs and fixed fee promotions can be looked on as buying promotional insurance. The client pays a lump sum which covers the complete cost of the promotion, including all premium, redemption and handling costs, regardless of the final redemption rate. The agency running the promotion underwrites all cost.

Whether the promotion over or under-redeems will not affect the client's balance sheet. This is attractive in several situations:

☐   where the client feels there is risk of over-redemption and has
       access to limited redemption history for the offer;
☐   where the business is small and wants to run a big promotion but
       cannot afford to carry the risk;
☐   where the management resources are small and no promotions
       agency is involved to carry the administrative burden.

Naturally, as with all insurance in the long run, the fixed fee agency will have covered their risk and you will pay for this. They will have to estimate and charge you for higher redemption rates if they wish to stay in business. For some organisations the convenience and risk free environment proves more attractive especially for a one-off promotion. Over a series of promotions this route may well prove more expensive as the buy-out company will err on the safe side for estimated redemption costs.

The extra cost of risk cover is sometimes amortised by the company making the fixed fee offer. For example, Fotorama run many fixed fee promotions and subsidise the cost by sending a further bounceback offer, or promoting their photographic services, in the redemption package to the consumer, eg England's Glory matches, who ran a sendaway offer for trees and a £1 voucher off Fotorama's processing prices accompanied the reward pack.

PROMOTION TYPES TO MATCH OBJECTIVES

It can be helpful to find a quick reference to some of the primary promotional devices that can address specific objectives. The following tables are designed to show some obvious matches and can, of course, be used the other way around to see if your chosen promotion usually fulfils the objective you have set.

Naturally these tables are not perfect in that promotional devices not shown as a match can work in some markets and situations. Likewise the matches indicated may not work well every single time. The media and creative positioning will be key to a successful outcome and may even help a technique address an objective that you would not normally expect it to. The unusual can do wonders, as it is the challenges to convention that gain attention, but this is a high risk strategy.

Only the main objectives are covered. Volume is conspicuous by its absence as it is a product of other more specific objectives.

Above we have looked at the rewards and how they can be presented to the consumer. From this I hope you will have gained some understanding of what the different techniques can achieve. The following chapter looks at this in relation to the objectives that are being addressed.

Technique vs objective checklist

	Awareness	Trial	Switching	Image	Purchase Continuity	Weight of Purchase	Display	Distribution	Stock Loading
Better Price									
Price Cuts		✓	✓			✓	✓	✓	✓
Multi-buys			✓			✓	✓		✓
Coupons:									
- Door Drop	✓	✓	✓						
- Press	✓	✓	✓	✓					
- In-store	✓	✓	✓						
- Cross-brand	✓	✓	✓						
- On-pack (MONP)	✓		✓		✓	✓			
- On-pack (MOTP)		✓	✓		✓	✓	✓	✓	
- Multiple Purchase			✓		✓	✓			
Cashback:									
- Collector	✓	✓	✓		✓	✓			
- Single Purchase		✓	✓			✓			
Extra Fill Free						✓	✓	✓	✓
Banded Pack Same Product							✓	✓	✓
Invoice Discounts							✓	✓	✓
Parcel Deals							✓	✓	✓
Retrospective Discounts							✓	✓	✓
Special Allowances						✓	✓	✓	✓
Staff Incentives	✓	✓	✓		✓	✓		✓	✓
Credit Deals		✓				✓		✓	✓

Technique vs objective checklist (cont)

Free (or nearly free) gifts

	Awareness	Trial	Switching	Image	Purchase Continuity	Weight of Purchase	Display	Distribution	Stock Loading
Banded Pack:									
– Gift/Other Product		✓✓✓	✓✓✓	✓✓✓		✓✓✓	✓✓✓		✓
– On Other Product		✓✓	✓✓✓	✓✓✓		✓✓	✓✓	✓✓	
GWP	✓✓								
FMI:									
– One Purchase		✓	✓✓✓	✓✓✓		✓✓	✓✓	✓	
– Multiple Purchase			✓✓✓	✓✓✓	✓	✓✓	✓✓		
SLP			✓✓✓✓✓						
Cashback:									
One purchase	✓	✓✓	✓✓✓	✓✓✓		✓✓	✓✓		
Container Offer									✓✓
Collector Scheme		✓✓			✓			✓	
Sampling							✓		
Trial Sizes	✓✓								

Technique vs objective checklist (cont)

	Awareness	Trial	Switching	Image	Purchase Continuity	Weight of Purchase	Display	Distribution	Stock Loading
Prizes									
Competitions:									
- On-pack	✓	✓✓✓	✓✓✓	✓✓					
- Off-pack		✓✓✓	✓✓✓	✓✓					
Free Draw							✓		
Instant Win:									
- On-pack	✓	✓✓	✓✓			✓✓			
- Off-pack		✓✓	✓✓✓	✓		✓✓✓			
Games:									
- On-pack	✓	✓✓	✓✓✓	✓	✓✓				
- Off-pack			✓✓		✓✓				
Cash Share Out									
Emotional Benefit (Image)									
Sponsorship	✓✓✓			✓			✓		
Charity	✓✓✓			✓			✓✓✓		
Character Merchandising	✓✓			✓			✓✓✓		
Personality Promotion	✓✓			✓					
Demonstrations	✓✓	✓✓✓		✓					
Money Back Guarantees		✓✓	✓	✓	✓	✓			
Service Enhancements	✓	✓✓	✓	✓		✓			

9
Creativity

This chapter looks at how creativity can be input to a promotion and how the process can be managed.

It is broken down into the following sections:

- ❐ the creative process;
- ❐ stimulating creativity;
- ❐ buying in creativity;
- ❐ managing creative resources;
- ❐ executional hints and tips.

The last section also deals with the fundamental day-to-day inter-relationship and management processes between promotion agencies and clients in addition to just the creative ones.

THE CREATIVE PROCESS

We have already stated that this is not just words and pictures, but is an applied combination of reward, technique, media and execution, eg design and copy.

The elements in the creative mix will all be subject to the same process as illustrated in Figure 9.1. It will stem from a clear vision of what the end goal is, and the brand and its environment. Idea generation is the next step, followed by selection, revision and development of the creative options, a final check and then in-depth development.

We can now explore how to progress the elements within this process in more depth.

The Brief

We have already discussed that the promotions that work best have ideas that are relevant to the brand, its marketplace and the promotional target at the time of the promotion. It is therefore important that this is understood by the creative team.

To do all of this the creative team needs to be fully briefed. A briefing checklist has been included below. This is a very full list designed to cover the briefing of an agency. The component elements are relevant whether an agency is established, or whether a new one is being used or not, but the depth of information required may alter.

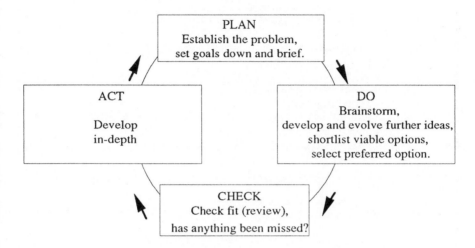

Figure 9.1 The Creative PDCA cycle.

Promotional briefing checklist

❑   *The market:*
- size and growth trends - volume and value;
- major brands and market shares;
- distribution - channels and characteristics;
- regional/seasonal characteristics.

❑   *The product/consumers:*
- brand sizes, variants;
- case/outer packings;
- prices - recommended, actual, trade;
- brand shares - current/previous, by size, volume and value;
- key brand benefits;
- production methods and characteristics;
- distribution - volume and value by trade sector;
- if retailer, structure of branch network;
- target audience profile - sex, age, class, purchasers and consumers, psychographics, pen-portrait;
- average rate of purchase - heavy/average consumer;
- purchase motivations and usage occasions;
- regional/seasonal characteristics.

❑   *Competitive activity*

CONT..

Promotional briefing checklist (cont.)

❏   ***The trade:***
- distribution information;
- major customers;
- methods of display;
- delivery methods.

❏   ***The sales force:***
- sales force or branch staff structure;
- trade sector coverage;
- sales cycle information.

❏   ***Markert strategy and support:***
- stated marketing strategy;
- advertising support - expenditure, media, creative strategy;
- stated promotional strategy.

❏   ***The campaign brief:***
  A.   Objective(s) (quantify)
  -      consumer;
  -      trade;
  -      sales force or branch staff.
  B.   Volume targets
  -      units;
  -      cases;
  -      by trade sector.
  C.   Timings
  -      packaging or other lead times;
  -      sales force or branch staff briefing;
  -      national accounts sell-in;
  -      promotional duration.
  D.   Budget
  -      maximum available;
  -      inclusions/exclusions;
  -      allocation guidelines.
  E.   Evaluating criteria.
  F.   Guidelines & constraints
  -      creative style;
  -      sacred cows;
  -      production constraints;
  -      packaging constraints;
  -      previous promotional
         redemption performance.
  G.   Support material (supply the following)
  -      product samples (inc variants);
  -      case/outer samples;
  -      examples of media advertising;
  -      examples of previous promos;
  -      other communication material (eg leaflets);
  -      any other relevant items.
  H.   The response
  -      agree date at the briefing;
  -      agree format/level of support material (colour or B/W
         concept boards etc)

Brainstorming and idea selection

Generating ideas

The brainstorming process is where a large number of ideas are thrown up. At this stage it is important that there are no barriers to the ideas coming out and the idea is to generate as many ideas as possible. Filtering out and developing the best can come later.

There are some simple rules that will facilitate this process in a small group of maybe five or six:

☐   *select a diverse group*;
☐   *choose a quiet, undisturbed, neutral, location*;
☐   *set the scene*
    - give a verbal brief for the session,
    - ensure the objectives are clear,
    - consider pictures or other prompts to relate to the target customer;
☐   *elect a leader*
    - their role is to keep order, ensure everyone obeys the rules and to draw out ideas from the group;
☐   *capture every idea*
    - have someone (the leader?) writing it all down;
☐   *make the ideas visible*
    - eg use a flip chart so that everyone can see the ideas and be stimulated to further ones by those already up there;
☐   *do not worry about proposing off-the-wall ideas;*
☐   *never criticise proposals*;
☐   *do not waste half-formed suggestions*
    - get them out and let others help concrete them.

Develop and evolve further ideas and short-list viable options

After the first burst of ideas the flow will eventually slow down. At this point it is often worth taking a break and leaving time for gestation. Come back later and have a brief session to capture any further thoughts.

Next, revisit the full list of ideas, cut out non-starters and identify a short-list of the most likely options. Some ideas may be good but have flaws in them. If such a problem is encountered, don't destroy the idea but isolate the concern and ask how can it be addressed. The group may be able to see a way through.

Select preferred option

From the short-list the preferred option, or a few options, will be selected for further work or research. Fundamental criteria include the following.

❏ *Fit*:
it is important that the concept fits with the brand, its environment and target audience.

❏ *Uniqueness*:
whether it is inimitable.

❏ *Campaignability*:
whether the basic idea can be used and adapted in the future.

❏ *Whether it is contemporary*:
fashions and promotional favourites change quickly.

❏ *Credibility*:
whether the idea is believable.

❏ *Delivery*:
offers should not overclaim, they must keep the customer happy, ideally giving them more than they expected.

❏ *Simplicity*:
is it easy to understand? A useful mnemonic is KISS 'Keep It Simple, Stupid'.

❏ *Immediacy*:
how easy is it to access the promotion?

The final preferred option will be checked for robustness by applying the criteria on reviewing to be found in Chapter 10.

BUYING IN CREATIVITY

Creativity may need to be bought in by an organisation because:

❏ there is no time available;
❏ creative skills are poorly represented;
❏ the organisational structure is not conducive to creativity.

Many big organisations are full of people with fixed roles in which they are highly skilled and knowledgeable, and who have been trained to minimise risk in their dealings. Such roles are adept at determining answers to clear-cut problems. They are not so good at finding innovative new approaches to problems.

Often these people are busy making decisions, analysing situations and performing their set tasks. Very little time is available for unfettered creative thought and additional resource is essential.

Required services

Often creativity is briefed out to promotion agencies or creative specialist agencies such as designers, games specialists or cardboard engineers.

It is necessary to decide the appropriate input or inputs to the situation and just what services are required and who can deliver. The need might be simply for the idea or for project management. Often promotion agencies have a fundamental input to brand strategy. Many are more than capable of this but it is important to remember that the actual responsibility lies with the brand owner.

Services that might be bought include:

- strategic/advisory;
- pure creative (ideas);
- design and artwork;
- copywriting;
- print buying;
- sourcing;
- project management;
- event management;
- sponsorship
- sales literature;
- consumer or trade promotions;
- staff motivation schemes;
- co-ordination between suppliers;
- locating and negotiating with third party contacts;
- administration;
- implementation;
- evaluation.

Direct promotion agencies may also be providing specialist services such as list broking, database design, building and management, laser printing, mailing and data analysis.

Selecting agencies

There are several different types of agency:

- the specialist working in a niche area;
- the ideas shop which is flexible and fast but has low staffing and resource, buying in all or many service functions;

❑   the one stop shop which has every service from print to database management in-house.

The above and all points in between can all be the right agency depending on the task required of it. The important thing is to match the resource to the need.
    The agency appointed will also depend on the following.

❑   *Past work and experience*:
    - look at their portfolio's;
    - their specialist skills and knowledge;
    - have they worked in your area before? If so why are they not doing so now?
    - have they won awards or do they have other demonstrable past successes?
❑   *Staff*:
    - quality, experience, capability and motivation;
    - will you be serviced by juniors or will you see the real driving forces?
    - are they just 'yes people' doing what you say as long as you pay the bills or will they challenge a poor decision or instruction?
    - what training do they get?
❑   *Interpersonal skills*:
    - does their chemistry work with you, are they team workers, what is their style? Different agencies will have distinct personalities.
❑   *Structure and size*:
    - have they the resource if they need to move quickly?
❑   *Recommendation*:
    - the views of others who have worked with an agency can be a good source of information on their capabilities.

One indicator of reputability is ISP membership. Many agencies who are ISP members are also members of the Sales Promotion Consultants Association. This is aligned to the ISP and is a register of ISP members who offer strategic sales promotion consultancy services.
    Many direct mail agencies are registered with the DMSSB, and major sales promotion agencies can offer experienced direct marketing input from internal specialists or divisions.
    Where a promotions agency is being appointed there are different types of relationship that can exist, examples are below.

❐ *Ad hoc*:
   where any agencies believed capable of delivering are pulled in for each project as it arises, no continuity of agencies being established.

❐ *Project*:
   eg agencies are used on a semi-regular basis working on individual set projects, agencies being pulled from a pool of preferred suppliers.

❐ *Retainer*:
   where an agency is appointed to work on all of a brand's business for a longer period of time, eg one year. A long-term relationship is established allowing better partnership development.

Whichever route is adopted, the value of a longer term relationship should not be underrated. Many learning curves will only have to be dealt with once, and unique systems and needs understood. Most importantly of all a good basis of trust can be established, sensitive data can be shared and commitment in one party will generate commitment in the other.

Pitching

A brief may be issued to several agencies on a competitive basis or just to a single agency. If you have a good known resource the need to pitch is reduced. If you are confident an agency can deliver, there is no need to brief out more widely. The times when a competitive pitch might be appropriate are if there will be no time to rebrief or work up proposals. In this case you will have need to get as many ideas in as quickly as possible.

It is important to realise that the more agencies there are in a pitch, the less the commitment and the greater the likelihood of receiving poor proposals back.

If you do decide to pitch:

❐ go for two or three agencies only;
❐ tell them they are in competition;
❐ brief equally;
❐ allow equal time to work up proposals;
❐ give them equal time to present;
❐ explain to a losing agency why it lost;
❐ if proposals overlap creatively explain this quickly;
❐ consider paying a refusal fee, eg to cover the cost of visuals. It is unlikely that this will cover the full cost of the presentation, but it does show commitment.

MANAGING CREATIVE RESOURCES

Briefing

The old adage 'rubbish in, rubbish out' was never truer. The quality of the brief presented to the agency will dictate the quality of the response.

Briefs should be written with relevant back-up information provided, eg samples, advertising, examples of past activity or house style, and any relevant research information etc.

Wherever possible agencies should be given a copy of the brief prior to the briefing meeting to encourage a more meaningful session.

Ensure the right people are there at the briefing session. That is, the ones who can answer any queries and who hold the budget and decision-making responsibility, eg:

- ❐ the hands-on brand manager;
- ❐ the budget holder;
- ❐ trade marketing input;
- ❐ the promotions manager (if applicable).

Agencies should confirm that they accept and are happy with the brief. If they feel the brief inadequate in any way they should make this clear so that it can be rectified. A good agency will reject the brief or at least ask for clarification if the briefing is inadequate. They should be given plenty of support to come back and ask questions of relevant sections of the organisation at a later stage, should it prove necessary.

Assignment of responsibilities

Make sure the agency knows the services you are buying up front, also who will buy other services, eg:

- ❐ design and artwork;
- ❐ print buying;
- ❐ sourcing;
- ❐ legal clearance;
- ❐ implementation;
- ❐ handling and fulfilment.

If the agency is buying services or items on your behalf, get and agree well in advance clear, unambiguous estimates in writing. Do this before the goods have to be committed and while there is still time to seek alternative sources.

Agencies can be expensive. Make sure you have alternative quotes to cross check with, but ensure you compare like with like. If the agency is still best and you have confidence in their ability to deliver, then all well and good.

Ensure both parties have a clear understanding of what the agency's liabilities are.

Response

A date for response should be agreed at the briefing. Agencies should make clear any concerns in this area at an early stage.

Responses should:

- ❒ normally take the form of a written document;
- ❒ demonstrate that the brief has been understood;
- ❒ provide a clear rationale for the direction proposed;
- ❒ come back with a sensible number of proposals, since too many shows they are not confident in their reply;
- ❒ respond with schemes which are legal and meet relevant codes of practice;
- ❒ have visuals as necessary. Guidance on the level of visualisation required can be helpful. Simple black and white visuals are often adequate and will be cheaper for the agency (and therefore you) in the long run;
- ❒ have outline costs (these will be estimates only);
- ❒ provide evaluation criteria;
- ❒ have an outline timing plan.

Beware when getting visualisations of concepts. A coloured picture may not represent the reality of what can be achieved. For example, the only way to be sure if an on-pack offer will work on-shelf is if the response is represented by a pack-sized mock-up, not an A2 concept board.

After the initial presentation, further work may be required. Ensure all parties are clear if this is being paid for. There may be costs associated with both time and design work.

Contact reports

All meetings and telephone conversations where decisions are made or concerns raised should be contact reported. Agree a fixed circulation. Contact reports should normally be with the client within 48 hours. After that the world will have changed and they will be redundant, apart from forming a historical record.

Agency remuneration

A good idea can be priceless. Do not be so mean as to save a few thousand pounds on fees when the optimal solution will make you tens or hundreds of thousands more.

Promotion agencies make profits in two key ways: by charging a fee and by making a mark-up on the services they provide. These may operate at the same time. Advertising agencies have traditionally charged 17.56 per cent on top of the cost of the services bought (the equivalent of 15 per cent of the gross cost). This can be very profitable if a lot of media space is being procured on the client's behalf. This rarely occurs in promotions, so quite large fees may be required.

Fees may be set on a retainer basis where the agency is retained for a fixed fee for a period of activity. Alternatively they may be set project by project or a combination of both. Influences on fee level include the following.

- ❑ *The purchase*:
  you are buying time, experience and concepts, and you should expect to pay a realistic market rate for the management time involved in the creative process, the implementation plus a premium for the idea.
- ❑ *The pitch*:
  very low fees may be just a pitch for access to the company roster. To establish a long-term relationship you need to understand what a true level of fee will be.
- ❑ *Time*:
  expect to pay more for rush jobs.
- ❑ *Complexity*:
  Some activity, eg roadshows, can demand higher levels of agency management time, and remuneration will need to reflect this. Also fees for doing several small jobs will be disproportionately large compared to single large tasks.

❏ *Scale*:
agencies generally charge a premium for managing larger activities.

❏ *Efficiency*:
if you keep changing your mind you will waste agency time and your money. Agreeing roles and responsibilities and having a timing plan will minimise this.

❏ *Level of input*:
creative time usually requires commitment from the more senior (and expensive) personnel.

❏ *Remuneration method*:
commission based remuneration can result in higher fees if a lot of goods or services are being bought for the client. This approach is dangerous as agencies will then have a commercial interest in buying the goods and services that offer best returns for them rather than what is best for the client.

Deal fairly with agencies, for example where a promotional proposal which has been initially accepted is cancelled for client reasons, then some compensation may be reasonable.

Make sure the principles of remuneration are understood up front along with what is included in the costings (eg extras such as taxis, couriers).

It is usually best to commit to fee payment in stages, eg a proportion on proposal acceptance and the rest on completion.

Agencies should be expected to keep within the set budget and be prepared to provide an instant update on expenditure made and planned against any project.

Contracts/terms of trade

The objective is to avoid ambiguities in the event of a dispute.

Carefully examine the terms and conditions often presented with proposals, eg in the back or on the cover of the document. Ensure your interests in terms of copyright and exclusivity are suitably protected.

Consider drawing up a specific contract spelling out the terms and conditions relating to the promotion.

It may be appropriate to provide written procedural guidelines so that all parties are clear on what is expected of them.

Feedback

Let agencies know how they are performing. Offer regular feedback. Give thanks for a job well done.

Dealing with clients

Essentially, the way an agency should be dealing with clients is exactly the same as the way a client should deal with an agency. The same things need to be agreed and a trusting relationship established. In the long run the well being of the client leads to the well being of the agency.

Agencies should pay attention to the management criteria listed above. They should also seek feedback from the client on areas of under- and over-performance.

EXECUTIONAL HINTS AND TIPS

Good copy

Promotional copy has very little time to register with the consumer.

Facets that contribute to good promotional copy include:

☐ *clarity on what the offer is*:
make the headline short and precise and the benefit clear;

☐ *clarity on how to take part*:
make it easily understood;

☐ *clarity on any restrictions or conditions*;

☐ *relevance*:
the detailed wording should be relevant to the brand and target audience;

☐ *lucidity*:
people not involved in the promotion's creation should be able to understand the copy;

☐ *minimal jargon*:
avoid 'marketing-speak' which normal people will not understand at all, use language people will understand;

☐ *avoidance of unnecessary cliches, adjectives and adverbs*;

☐ *keep it short*:
edit hard, then go back and edit again;

❐   *be easy to follow, have flow*:
    let one point lead on from another, think about putting copy into
    clear blocks and use colour and pictures to help understanding
    and clarity, use short sentences and paragraphs, think about how
    the consumer's decision process will work;
❐   *by not clouding the main points*:
    eg where there are application forms, consider getting as much
    of the administration as possible on to it and out of the way of the
    basic message;
❐   *being straightforward*:
    make sure the offer does not mislead in any way, do not try to be
    too clever;
❐   *making it enthusiastic and interesting*:
    give a sense of urgency and a reason to act.

Note that direct mail copy requirement may be slightly different to some of
those above, because of the physical properties of the medium, because
consumers can be addressed as individuals and because consumers may
interact longer. For example there may be many points of contact, such as the
envelope it is delivered in, a letter, the reply device, the offer, any brochure etc.

Design

Make sure brand recognition is high throughout the execution - use logos and
relevant colours, since these are more recognisable and noticeable than just
words.
     Use photographs in preference to illustrations. Photo-libraries can be
used and they are cheaper than hiring a photographer. Book early, for if they
know you're in a spot the price may be less negotiable.

Subjective comments and practical hints
Design is the area where subjective comments are most rife. Therefore I shall
follow the tradition and interject a few of my own opinions and observations,
along with some practical tips in developing print:

❐   keep the number of typefaces to a minimum, more than three and
    it tends to look a mess;
❐   do not make the execution too busy;
❐   many logos have a higher recall than names;
❐   use the correct colour for logos;

❏   use the correct colour and a consistent typeface for names;

❏   do not use too many capitals;

❏   apart from logos use special colours sparingly;

❏   avoid white-out type, especially from colours, toned areas and when using a small typeface;

❏   discuss the leaflet size with the printer. Most things are printed several to each sheet going through the press, and thought can save paper waste and costs;

❏   do not make artwork changes at proofing stage;

❏   rush jobs are very, very expensive, good design cannot be rushed;

❏   do not use unnecessary transparencies, as they cost more to reproduce;

❏   larger transparencies are better quality and allow more room for touching up, but transparencies the right size can be cheaper to use - use big transparencies for bigshots, eg posters, to ensure quality.

Having looked at the creative process, we can now go on to the final check before the implementation of the idea.

10
Review The Selected Promotion - Check

By now the promotion will have been decided upon in principle or a short-list selected. Hopefully all concerned will be keen to see one promotion acted upon and implemented. However, in practice there may often be some dissent as to which is the best of the short-listed ideas or the need to win over some people in the company. In the TQ company there is a step prior to implementation, the one that will provide the groundwork to win these arguments and will often save the organisation a lot of money and the promoter a lot of embarrassing mistakes. This step is the check in the PDCA cycle.

Whether or not there is a point to argue or promotions to decide between, the application of this check is vital before committing your company and its resources. This is the stage of making sure out of all the creative possibilities to fulfil the promotional need, you have chosen the right one for the job. It is effectively a pre-evaluation against expectations for the promotion and will mirror the steps taken when the activity is evaluated after the event.

This chapter is structured in five sections.

- ☐ A review of the four key check questions.
- ☐ The implications of the chosen promotion.
- ☐ Checklist on promotional standards.
- ☐ Pre-evaluation modelling.
- ☐ Research.

THE FOUR KEY CHECK QUESTIONS

It is essential that four key issues are reviewed.

Q1. Have you been true to your objectives?
Q2. What are the implications of the chosen promotion?
Q3. Is the chosen promotion the best one for the job?
Q4. Is it expressed in the best possible way?

This is effectively a filter that ensures only the best and most appropriate promotion gets through to the implementation phase.

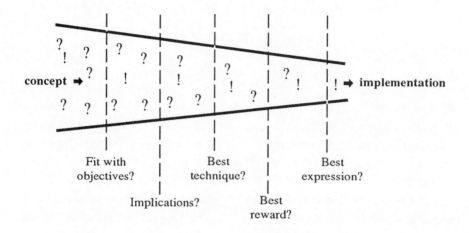

Figure 10.1   The review filter

Q1. Have you been true to the objectives?

This means revisiting the 'SMART' objectives you will have written down at the start of your promotional planning exercise. Go back to the brief and think hard and long. Have you addressed the who, what, why, where and when issues inherent in that brief?

Q2. What are the implications of the chosen promotion?

The promotion you have chosen or short-listed will have effects on a wide number of issues, both to do with the promotional target, any intermediaries and your own organisation. You will therefore need a very comprehensive checklist of issues to ensure that nothing unexpected crops up later to scupper or damage the planned activity, and one to start you off is included here. Your own special circumstances may dictate additions to this list.

Promotional implication checklist

❏   *Customer effect:*
how the final customer will react and how the promotion will affect them.

❏   *Trade effect*:
how any intermediaries will react and be affected.

❏   *Profitability*:
does the proposed activity give an acceptable return?

❏   *Company policy*:
whether there are internal policy issues that need to be complied with or challenged.

❏   *Timing*:
whether it can be done in the timescale available and is it still the best time for the activity?

❏   *Redemption history*:
what has happened before?

❏   *Budgets*:
whether the costs and risks are still affordable.

❏   *Resources*:
what is required to make it happen well?

❏   *Factory and production implications*:
can they still make and deliver, including any special pack needs?

❏   *Safety*:
are premiums or promotional items safe for the consumer and all intermediaries?

❏   *Environmental issues*:
have these all been covered off and a sensible long-term view taken?

❏   *Taxation:*
have you a nasty surprise awaiting you if you go ahead?

PLUS:

❏   *Anything else?*

❏   *Legal and codes of practice*:
are you allowed to run the promotion at all or are special provisions required?

Q3. Is the chosen promotion the best one for the job?

This means checking to ensure that there are no better options to your chosen direction. You need to be confident that there are no better promotional techniques that you have overlooked, that yours is the most cost-effective solution and that other directions such as advertising or PR would not better meet your objectives.

It is important to base decisions on factual information and to have hard measures of your expectations. These are the foundation upon which the soft opinions can be overlaid. Soft opinions alone will rely on gut feel, and the experience and personalities of the people involved in putting the activity together. While such factors have their place they must not operate alone if the business is to learn and improve its performance. The TQ company will want, and will benefit from, objective measures. These will be based on evaluation and research. Research is covered in the final part of this chapter.

Q4. Is it expressed in the best possible way?

Promotions that work will be more than robust mechanical devices that will deliver the promised rewards on paper or a computer model. They will need to be expressed effectively if they are to work in practice. It is no use being strategically sound if the activity is expressed badly.

Poor physical execution, bad placement or poor choice of partners will destroy a promotion. The key aspects to consider are whether the proposed activity is the best to fulfil the criteria listed in the promotional expression checklist that follows.

Most of these issues simply require a few moments' considered thought or input from colleagues. Others might benefit from research as discussed below.

Support

Part of the expression will be the exposure a promotion gets. Sometimes it requires specialised additional support activity not crucial to the working of the promotion to get the best effect, eg display or feature. Good display will boost a promotions visibility and therefore its effectiveness. There may be other types of awareness build that can be incorporated. For example, an advertised sendaway promotion will redeem much higher than one that is just carried on the pack. The quality of the participant may be different too. Figure 10.2 illustrates how visibility can affect sales.

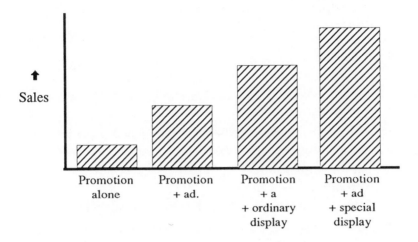

Figure 10.2   The benefits of increased support

THE IMPLICATIONS OF THE CHOSEN PROMOTION

Here we expand on some of the issues covered in the promotional implication checklist.

Customer effect

To judge this without testing you need to try and become a customer. If you have a reasonable understanding of your customer, consumer or trade, simply putting yourself into their shoes and imagining their response will eradicate a large number of your errors and oversights.

Is the promotion credible? What will be the result of customer action, inaction or, worse still, will there be any adverse reactions? It is far easier to disgruntle a consumer with a promotion than it is to please them. Consumer customers will remember this and hold it against your brand. Trade customers are also likely to remember the negatives and use them against you in future negotiations.

Total quality is about having an informed and balanced view, and a compulsive obsession with customers in isolation is restrictive. They must be viewed in a broader context and it is essential to consider the competition and how they are approaching your customer if you are to counter their efforts effectively.

Promotional expression checklist

☐ *Appeal:*
has it maximum emotional appeal to the target audience? Will it meet or, better still, exceed their expectations?

☐ *Visibility*:
does it maximise visibility to the target audience? Has it adequate support, eg is a special media campaign called for, and is it being sold hard enough?

☐ *Brand values*:
does it strengthen, or at least maintain, brand values?

☐ *Harmony*:
does it work in harmony with the rest of the marketing mix?

☐ *Focus*:
does it give adequate attention to the message?

☐ *Novelty*:
does it appreciate the scarcity value of a promotional device?

☐ *Uniqueness*:
techniques are rarely truly unique, but how they are creatively used and expressed can make them so. Has your promotion this quality that will make it stand out from the crowd?

☐ *Timeliness*:
is it timed to coincide with any advertising? Is the offer topical and is the mechanic tired or all the rage?

☐ *KISS*:
does it adhere to the KISS ('Keep It Simple Stupid') mnemonic? The promotion should be no more complex than the target audience can grasp in the time they are likely to have available.

☐ *Expression*:
can it be clearly and easily expressed in design and copy terms?

☐ *Accessibility*:
has it the minimum barriers to entry possible?

☐ *Reward*:
in the best promotions, everyone who is involved benefits. All parties from the end user, intermediaries, agencies and the promoting company should benefit from the promotion.

Trade effect

The retail trade or other distributive channels are customers in addition to the end consumer, even if the promotion itself is directed at the consumer. The best way to look at this is from the TQ premise that you are serving the customer's customer. Only then can you be sure you are meeting everyone's needs. With the rise of category management the promoter needs to understand all the market dynamics and be sure the promotion is driving the category forward profitably, for the account as well as the supplier.

Consequently, it can be well worth sharing promotions with the trade at early stages of development to help you understand their views. These contacts need not be restricted to the the buyer/seller interface. With partnership working communication is at a multi-functional level. The buyer may not be the appropriate person to help you understand logistics issues or company merchandising policies. Their corporate marketing department may be able to give a company view on preferred promotional techniques unhampered by any negotiation issues. They may also give information on special restrictions in design, message or other implementation issues that will affect the promotion's viability.

To show the effects on a customer's other departments, consider supplying them with a banded pack. It will have fundamental effects on the retailer's supply chain. Figure 10.3 illustrates the potential influences on profit for the retailer. If a pack is larger it may mean more pallets, more warehousing and transportation costs, and merchandising difficulties if it takes up different shelf space. It may even detract from other, more profitable sales. All these issues and costs are likely to be considered by the retailer and used to challenge the validity of the offer. A suitable argument must be constructed to justify the activity in the light of likely objections.

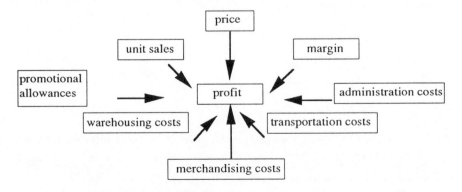

Figure 10.3 Promotional influences on retailer's profit

The trade may also be a valuable input into sales expectations. You will need their input to ensure you are going to sell enough product to make the promotion worthwhile, or whether out of stocks are likely on your projected volumes. You will also need to discuss with them any special merchandising requirements and timing issues.

Naturally retailers want manufacturers to spend their promotional money with them directly. For this reason you can expect cautious or disinterested responses on most off-pack, out-of-store activity. Responses will always have to be tempered by your understanding of what the retailer is looking for in a promotion, not just what the consumer benefit is.

This check must include consideration of whether you have planned the best way to sell your promotion and, if appropriate, how to counter the established views and policies of the buyer and customer's organisations.

Company policy

Structured and disciplined organisations may well have set policies and guidelines about what can and cannot be done. These policies may be internal, ie the promoter's company policies, or external, ie supplier's policies. These are usually robust, borne from the experiences of the past and have come from a higher level than the buyer/seller interface.

Internal policies should be guidelines to prevent waste, inefficiency and the repetition of errors made in the past. They should be designed so that something falling within policy can proceed with the minimum of difficulty. When the company's environment changes so policy needs to change with it. Policies should not be so rigid that they can never be challenged and change.

Timing

There are three timing issues:

- ❐   lead times;
- ❐   phasing;
- ❐   longevity.

Lead times
The outline timing plan should already have been prepared, but now the promotional direction is more clear, detailed options need to be worked up to ensure you can bring the promotion to market in the time available.

There is no point in planning a gift with purchase promotion in 12 weeks' time if the sourcing lead time is 16 weeks. However, now is not the time to give up, but to challenge the rules. For example if the lead time includes four weeks to make a special production tool, can you buy a stock line? If there is six weeks for sea shipment what is the extra cost to air-freight?

Rushed activities are more likely to fail and cause strain in other parts of the business than properly planned activities. Embark on them with your eyes open and at your peril. Make sure all involved are aware of the risks and issues.

Timing plans are dealt with in detail at the start of Chapter 11.

Phasing

Timing issues may also be about phasing. It is often very important to ensure promotions link into other activities such as advertising. When a product is being promoted and advertised at the same time you can expect greater sales and participation than when it is being promoted in a non-advertised period.

Phasing may also be about avoiding promotional overlaps. For example it may be uneconomical to double-discount your product in which case you will want to ensure consumers only have access to one offer at a time. If you are running a number of activities at a national level or more typically one at a national level and others locally, will their coincidence be beneficial for the brand? You may wish to ensure you are not running, say, a coupon door drop when you are offering special packs in-store. Sometimes this double-discount may be part of the strategy, eg buying feature with a low level discount to ensure brand visibility coincides with a door dropped coupon.

Longevity

The other aspect of timing is longevity. Is the promotion going to be around long enough for the optimum number of people to see it? Are the special tokens going to be on-pack long enough for the participant to collect enough to qualify for the offer and will the closing date be sensible?

Redemption history

Examples of redemption expectations are included in Chapter 8. The ability to predict the number of redemptions will be vital. In the TQ company this will be driven by the amassing of information through the evaluation process.

As far as the principles are concerned, there are two arms to the redemption issue, scale and efficiency.

Scale

Understanding the redemption expectations is key to selecting the best promotion. The number of participants or scale of the activity can be related back to the objectives to see if you are really achieving worthwhile results. Supposing the market is saturated with 10 million units selling in your promotional period. If you have a 10 per cent brand share (ie a million customers) which you would like to drive up to 15 per cent on a promotion, there would no point in running a promotion which only had 300,000 opportunities to participate and expect 100,000 to do so.

You will need to relate the total number of participants to the number represented by the promotional objectives. Accepting that there may also be the hidden benefits of slippage and motivation to non-participants through greater visibility, it is important to see if the scale of activity is right.

Efficiency

The aim of most promotions is to get the maximum number of participants at the lowest possible cost. The more participants per pound spent, the better the cost effectiveness of the event. Proposals will often have redemption costs in them, eg the cost of couponning, application handling and premium rewards, and these need to be checked through carefully for robustness.

Budgets

In the ideal world for promoters, budgets would be flexible to meet the needs of the brand. In the real world they have to be planned for as part of a company's whole business planning process. Therefore budgets tend to be semi-fixed, flexibility usually meaning that some other brand or part of the business has to suffer. It is important to have a clear grasp as to whether there is any budgetary flexibility, since promotions may work but require a different scale to make them efficient or viable.

The costs of running a proposed promotion will rarely match the budget set for it. Hidden or unexpected costs, high redemptions or low redemptions will all throw the budget out unless it is a fixed fee or buy-out activity. On the planning side, elements of a proposal will often have to be cut out or the whole activity scaled down to make plans match the budget.

Agency pitches should come in on budget. In my observations I have noticed they tend to come in slightly over. Realism is the order of the day, with the understanding that some elements like redemption related costs, eg premiums, print, handling and postage, will be subject to up-side and down-side risk. Beware of the agency proposal that conveniently leaves out the fees and design costs, or predicts unrealistic handling or print costs. Some agencies suffer from optimism, eg high redemption rates that make the promotion look good, or special print or premium cost prices that cannot be achieved at the implementation stage. Others suffer from pessimism and underestimate redemption rates or quote high premium or print costs (sometimes this is a hidden mark-up).

Internally and externally produced budgets need to be scrutinised very carefully. They will rarely be accurate first time around and should not be taken at face value. Check them through carefully against the assumptions, specifications, cost of things in the past and any redemption history you have experienced before. Ask colleagues about their experiences and costs. You still may not get it right, but you should be closer, and have identified the areas and degree of risk.

Apart from the absolute budget criteria, there is a cost to implement as far as the business is concerned and you should seek to minimise the cost of implementation through all means, for example all other things being equal, select options with lower level of complexity.

The budget checklist included below should catch virtually all promotional costs but think carefully about the individual situation in case there are special considerations. Try to avoid budget changes after creative input.

Resources

In addition to the financial resources there are physical resources to be checked off if you are to be able to make the promotion happen effectively. These will include the list below, but you may have others peculiar to your situation.

- ❑ *Creative resources*:
  to refine ideas, visualise and write copy.
- ❑ *Implementation resources*:
  to do the leg-work, to make all the calls, contacts and arrangements to make things happen.
- ❑ *Fulfilment resources*:
  to send back promotional rewards, collate competition entries and deal with queries.
- ❑ *Sales resources*:
  to sell the deal in. Has the salesforce the right tools, number, strength and balance of different promotions? Are there too many things for them to do at once? Are they prioritised correctly and are they simple enough?

Budget checklist

☐ **Creation costs:**
agency fees;
concept boards and mock ups;
research;
design;
artwork, illustrations, photography charges;
legal fees.

☐ **Implementation costs:**
print;
labour and materials for special packs (primary and secondary packaging);
delivery/distribution;
managment costs;
data costs;
media space;
trade payments, margin concessions, display costs, other discounts and payments;
premium items (on-pack, gift with purchase);
rush charges if late;
sales aids and incentives;
bike charges.

☐ **Fulfilment costs:**
promotion set-up and storage;
handling, including prize distribution;
judging;
postage;
rewards, premium items, samples, refunds, prizes;
mailer and/or communication package;
telephone or other response media;
insurance;
datacapture.

☐ **Opportunity (hidden) costs:**
time spent on the activity;
lost sales, eg cannibalisation of another brand or size, wasted sales through unintended buy-forward.

❐   *Factory, production and transport implications:*
      Can the factory and supply chain make it and get it physically
      delivered? Ensure they understand that failure to provide what
      the customer wants means failure for the promotion and the
      company's future demise as competitors step in. Brief them
      well and in good time.

Safety

It is essential that all gifts, premiums, samples and promotional packaging and
materials of all types are carefully checked to ensure they are safe for the
supply chain and the trade to handle, and most importantly, for the consumer
to participate in. A reward for a consumer needs to be checked very carefully
to ensure it comes up to approved standards and is presented in a suitable
format, environment and with suitable cautionary messages. It is particularly
important to do this if the reward is likely to be eaten or to come in contact with
skin or young children. There are independent safety assessors who can test
goods against international and EC standards. The Post Office can advise on
goods which cannot be mailed.

Door dropped samples warrant a special note. There has been some
adverse publicity about unsolicited samples with concerns for children who
may come into contact with them. The sensible thing is to ensure the samples
are tested to be safe for children to come into contact with.

Significant legislation in the safety area includes the Consumer Safety
Act 1978. As always, being practical and putting yourself into the the
consumer's shoes should avoid most problems.

Environmental issues

The importance of environmental issues

The environmental argument may go quiet occasionally but it will not go
away. It has fundamental bearing on all promotional activity at all levels: in
production of goods and promotional materials, in the packaging and delivery
of these materials, and in the way a brand is perceived by the consumer.

Anyone who doubts that should note that it is on the agenda at the highest
levels of government. The British Standards Institute has an environmental
standard BS7750 to which many companies aspire.

More and more consumers are environmentally aware and promotors ignore
this at their peril. Research carried out by the HPI Research Group (*Super
Marketing*, October 1992), breaks consumers into four categories: activists (26
per cent), waverers (36 per cent), apathetics (21 per cent) and the ostriches (17

per cent). Promoters cannot afford to risk alienating these large sections of the population with environmentally unfriendly promotions. The indications are that today's youth, tomorrow's mums, dads and heavy shoppers are even more environmentally aware.

The environmental issues for promotions are primarily in the packaging and sourcing areas.

Packaging

Much of industry has only just started to consider the environment in real depth. They are being driven by legislation. Packaging is the most visible example of this and some countries have taken the route of using the consumer to drive it forward. The Topfer decree in Germany requires manufacturers to take back and recycle most packaging, and shoppers can return it or even leave it behind in supermarkets. Naturally the hassle of clearing this up has led to a reduction in excessive packaging.

The EC's proposed Directive on Packaging and Packaging Waste will eventually require member states to recover 90 per cent of waste and recycle 60 per cent. However, according to the Friends of the Earth, this does not effectively tackle the basic environmental issues which are unnecessary over-packaging and how the packaging is recycled, eg incineration and recycling are viewed as equal in environmental terms.

Reducing the amount of packaging is the environmentalists' first priority followed by re use and then recycling. The correct balance between necessary and unnecessary packaging needs to be sought. In the long run, the winners will be those that think of better ways of getting the promotional message across without high levels of waste.

Supplier choice

Many big retailers recognise that environmental issues are fundamental to their choice of long-term suppliers. In the future, only those companies who address environmental issues in a responsible and forward-thinking way will be selected as partners. Environmental measures need to be looked at in a 'cradle to grave' approach, not just the product, but manufacturing, secondary packaging, distribution and of course promotions. Environmental auditing is becoming more important at all stages in a company's business. An environmental audit is likely to extend well beyond a company's production sites, to associate companies acting as agents, distributors and suppliers in their own right. It is no use preaching environmental awareness if your premiums are from dubious sources.

Environmental opportunities

Smart promoters are using environmental issues to their advantage by linking up with environmental agencies and running co-operative and fund-raising activities. Charities such as the World Wide Fund for Nature are experts in this type of promotion. Some companies have promoted pushing the recycling angle. For example, Duckham's ran a promotion offering a free oil tidy which allowed motorists changing their car's oil to save the old oil. To ensure it was safely disposed of, applicants were given the addresses of local authority sites accepting waste oil.

There must be a lot of potential in promotional activity linked to reusable containers and I for one eagerly await promotions based on this principle.

Taxation

Taxation, particularly VAT, can affect the costings and viability of promotions, and the promoter needs to be aware of commitments in this area.

Taxation problems do not stop at VAT. Care is also needed when offering gifts and incentives to customers and employees. Employees cannot accept gifts without the risk of being accused of bribery and corruption. A sole trader can accept a gift but where the recipient is an employee they must have their employer's approval to accept. Depending somewhat on the exact circumstances, the donor would be well advised to get written permission from both the recipient's and the donor's companies to make the gift.

It is against the law to offer gifts to public sector employees.

Any gift of material value (over £10) will have to be assessed for personal income tax assessment. Even a trade promotion offering the chance to win a free holiday acquired by the winner by reason of their employment runs the risk of making the winner liable to tax on it. It is possible that the Inland Revenue can provide some special arrangements where the tax liability can be paid by the donor contact: the Inland Revenue Valuation Unit is a contact for guidance notes. All gifts and incentives should be carefully checked legally. Your local VAT and Inland Revenue offices can often offer information, although there may be some regional interpretation of the legislation. Specific legislation includes the Income and Corporation Taxes Act 1988 and the Prevention of Corruption Acts 1889 to 1916.

There are specific EC issues impinging on VAT payments and collection when goods cross borders between EC countries. Refer to your tax expert.

PROMOTIONAL STANDARDS

Planned promotions should adhere to the checklist below:

Promotional standards checklist

☐   *Legality*:
promotions should be legal (see Chapter 4).

☐   *Decency*:
promotions should be decent, ie should not cause offence and care should be taken over distasteful approaches.

☐   *Honesty*:
promotions should not exploit consumer's credibility or lack of experience or knowledge to the detriment of their interests.

☐   *Truthful*:
they should not mislead.

☐   *Principles*:
they should be executed in the spirit as well as the letter of the code.

☐   *Competitively fair:*
they should adhere to the spirit of fair competition, ie they should not unfairly or innaccurately denigrate or compare competitors' products, imitate or exploit their goodwill.

☐   *Fairness*:
they should be structured to deal fairly and honourably with the consumer;

☐   *Happiness*:
they should be structured to avoid disappointment.

☐   *Reasonable*:
they should be fair to all concerned and in the public interest.

☐   *Responsible*:
they should not play on fear or distress, or condone or incite anti social behaviour or violence. They should look out for the interests of children and not exploit them.

☐   *Appropriate*:
they should be constructed to ensure that advertising or promotional material does not reach those for whom it is inappropriate.

☐   *Open*:
they should be presented so that any rules and conditions are clear before purchase.

☐   *Efficient*:
they should be administered effectively to provide no grounds for complaint.

☐   *Respectful*:
they should be respectful of privacy and regardful of safety.

MODELLING REDEMPTION COSTS AND PROMOTIONAL EFFICIENCY

The computer-literate marketer or agency has a wealth of simple tools at their disposal to build easy-to-use spreadsheet models of the planned activity. These can be used for such things as:

❐   redemption costing;
❐   cost per trialist;
❐   cost per new purchaser;
❐   breakeven analyses.

These models make the comparison of different costs and response rates easy. However, it is important to keep the numbers in perspective and remember that this is a model to help decision making. It is not a set of facts, since these can only come after the event when the promotion is evaluated. While some inputs may be reasonably firm, others such as response rates, the number of current users who will apply or the number who will convert to the brand can only be estimates unless comprehensive research has been carried out.
The true value of this type of modelling is to assess such things as:

❐   whether the proposal is viable against expected costs and re-
       sponses;
❐   what happens if we alter the reward or other cost elements;
❐   what happens if the response varies;
❐   which is the best out of a set of alternative proposals;
❐   whether the activity is highly risk sensitive, if one or more
       assumptions prove to be wrong:
       - how far out you can be before the activity becomes non-viable;
       - up-side risks and down-side risks to numbers of participants;
       - what the financial risks might be;
       - whether the maximum redemption level is too high to physic-
         ally handle;
       - whether it will affect premium purchase decisions;
       - what the most risk-sensitive elements are (can they be re-
         duced?).

Redemption or cost to trial model

The model in Figure 10.4 shows how to determine the cost per participant in a promotion. The principle will work for a free mail-in, a coupon or a sampling activity and shows how much it costs you for each participant.

INPUTS:
>   A Number of communications, ie how many opportunities to participate.
>   B Fixed communication costs, eg design, artwork, fees etc.
>   C Variable communication costs, eg delivery, packaging, leaflets etc.
>   D Percentage participation, ie redeemers, those taking up the offer.
>   E Fixed reward costs, eg prize.
>   F Variable reward costs, eg premium, handling, packaging, postage
>   etc, any financial inputs, eg postage contribution or SLP payment
>   can be taken off the reward costs.

CALCULATION:
>   Step 1: Communication Costs = B + (A x C) = G
>   Step 2: Number of Participants = A x D = H
>   Step 3: Reward Costs = E + (H x F) = I
>   Step 4: Cost/participant = $\dfrac{G + I}{H}$ = J

OUTPUT: The cost ascribed to each participant.

Figure 10.4   Redemption or cost to trial model

Cost per new user model

This model is designed for promotions where the objective is to get new users into a brand. In this case we are not simply interested in the cost per participant but want to know the cost per new user or first-time trialist. By discounting the participants on which the reward is wasted you can see how much it is costing to get at each new user. It does not measure what happens after this initial trial.

The same modelling advantages apply and different scenarios can easily be tested.

INPUTS:

    A to F as above

    K Current users among participants. The offer is wasted on those who already use the product.

    L Participants who do not get their reward because it goes astray, eg someone else in the house who is not a prime target uses the sample.

    M Participants who receive but do not try, eg receive the sample but forget to use it.

    N Cheats - those people who misredeem the offer, eg misredeem the coupon, or send off for the gift using someone else's proof of purchase, ie without trying the product.

CALCULATION:

    Steps 1 to 4 above

    Step 5: Worthwhile participants = H - (K + L + M + N) = O

    Step 6: Cost per worthwhile participant = $\dfrac{G + I}{O}$ = P

OUTPUT:

    The cost ascribed to each new user.

Figure 10.5 Cost per new user model

Conversion analysis for sampling activities

This looks at the conversion of the new users to the brand after a sampling activity. If the promotion was seeking purchase of the product as the first trial of the product then the cost per worthwhile participant (P) above represents the cost to get the customer in on your brand for the first time.

However, in a sampling operation where the product has been tried free of charge, not all 'worthwhile' users will go on to buy the product and some will drop out. The cost per new user is inappropriate, what is required instead is a cost to get to the next stage, new purchasers.

Trial activities require information or assumptions about the likely conversion of trialists to purchase and their subsequent loyalty to the brand. This is likely to be difficult to obtain without specific research input.

INPUTS:

   A to P Above.

   Q The percentage conversion of trialists to purchase

CALCULATION:

   Steps 1 to 6 as above

   Step 7: Number of converts to the product = O x Q = T

   Step 8: Cost per convert (purchaser) = $\dfrac{G + I}{T}$ = U

OUTPUT: Cost per new purchaser.

Figure 10.6 Conversion analysis

Breakeven analysis

Applicable for trial, and volume driven activity, this model looks at when the activity will have paid off. It gives some scale to the activity.

By inputting the value of each sale and the likely number of market purchases per year (the number of times a consumer buys into the market) the model can easily calculate the point in time when the activity will break even, ie when the costs of the activity will have been paid for by the profit from the new sales.

This is a very stark model about which it is difficult to be accurate. It also ignores such benefits as the extra noise and awareness created by the activity which will help trigger off a purchase at a later date. It is therefore important not to use such a model verbatim, but merely to provide scale, ensure an insight into what the consumer is likely to do and to offer a way of comparing alternative activities.

INPUTS:

    R The profit from each sale

    S The number of market purchases per year

    T A loyalty factor, ie the percentage of future market purchases that
        will be of your brand (NB loyalty may decline over time)

CALCULATIONS:

Step 9: Number of purchases to breakeven $= \dfrac{U}{R} = V$

Step 10: Number of years to breakeven $= \dfrac{S \times T}{V} = W$

OUTPUTS:

    Number of purchases to breakeven

    Length of time to breakeven

Figure 10.7 Breakeven model

PRE-PROMOTIONAL RESEARCH

Modelling is fine as a theoretical exercise but it is most valuable when based
on the evidence from evaluation and research. Here we look at some of the
options for research.

- ❑ Inputs.
- ❑ What it can offer.
- ❑ Necessary qualities of research.
- ❑ Limitations.
- ❑ Planning.
- ❑ Types.
- ❑ Commissioning.

Inputs

Research provides the opportunity for fact-based decisions or at least enhanced opinions. There are a wide range of inputs to an assessment of promotional expectations and these are illustrated in Figure 10.8.

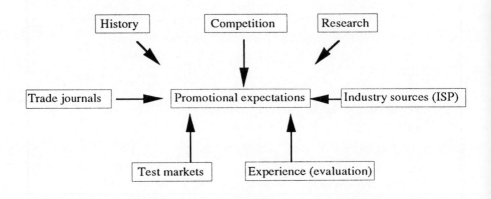

Figure 10.8 Inputs to promotional expectations

With an increasing tendency towards fewer bigger promotions, the commitment is very high, consequently promoters want to be reassured that their investment is sound. Research is one way of corroborating the promoter's views. Research can greatly help in the decision-making process, but it must be remembered that it is only one input and is unlikely (except perhaps in direct marketing) to replace it.

Joint research commissioned by *Promotions and Incentives* magazine and the ISP confirmed that the big spenders view promotional research favourably (*Promotions and Incentives*, June 1992). Around half of companies who run promotions claimed to carry out research into them, which is a long way behind advertising and direct marketing. If you are not one of the half that do research, why not? Sensibly the big spenders are making sure their money is well spent and doing more resesrch, perhaps others should too. Big promoters like cereal manufacturers and oil companies regularly put concepts into research to help them select from-short listed ideas.

What can research and pre-testing offer?

Research and pre-testing can offer input to:

- ❒ choice: a way of choosing between proposals;
- ❒ focus: on who to aim the promotion at;
- ❒ relevance: confirmation that the proposal is relevant to the target;
- ❒ realism: compared to expectations;
- ❒ creativity: assistance to agencies in their creative work, access to the emotional content of research can be a fertile idea source;
- ❒ the avoidance of blatant mistakes;
- ❒ on where/how to refine a proposed activity;
- ❒ identification of poor ideas;
- ❒ a decision on whether to run the promotion at all;
- ❒ a sales argument for the trade.

Promotional responses are vested in the consumer (or customer for trade activity), not in the promotion. It is the consumer that makes the decision to participate or not. A strong but inappropriately constructed offer either will not generate responses or will generate responses from the wrong people. It therefore follows that trying to pre-guess the response is very difficult unless you know the consumer very well and have a great deal of historical information.

It is clearly important to understand this dynamic to achieve a quality promotion that hits its objective. We can test the following at any of the steps along the chain of promotional participation:

- ❒ awareness;
- ❒ comprehension;
- ❒ attitude;
- ❒ intention;
- ❒ purchase/trial likelihood;
- ❒ repeat purchase likelihood.

Research and pre-test qualities

Effective research needs to:

- ❒ be designed or selected specifically for the need;
- ❒ be diagnostic to discover the reasons for the effects;
- ❒ be worth the investment (if not why bother with such a small promotion?);
- ❒ provide easy to understand results;
- ❒ have results that can be acted upon.

Limitations

Naturally promotional research does have its limitations:

❑ what is true at the time of asking may not be true later, environmental issues and brand perceptions may have changed, the marketing mix may have altered and competitors may have done something unexpected;

❑ people will say one thing and do another. They frequently respond in the way they think they should or what they believe they would do, but their behaviour does not match the claim;

❑ beware and monitor for competitive spoiling tactics in regional and store based testing.

Planning research and pre-tests

Effective research and testing needs to be well planned:

❑ it must have clear objectives and action standards. Research is unlikely to answer questions you do not ask and answers may be ambiguous if the research is not well structured;

❑ there generally need to be control groups who are not offered the promotion and form a basis for comparison;

❑ comparisons must test like with like;

❑ only test significant things, not irrelevances;

❑ test only changes to one element of the mix at a time or test completely different things, otherwise you will not know what changes have caused the different responses;

❑ ensure you have effective stimulus material - illustrations may be fine, as may unfinished work for rough tests. This is especially true if dealing with factual comparisons, but if softer emotive issues are involved then the physical creative execution will have greater influence, and testing will be more difficult and will require more finished materials;

❑ it must have the right sample eg users of the competitive brand you are attacking;

❑ for qualitative research, ensure the sample size is big enough and the response rate high enough for the results to be statistically sound.

Types of research and pre-testing

There are four approaches to finding out what your planned promotion will do.

- ❐ Desk research.
- ❐ Qualitative research.
- ❐ Quantitative research.
- ❐ Testing.

These approaches are not alternatives, they are complementary and which ones to use will depend on the questions you need answers to.

Desk research

There is a wealth of information already available in most companies. Often this is lying around unused, or it may be in an unfriendly format that needs your analytical input. Get it out and dust it off, it is a valuable tool to help you choose and fine tune your promotions. The information will usually be in the following forms.

- ❐ *Verbal history*: soft information on past experiences residing in older members of the sales and marketing community. This runs the risk of bias, questionable factual basis and selective memory problems. Go out and ask but use with caution.
- ❐ *Redemption data*: somewhere the response rates to past promotions are likely to be recorded, in an easy-access system in TQ companies, all over the place in most. This will show trends and scale even if it will not give precise measure or the reasons behind response rates, eg the design was poor, there was high competitive activity etc.
- ❐ *Guard books*: companies used to keep full promotional histories of their brands' activities in guard books. If these exist or the brand office has good records this may help resolve some of these practical questions.
- ❐ *Evaluation histories*: the best source of factual data, especially if backed up by concurrent or post-promotional research.
- ❐ *Competitive analyses*: ideally there should be an ongoing recording of all competitive activity. This may be augmented by specific analysis on the most relevant and impactful activities. Understanding competitors gives you access to the powerful TQ

tool of benchmarking. It allows you to ensure you do not over- or under-pitch your promotional proposition.

❒ *Panel data*: there is often a wealth of panel data but the skills to interpret it may not be present. Get them. Where robust information is available such sources can be very revealing about your and your competitors' promotional histories. This can often help to show the affects of an activity on sales, penetration, loyalty, awareness and purchasing habits. Very specific and practical analyses can be done, eg sales movements versus price analysis of panels can determine the price elasticity and help decisions on how much to discount for optimum effect.

Qualitative research

Here research is planned to investigate the effect on the softer issues such as the consumer's attitude to the promotion and their motivations for paticipating. The research does not use a structured questionnaire and the sample base is small, ie it may well be typical but it is not going to be statistically sound. Consequently the findings cannot be used for any quantitative decisions, eg sales increase or redemption rates.

The abilities of individual researchers running these tests is important, since good ones can probe behind the viewpoint expressed to find the underlying reasons for a particular attitude. This research can check for gross negatives and give valuable developmental information to select an offer on its appropriateness or refine the proposition, but they rarely provide a clear yes/no decision.

Qualitative research can provide soft measures and insights into such things as:

❒ *awareness:* the impact, attention and recall a promotion will command;

❒ *comprehension*: a response to the creativity elements, an understanding of what is being communicated and whether the panel can easily describe and access the promotion;

❒ *attitude*: the reaction to the proposition, eg relevance, image fit, credibility, negatives, irritations, whether it has reached wear-out point and its fit with other marketing activity such as advertising. These studies will not indicate whether a promotion will work, just whether it 'fits'. Promotions that do not fit may still pull in good responses but they are likely to erode the brand's uniqueness over time;

❒ *intention*: have they been persuaded by the proposition, will it affect their response or purchase propensity?

Qualitative research is quick, cheap and easy to set up. Types of qualitative research include the following.

- ❑   *The straw poll*: where the brand manager goes around the office asking all the secretaries and/or colleagues what they think of this or that promotion. This is a disaster as far as true decision taking is concerned. It may point out a few glaring mistakes or practical points and is worth doing on that front, but it cannot tell you how your target audience will react in the real world.
- ❑   *Discussion groups*: here small groups of around six to eight consumers participate in a general discussion on a particular topic. The researcher acts as a catalyst and also steers the conversation towards areas of interest but without giving any bias to the views. These are one of the commonest ways of pre-evaluating promotions, however they are not suitable for very complex or private brands or promotions. Discussion groups will be just that, people discussing the issues between each other, and this is a much more rich information source than a question and answer session.
- ❑   *In-depth or extended interview studies*: one-to-one interviews can probe more deeply into the decision-making process and can get at sensitive issues that might be masked by group dynamics. On the down-side such interviews tend to have more interviewer generated responses. In-depth studies are often a good follow up to discussion groups.
- ❑   *Others*: there are others, eg observational studies and conflict groups, but these are less often used promotionally.

Quantitative research

Quantitative research in a pre-testing situation is in effect a mini-test but under controlled circumstances. It can provide information on similar topics to qualitative research but has some numbers attached. It may appear that quantitative research is better than qualitative as it potentially provides a numerical basis for financial decisions. This is not necessarily so, it is just different from qualitative research and provides different types of answers. Both have their place.

Quantitative research is more structured and will require specific answers laid out in a questionnaire. These may be lead by a researcher using prompts and visual aids or may be performed at a distance, eg by telephone or post. Because of the scale of information required it tends to cost more than qualitative research.

However, it is unlikely that the numbers from quantitative research will be perfectly accurate. Their accuracy can be enhanced by ensuring that there is a big enough sample. What is important is to structure the research carefully and ensure you ask the right questions for the situation in hand. An offer may generate a high response but it may be from the wrong people or it may be scoring low simply because the offer is not clearly expressed. Quantitative research may not always tease these answers out, you only get feedback on the content of the questionnaire. Low scores should be revisited to understand the reasons why. They might be simply remedied.

The types of things that can be tested for different offers (rewards and mechanics) and products include:

- interest;
- awareness;
- recall;
- comprehension;
- credibility;
- relevance;
- purchase likelihood;
- influence of the promotion on purchase;
- repeat purchase likelihood;
- thresholds for multiple purchase offers;
- response to offer;
- value for money (vs other brands/offers).

The types of quantitative research that might be carried out includes the following.

- *Hall tests*: where groups of consumers are brought in to answer questionnaires.
- *Panels*: where fixed or rolling panels of consumers are set up to act as a sounding board for ideas. Sometimes these panels are put into simulated buying situations where they have to chose products to purchase, including the promotional items on test.
- *Past customers*: contacting past responders/purchasers to find out their views.
- *Street surveys*: where shoppers or people passing are stopped and their views polled.

❏   *Door to door surveys.*
❏   *Regional/localised tests*: for example around supermarkets and other discreetly located businesses such as restaurant chains.
❏   *Exit interviews*: eg of customers leaving a shop.
❏   *Observation tests*: where behaviour is recorded.

Testing

Testing means putting your promotion into the field, usually in restricted availability, to see how it responds. The results obtained will be better than research results, in that they are representative of actual consumer behaviour in the environment where they would normally access the promotion, rather than measures of what consumers might do. Tests give some real numbers to the proposed activity.

Testing is restricted. In purely commercial terms you will be able to calculate costs much more effectively but supportive qualitative research information will be required if you are to understand the reasons behind consumers' actions.

Even tests are not completely accurate. They are subject to the laws of probability and the statistical robustness of the sample, plus any changes in the environment between test and roll-out. Testing frequently cannot replicate in-store and medial exposure. Testing along with appropriate support research is typically used when very large and expensive activities are to be run, eg a major sampling campaign.

Types of restricted tests include the following.

❏   *Geographical*: for example TV or sales region tests or those around supermarkets or other discrete areas.
❏   *Store tests*: specialist research agencies can arrange for promotions to be tested in representative retailers' stores. These can offer very specific information on potential brand share movements, brand switching, absolute and relative rates of sale and any incremental market opportunity. Some stores are very co-operative, even running their own testing service and making EPOS data available, usually at a cost.
❏   *Media based*: what is the best media to put the offer out in.
❏   *A/B splits*: where different executions are run in each half of the test run. This is typically used in magazine promotions with half the titles running one ad and the other a different one. The types of things that might be changed in a split run test include:
    - the presentation of the offer, eg design, copy, format, size,

layout, number of elements (eg direct mail pieces) and loca
tion;
- the content, eg the type of offer and reward;
- the response mechanism, eg the number of proofs of purchase,
method of application, incentives and prizes to support the
reward structure.

Commissioning research and tests

The professional association for those involved in compiling or using market, social or economic research is the Market Research Society (MRS). The MRS produces a year-book which provides information on researchers and research related topics. Researchers registered with them have to adhere to the guidelines laid down by their Professional Standards Committee in their Code of Conduct. The MRS also has specific interest groups and provides an information service to members.

MRS members should be able to offer much more comprehensive and specific advice than that offered here. The purpose of exploring research here is not so that you can go away and plan and implement your own research programmes, but to give you some familiarity with the types of resesrch available and the issues that may arise.

Once research and other checks have validated your proposition, you can proceed with the implementation.

11

Implementation Processes

By now you will have a promotion you wish to run with. To date most things have had a theoretical slant, but implementation is about commitment, or to put it another way actually spending money to achieve your goals. In terms of the PDCA cycle, implementation is the 'do' of promotions.

No matter how good the idea is, it will fail if poorly implemented. Failure means not meeting your customer's needs, and probably getting trade and consumer complaints along with a loss of franchise.

Implementation can be looked upon as a difficult chore and is often under-resourced, low profile and the issues avoided as much as possible. This is because:

❐   it requires different skills (eg completer finisher) to those required in the creative and strategy defining processes and is not seen as exciting enough by the people starting the promotion off;
❐   it looks horribly complex;
❐   it takes a long time;
❐   people do not know what they have to do, and there are often no simple systems and instructions.

The next two chapters seek to demystify some of the implementational issues and make this vital step easy to deal with.

The PDCA cycle for the implementation phase is expressed in Figure 11.1.

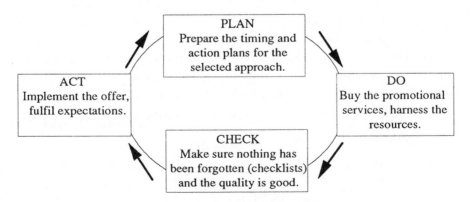

Figure 11.1 The implementation PDCA cycle

In line with this, implementation is broken down into two sections. Chapter 12 deals with checklists and notes for specific promotional types, while in this chapter we look at the more general processes:

- ❏   *planning the implementation*:
- ❏   *design, artwork and print*;
- ❏   *sourcing*;
- ❏   *agreements with other parties*;
- ❏   *targeting*;
- ❏   *handling and fulfilment*;
- ❏   *insurance*.

PLANNING THE IMPLEMENTATION

To make sure your promotion is implemented in a TQ way a thorough and detailed plan of what must occur to bring the promotion to life is invaluable. This plan can be expressed in a number of ways but there are essentially two formats, both of which need to be communicated effectively to all concerned.

Process maps and networks

There will be many detailed steps on the way to completing a promotion and these can be expressed in pictorial forms that help show the order in which activities need to be done and the process by which they should best happen.

Process maps
Determining the constituent parts of an activity requires detailed analysis, especially where a new type of activity is being implemented. One TQ tool to help this is to process map the steps.

Process maps use simple flowcharting principles to describe processes. In a process map step actions are written into bubbles and lines connect these to show the order of activities and how they are inter-connected. The different steps will include a start point and a goal, a series of activities and decision points on the way. These can be represented by different shapes, as shown in Figure 11.2, opposite.

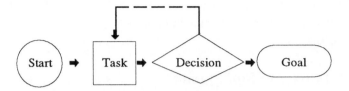

Figure 11.2 Process map symbols

The first thing to do is determine all the tasks or steps necessary to complete
the particular process. For each step there will be up to four types of linkage:

- input from previous steps;
- feedback to previous steps;
- output to the next step;
- feedback from the next step.

For each step you need to be sure there are suitable standards, measurements
and resources to ensure a quality output. Figure 11.3 shows a process map for
artwork preparation. This is a simplified model for the sake of illustration.

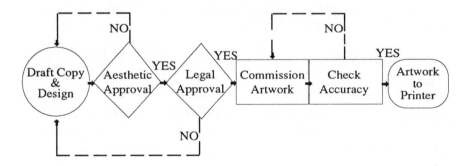

Figure 11.3 Simplified process map for artwork preparation

Process maps are particularly valuable to help identify tasks, spot weaknesses
in a process and identify improvement opportunities.

Networks

These are often factory tools to describe the sequence of events to achieve
completion of a manufacturing project, but they can be used for any activity.
They are schematics where the series of actions required are drawn up
pictorially to show the connections between events and to put a time measure

on chains of activity. This provides earliest and latest dates for activity steps to occur and also show up which activities are dependent on the completion of another step in the process.

Action plans and timing plans

These are effectively the same thing. Here the network can be expressed in a more friendly format and more detail may be included. The task to be performed is expressed as a specific action required, the ownership ascribed and the date by which it is due recorded. It is a good TQ check to include another column recording when it was achieved. Later analysis will throw up problem areas that need addressing.

An action plan is the single most useful quality tool to achieve effectively implemented promotions. They may seem like an effort to prepare but they will repay the time spent in putting them together many times over. Anyone who does not prepare an action plan is foolish.

The content can be derived by thinking through all the steps to implementing a promotion. Use the various checklists in this book and overlay your own organisational needs. I have illustrated this with an imaginary action plan for an on-pack sendaway offer showing how the actions due might be expressed and shared. Remember to build in extra time for unforseen eventualities.

Communication

Ensure all parties involved see the whole action plan and understand their responsibilities. Gain feedback and consider the best way of communicating changes and progress to all parties. Consider any other softer inputs that are not necessarily core to the process but valuable in ensuring a quality output that meets customer need, eg ensure you tell the salesforce and key customers of your main decision points so that they know the date by when they have to comment if they wish to influence the outcome.

Once your plans and communication systems are in place you can start to implement.

ACTION PLAN NO 1
PROMOTION: Free rolling pin with brand X.   DATE: Week 1

IN FIELD DATE: W32   PROMOTION OWNER: Brand manager.

ACTION	OWNER	DUE BY	DONE BY
brief agency	brand manager	w1	
initial agency response	agency	w4	
feedback to agency	brand manager	w6	
final agency response	agency	w8	
rough designs in	agency	w9	
premium samples in	agency	w10	
brief handling house	brand manager	w10	
brief for special packaging	brand manager	w10	
determine draft sales estimate	sales/marketing	w10	
initial quotes: - design/artwork	agency	w10	
- handling	handling house	w13	
- packaging	factory	w14	
- premium	agency	w11	
- other			
draft copy	agency	w12	
enhanced designs	agency	w12	
feedback: - production	factory	w14	
- legal (principles)	legal	w12	
- commercial	commercial	w12	
- sales	sales	w14	
- handling house	handling house	w13	
- marketing director	MD	w14	
check practical handling issues	brand manager	w15	
production confirmation	factory	w16	
formal go-ahead	committee	w18	
appoint handling house	brand manager	w18	
final copy	agency	w18	
final designs	agency	w18	
order materials/premiums	brand manager	w18	
artwork due date	agency	w20	
legal approval of artwork	legal	w21	
brief printer	brand manager	w22	
brief trade	brand manager	w22	
brief consumer research	brand manager	w22	
prepare sales aid	agency	w24	
proof print	brand manager	w25	
print due date	printer	w27	
premiums due in date	agency	w30	
premium packaging due date	handling house	w30	
contract packing of offer pack	factory	w29	
on-shelf date	sales	w32	
evaluation date	brand manager	w48	

NB: Ownership is likely to be variable, particularly between brand manager
    and agency, depending on organisational structures.

DESIGN, ARTWORK AND PRINT

This is an enormous area, easily justifying a book in itself. However since print is almost invariably involved in promotions it is appropriate to cover this at a very top-line level. It should be noted that there are many new developments in print technology and many of the older preparatory stages in design and print are being replaced by computer-based systems, eg computer-aided design and digitised artwork.

Basic print process

The basic steps towards printing, say, a leaflet are illustrated in Figure 11.4.

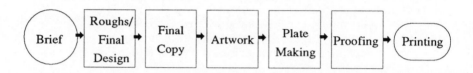

Figure 11.4 Basic print steps

Design briefs

As with all briefing, the better and more thorough, the better the results. Refer to the checklist for brief contents.

Design brief checklist

❐   *Market background*
❐   *Product information:*
    - usage, place and purpose;
    - purchase habits and place;
    - brand positioning statement.
❐   *Target audience*:
    - geodemographics;
    - socio-economics;
    - behaviourgraphics;
    - attitudinal qualities;
    - any research background, including design and packaging.
❐   *Other marketing activity*:
    - advertising;
    - promotion;
    - publicity.
❐   *Retail/distribution issues*:
    - place final item will be, outlet;
    - merchandising;
    - shelf/display position
    - special display issues;
    - storage.
❐   *Production issues*:
    - quantity, in total and print run;
    - size of finished item (dielines);
    - reproduction method;
    - materials;
    - outer packaging;
    - transportation and handling.
❐   *Cost limitations.*
❐   *Design objectives*:
    - what is the promotion trying to do?
    - what is this particular piece of print trying to do?
    - where will it happen?
    - what does the target audience need to take out of the design?
    - state priority of any different messages;
    - state any need for future copy to be added or whether the design
     produced will be adapted for other purposes;
    - need to match to the brand personality.   CONT...

Design brief checklist (cont.)

- ☐   *Tonal quality*:
  - mood, feel and look of design;
- ☐   *Promotional objectives.*
- ☐   *Copy*:
  - the draft copy for the activity;
  - any theme or headline;
  - rules to be included;
  - cautionary information;
  - legal requirements;
  - fill, weights, sizes;
  - ingredients, contents;
  - manufacturer details;
  - special messages;
  - bar coding.
- ☐   *Restrictions*:
  - sacred cows or corporate rules on what must or must not be done in all cases;
  - necessity of conforming to existing design styles;
  - materials;
  - inks, colours, including special colours for logos etc;
  - sizes;
  - shapes;
- ☐   *Response time*:
  - roughs;
  - final design;
  - artwork.

Design and artwork progression tips

- ☐   Design - do not go to the expense of colour if black and white roughs will do.
- ☐   Anyone with power of veto over the final item needs to agree the design before before you progress to artwork.
- ☐   It is essential that every part of the artwork is checked through very thoroughly. Copy should be checked not just word by word but letter by letter, ideally by someone not involved in the promotion.
- ☐   Get the artwork legally cleared. It is far from unknown for

changes to be made between 'final' copy and artwork.
❐ Transparencies can add to origination costs.
❐ When getting print quotes, provide the printer with a mock up or rough.
❐ Larger transparencies provide better quality, eg for larger display pieces, and also provide more room for retouching.
❐ It is helpful to the printer to include a colour mock-up or visual with the artwork.
❐ Use special colours if a specific colour is required. Here a specific colour reference (eg a Pantone number) is given for the printer to match.
❐ Keep the number of special colours to a minimum to save on cost.
❐ Where the same basic artwork is being used for a number of similar applications with some specific changes, eg a door drop leaflet with each area's leaflets being printed with the local shop address, use overlays for the replacement parts of the artwork.
❐ Avoid artwork changes once the printers' plates are made, ie at proof stage. It is expensive and will cause delay.
❐ The person commissioning the print job should approve the proof.
❐ Consider using 'cromalins' instead of proofs. These are higher quality photographic representations of the final job. They are good for checking appearance and detail but the colour balance will not be the same as a proof.

SOURCING

Choosing items

One of the most important qualities of premium items is their uniqueness and inimitability. Many advertising gifts are typified by the relatively turgid list of pens, diaries, calculators, calendars, T-shirts and desk pads that account for the vast majority of these items. However some gifts and the best premium items for consumer rewards are much more varied and tend to be more specifically chosen for the task and recipient.

Sourced items may be:

❐ totally bespoke, ie designed and made specifically for the promotion;
❐ adapted from existing items but personalised in some way;
❐ totally off the peg, with no special properties.

The very best premiums are unique and cannot be copied, and will be uniquely linked to the brand being promoted. Ideally they will add value to the brand proposition and become a unique property of it. They must never detract value from the brand. Novelty has the added advantage of increasing a premium's perceived value.

In reality true uniqueness is difficult (but not impossible) to achieve. Depending on the final use it may be more appropriate to offer a regular line but present it in a way that is exclusive to you. For example, existing material in a book can be freshened and represented to provide a product that, while constructed from a stock of background material, by the use of a little editing, page inserts and cover personalisation, can appear specifically written for that promotion. The same principle can go for most other premium items from clothing to mugs. You buy the basic model and have it adapted to your specific needs.

Originality may not be down to production but to print. Printing the logo (in the right colour) can make for a highly memorable premium. Therefore it is important to ensure that you can print on the material to a suitable level of quality. Taste is also important, do not emblazon the logo so strongly that people are put off, say, from wearing an item of promotional clothing. However, a discreet message can provide an effective, long-term reminder. For some brands with a strong cachet, personalisation is not problem but a boon and for others it provides a fun air of collectablity, eg corporate tea mugs.

Totally original items tend to be more expensive because there are start-up costs such as tooling that need to be amortised over the production run. For example, if you are buying bespoke plastic widgets (the generic slang for premiums) you must be guaranteed a certain volume to justify the high cost of making the moulds from which the items are made.

Suitability of premiums

Fitness for the purpose is a definition of TQ itself. The process of the supply of premium items is well matched to being a TQ operation and ensuring the premium is the best possible one is absolutely vital.

Successful premiums will have the qualities described in the suitability checklist on the next page.

Briefing suppliers

Normally you will be using some kind of supplier to provide the premium item. In this case they will need a thorough briefing on the type of item you want and what it is to be used for. Use the briefing checklist to make sure they are in a strong position to respond with the most appropriate item. Good briefing will save you time and money.

Premium suitability checklist

☐   *Uniqueness.*

☐   *Enhancement/consistency*:
       - with the brand image.

☐   *Suitability for the recipient*:
       - especially on items designed for children or with which
        children may come into contact.

☐   *Suitable quality*:
       - should be consistent with or exceed that in the marketplace;
       - weigh price and quality;
       - ensure production quality is consistent.

☐   *Objective value not subjective interest*:
       - subjective qualities of an item may cut redemption rates even
        if the item is good quality, eg colour or fashionability.

☐   *Good value*:
       - the best advantage is often from products that have high
        perceived value but low cost, eg clothing and jewellery can
        have good mark ups, especially if bought from abroad.

☐   *Personalisation*:
       - eg can you print on it or attach a label?

☐   *Ease of description or illustration*:
       - must be done in a way that will not mislead;
       - the likelihood of any variations, eg colour will need to be
        specified.

☐   *Safety in presentation and use*:
       - especially important if the item comes into contact with the body
        or food, eg will it taint or become tainted, and in the case of
        electrical goods.

☐   *Unrestricted use*:
       - is it free of copyright and patent restrictions? Promotions
        agencies often propose ideas based on high street products, so
        ensure you are entitled to use, advertise and have the item
        manufactured.

☐   *Consumer friendliness*:
       - any necessary instructions and warnings must be supplied.

☐   *Easy storage and transportation.*

☐   *Physical suitability*:
       - eg not too fragile or heavy for dispatch.

☐   *Guaranteed by the supplier.*

☐   *Appropriate after-sales service*:
       - any required should be available, eg provided by the supplier.

The type of supplier you use will depend on the item you need and the resources you have available.

Briefing checklist for sourcing

    ❒   *Rough idea of type of item.*
    ❒   *Budget.*
    ❒   *Number required.*
    ❒   *Delivery timing.*
    ❒   *Delivery location.*
    ❒   *Offer details.*
    ❒   *Target audience profile.*
    ❒   *Brand positioning.*
    ❒   *Description of end use.*
    ❒   *Personalisation required.*
    ❒   *Special print/personalisation requirements.*
    ❒   *Early sample requirements, eg trade sell-in samples.*
    ❒   *Lead time and minimum quantities for repeat orders.*

Choosing suppliers

There are a number of ways of sourcing premium items:

    ❒   buying yourself direct from the specialist supplier, manufacturer or agent;
    ❒   using the promotions agency;
    ❒   using specialist sourcing houses.

Going it alone

If going it alone be aware. There are a thousand pitfalls out there for the unwary and the inexperienced. Large organisations which buy a lot of premiums may have the resource and expertise to cope with this. The average brand manager does not. For small purchases and very distinct items for which there are established specialist sources, eg pens, calendars, pottery or glass-ware, these suppliers may be geared up to provide the level of service that may enable you to buy direct. However, be sure you know what you are doing.

Seeking out a manufacturer or agent from the dozens of likely sources will take up more time than you have available and you will never be confident you have the best price or most reliable supplier.

One possible source of reliable direct supply is using the resources of existing major premium purchasers. For example, there are mail order companies who have their own catalogues and sourcing organisations already set up. This is a bit like buying off the peg. It probably won't be the cheapest but it is likely to be easy and someone else is taking all the strain for you. This route is ideal for lower level redemptions and where you want to make a choice of premiums available. Frequently a lot of the back-up material you need, such as visuals, catalogues etc, already exist, just waiting for you to tap in.

If you insist on going it totally alone there are sources of information which may provide suppliers and ideas.

❐   *Annual buyers guides*:
     eg *Incentive Today* magazine's 'Buyer's Reference
     Book', *Promotions and Incentives* magazine's 'Buyer's Guide',
     BRAD's 'Premium and Incentives Price Guide'.
❐   *Magazines*:
     eg *Incentive Today, Promotions and Incentives,*
     What's New in Marketing, Marketing Week, Marketing.
❐   *Promotion exhibitions, gift and trade fairs.*
❐   *The British Promotional Merchandise Association (BPMA)*:
     has a library of merchandise suppliers and issues a publication
     BPMA Promotional News which has lots of ideas and contacts in
     it.

The Institute of Purchasing and Supply runs training courses, has an ethical code of practice and publishes rules for trade promotions. The BMPA also has a code of practice.

There is one other category of going direct and that is for joint promotions with another company. There is a joint promotions checklist in Chapter 12.

Using the promotions agency
If you do go via your sales promotion agency be aware that many of them are going via a sourcing house anyway and if they are not, be very confident that they have the knowledge, experience and contacts to ensure they deliver a quality result before you proceed. Some do and have their own buying departments or sourcing businesses.

Most agencies would prefer to source themselves because they can take a commission or mark-up on the goods they buy for you. Some agencies are happy to propose ideas, and take the creative and implementation fee, accepting that a sourcing house or your buying department will take over, providing they know this is the way it will operate in advance.

The fairest way, if you are confident in their abilities in this area, is probably to let them cross-quote, and if they come up with the best price then fine.

Sometimes the premium cost is not that great and other payments are paltry in relation to the work the agency has to do. In these one-off cases it might be as well to let the agency run with it. If the organisational complexity of the sourcing operation is very high you may wish to pay the agency a fee to manage the buying process.

The sourcing house

These are the true professionals in the premium buying area. They often have worldwide networks of contacts and some even have interests in factories overseas to enable them to get the best prices.

The vast majority of these suppliers work on a commission basis, although a few do work on a fee-only approach. Some sourcing agencies are setting themselves up in more of a consultancy role, challenging the promotions agency. I would advise caution in adopting this route if only because at least a worthy promotions agency would try to steer you away from a premium based promotion if it was inappropriate.

Reputable sourcing houses are likely to be members of their trade organisation, the Promotions Sourcing Association (PSA). The best suppliers will be able to work in long-term partnership with you, removing the learning curve associated with new suppliers and benefiting all concerned.

When selecting your supplier, be they a sourcing house, direct or whatever, note the supplier quality checklist opposite.

Getting quotations

It is advisable to get more than one quote. Three is often a good number.

However, the quotes might not always be against the same specification regardless of how tight your brief is. Make sure you are comparing like with like.

Remember you can negotiate. There are a number of ways of doing this, eg ask for volume discounts, special prices for improved payment terms (speed of settlement or money up front), sale or return (SOR) and forward buying discounts for agreeing to future orders. When running joint promotions or buying branded goods, remember any visibility you are giving has value for the third party. In the same way, as it is quite feasible to get holidays and cars offered free as prizes, if your premium offer has high visibility and

---

Supplier quality checklist

❐   *Reliability*:
the cheapest supplier is not always the best.

❐   *Commitment*:
are they prepared to invest to sort out problems to protect your
and their reputation, even if it means a short-term loss?

❐   *Professionalism*:
how do they operate, do they have reliable and efficient systems?
Some are now registering for BS5750.

❐   *Experience*:
are they established and have they worked on the type of things
you require before?

❐   *Creativity*:
the ability to come up with genuine innovations.

❐   *References*:
can they supply the names of satisfied customers that you can
talk to?

❐   *Speed*:
can they supply or mock-up samples quickly and efficiently,
eg for selling-in or research?

❐   *Financial soundness*:
will they go bust while your order is on the way? Ask for bank
references, or better, a credit rating.

❐   *Flexibility*:
can they respond to demand surges and give a rapid response to
reorders at smaller run lengths?

---

may result in incremental sales for the supplier, then this has value in your
negotiation. Do not expect too much, for if you are only buying small volumes
you are unlikely to beat the prices of the high street majors with their enormous
buying power.

Sourcing often seems to be done in a hurry, whereas leaving adequate
space in the timing plan can result in both a better price and a better quality
product as suppliers have longer to find the best source.

Longer lead times also allow for more economical delivery methods:
sea is much cheaper than air -freight, but takes longer. Air-freight may not be
a viable alternative at all for bulky items.

If the promotional response is unknown and a quick adjustment to volumes is required, consider a UK or EC source rather than a long-distance supply, even if it does cost a little more. The latter may have prohibitive delivery times which may prevent you satisfying customer needs in the time agreed in the offer. Discuss your requirements with your supplier.

The last check

Before you actually buy your premium, you should double-check:

☐   *that the item is safe*:
the item should meet UK and EC safety regulations and conform to the Consumer Safety Act 1978. There are independent safety laboratories that will carry out these tests for a small fee;

☐   *that the packaging is safe*:
eg polythene bags may require warnings and air holes;

☐   *that it works*:
use and abuse the item and see what happens;

☐   *that it mails or can be dispatched as intended*:
actually post it to yourself;

☐   *that it can be delivered right first time*;

☐   *that everyone has signed on for the item*:
a lot of money is spent on premiums and yet the buying responsibility is often held at low level, so make sure higher levels are happy too.

☐   *that all other involved parties are happy*:
eg the handling house;

☐   *that the supplier understands all your needs, for goods and services*:
is there anything else the supplier needs to know? For example, perhaps they would benefit from a visit to the factory if the items are going to end up on-pack.

☐   *you have thought about insurance*:
from product liability, to trade disruption and over-redemption;

☐   *the goods originate in a politically stable country*:

☐   *the duty situation*:
what is due now and during the life of the promotion;

☐   *the exchange rate*:
what was used in the quote and that the supplier guarantees the price regardless of fluctuations;

❏   *you have ordered the right amount*:
      do not over-order or under-order; remember suppliers may work
      to +/- 10 per cent tolerances on order sizes so check the position
      carefully; use evaluation to anticipate redemptions; set up a
      monitor for redemptions and compare past performance to esti-
      mate reorders;

Accepting quotes

Acceptances of suppliers' offers can be in writing, verbal or by action. It is best
to ensure they are always written. Quotation acceptances or orders need to be
fully detailed to avoid confusion or disappointment and a detailed specification
should be a part of this.

It should be noted that where conditions are laid down, failure to comply
means the aggrieved party can back out of the contract. Contract law is highly
complex and there are different levels of commitment and liability, eg
warranties are different from conditions and only allow the aggrieved party to
sue rather than cancel the whole contract. Because of this complexity it is
important to be detailed and specific in your agreements. Contracts should be
vetted by your legal adviser or with due regard to pedantics and realism.

When you do accept a quote or offer using the order specification
checklist should help you avoid most problems.

Order specification checklist

❏   *The supplier.*
❏   *A full description*:
      - of the item and if appropriate the materials and appearance.
❏   *Quality and safety standards*:
      - quality assurance (guarantee of quality) versus quality control
        (checking to assess level of quality);
      - what checks are required and approval systems to be used?
❏   *Price*:
      - specify VAT, duty and shipment costs;
      - who will carry the price of any material cost increases or ex-
        change rate fluctuations?
      - are you expected to pay for overages?
❏   *Packaging*:
      - how each item is to be packed.
❏   *Delivery method*:
      - eg sea or air-freight, the high cost differences demand clarity.
❏   *Delivery format*:
      - outer packaging size and specifications, palletisation, special
        instructions.   CONT.

Order specification checklist (cont.)

❐   *Delivery place:*
   - any contact, special times or booking in required.

❐   *Delivery date(s):*
   - specify any need for early samples or phased deliveries.

❐   *Insurance:*
   - eg for damage in transit;

❐   *Indemnity and risk:*
   - eg any damage the premium might do to third parties.

❐   *Guarantee:*
   - eg for the replacement of damaged or faulty goods, especially important if the item has moving parts.

❐   *Contingencies:*
   - if there should be supply problems, failure to supply on specification, the factory goes bust or delivery is late, what will you offer the customers and who will pay?

❐   *Continuity of supply:*
   - guarantees of availability for future orders.

❐   *Reorders:*
   - what the terms, minimum order size, lead times and delivery specifications are.

❐   *Exclusivity:*
   - degree of exclusivity, eg timescale and product areas.

❐   *Copyright:*
   - liability if copyrights or patents infringed.

❐   *Payment terms.*

❐   *Confidentiality.*

❐   *Insolvency:*
   - what happens in the case of insolvency?

❐   *Arbitration:*
   - what arrangements if there are disputes? Arbitration is cheaper than lawyers, advice can be given by the ISP.

❐   *Termination arrangements:*
   - especially important for long-term promotions where suppliers might be taking measures to secure long-term delivery. They need to know how long the commitment of the purchaser will be guaranteed.

❐   *Residuals:*
   - what happens to residual goods or material? Specify any sale or return (SOR), buy-back agreements or discounts for unmade up materials that cant be reused elsewhere.

Disposals

Sadly there are always too many or too few items bought unless they are off the peg items held in stock, in which case you are less likely to get a good price. Residuals can be returned if you can negotiate SOR, great if you can get it but rare for most things. Try to use stock up if possible, eg to get good PR, maybe give away to charity, but whatever you decide do it as quickly as possible. If dealing the residuals off it will be at a loss, but keeping the goods for another promotion will, in my experience, rarely work, and just costs for storage and wastes time while you try to find a suitable use.

AGREEMENTS WITH OTHER PARTIES

Many promotional situations will require agreements with external parties, from sourcing premiums and services to joint promotions.

It is essential that these are made formally to ensure everyone has clearly defined responsibilities. This not only aids clarity but provides a start point should there be a dispute. Agreements should not be so laborious as to detract from the task of getting on with the promotion, or to dampen enthusiasm.

Agreements checklist

❏   *Funding:*
    - who is paying for what?

❏   *Volumes:*
    - how much service or how many goods are required?

❏   *Timing;*
    - what are the key timings, commitment, delivery etc?

❏   *Approvals:*
    - who has to approve any action or artwork etc?

❏   *Support:*
    - do support levels, eg advertising, PR need to be agreed?

❏   *Exclusivity:*
    - is it necessary to protect in this way?

❏   *Data ownership:*
    - who owns any databases generated?

❏   *Liability:*
    - who is liable for what errors or for recompense if part of the deal is not fulfilled?

❏   *Legality:*
    - avoid the lawyers' battle of words but get a firm letter of agreement or contract signed by both parties.

❏   *Authority:*
    - ensure the person has the authority to make the deal.

❏   *Double-check:*
    - cross-reference with other appropriate sections in this book, eg the sourcing , joint promotion and managing creative resources sections.

IMPLEMENTING TARGETING SYSTEMS

Producing profiles

This is where a profile of the target audience is determined and described in the terms of the the targeting system being used.

Profiles can be developed from any suitable data sample containing names and addresses of the target audience, eg:

☐ lists of known product users;
☐ promotional respondents;
☐ databases with branded information, eg TGI;
☐ lists of other similarly profiled product users.

The geographical location of the individual address records (usually via the postcodes) of the target consumers are compared to the geodemographic system and a profile prepared. Each address can be ascribed on a geographical basis to a segment of the targeting system. From this, a score for each segmentation type can be drawn up, showing the penetration of the target within the segment. This is then indexed against the average expectation so that a full profile of the target group can be drawn up.

Graphic representation of the findings can easily show targeting classifications where the sample is over or under-represented. This can be used either as the basis on which to plan a promotion, or by profiling respondents as a form of evaluation.

Using targeting for door drops

Here the profiled information is used to select the best areas to drop. Typically but not exclusively a geodemographic system is used for door drops.

A campaign potential report is produced. The computer aggregates the information into door drop units, ie postal sectors of around 2,250 homes and provides information against various sizes of distribution on:

☐ an index of the degree of targeting achieved versus a non-targeted drop;
☐ an estimate of the percentage of households in the drop that will actually match the target profile exactly;
☐ the number of non-targeted households that would have to be dropped to reach the same number of people in the target profile.

This report allows a decision to be made on how many items to drop. The cut-off can be made two ways:

- ❏   at a set number that matches your fixed budget, while making sure you get at the best mix of people;
- ❏   by cutting off when penetration of the target market drops below a predetermined level below which the reduced likelihood of the right person getting the reward makes the activity uneconomic.

Clearly, when dropping expensive items such as samples, targeting is a relatively cheap and highly useful tool in reducing waste. Even for leaflets the costs are usually easily more than covered.

The reports can be numerical or can be produced in map form to show exactly where the target market can be found and where the drop will occur.

Once the decision on how many items has been made a postal sector ranking is produced and this details by postal sector which precise areas will be dropped and how many items will be required for each area.

Targeting individuals

This is done for many direct marketing applications, eg direct mail or telemarketing, to find the best prospects from lists. A profile is produced as above, usually from a list of known responders for people you are trying to access or even of non-responders to isolate people you are trying to avoid.

The profile can then be applied to the unknown larger database and matched up to find people with the same characteristics. This will usually be done at the individual household level rather than postcode sectors and the sophistication of the targeting system selected is likely to be higher, eg the lifestyle questionnaire based systems.

HANDLING AND FULFILMENT

Offer fulfilment should be barely noticed by the customer unless it is to comment on how thoughtfully and considerately it has been performed. Your aim should be seamless fulfilment of the offer within the specified period, ideally a lot quicker if appropriate, eg within one week. The goal should be to exceed customer expectations and provide faultless service.

Failure to provide this will mean a lack of customer satisfaction and the risk of losing your valued customer base. Remember it costs more to get a new customer than to keep an existing one. I can illustrate this with a prize I won. The prize arrived over six weeks after my claim. It was left outside, in the wet as a gift to neighbourhood burglars, with no letter inside, not even a compliments slip. To compound my disappointment over the prize of a year's supply of free product, no one had asked me about which products in the range I used and no way was a full year's supply provided. Hardly a quality result and my enthusiasm for that manufacturer has totally evaporated.

In most cases the contact with the promotional respondent is arranged and performed via a third party who specialises in this. This is so whether the offer is a simple free draw, a sendaway, a telemarketing operation or a complex database activity. These agents are acting as your representative and how they perform will reflect directly on your brand. This is a classic case of a chain being as strong as its weakest link, so you cannot afford to skimp on attention to detail that may result in a poor quality offering.

The biggest problems associated with handling most promotions are:

- ❏   late delivery;
- ❏   sub-standard packaging;
- ❏   sub-standard accompanying materials, eg compliment slips;
- ❏   inaccurate information.

Fortunately many of the handling and fulfilment specialists have much improved over the 1970s and early 1980s but problems can still arise, often as a result of oversights and poor briefing by the promoter. This section highlights key areas that need to be covered off for effective offer fulfilment.

This section covers:

- ❏   dealing with fulfilment houses:
  - choosing and appointing;
  - briefing;
  - administration and reportage;
- ❏   sending promotional material;
- ❏   dealing with money;
- ❏   postcodes and mailing economy;
- ❏   the redemption package;
- ❏   stock control;
- ❏   queries and complaints.

Dealing with fulfilment houses

Choosing and appointing

Handling and fulfilment are to all intents and purposes the same thing. Handling infers more handwork but effectively the suppliers will usually be offering a range of services. There is a great diversity of supplies from the high technology, highly computerised organisations offering database and telemarketing facilities, to the smaller outfits set up to do small jobs with more flexibility, speed and precision.

Do not try to do handling yourself or by your agents unless this is a fundamental part of your or their business, eg mail order. There are many stories of companies being swamped by responses and having to call in the experts at short notice and high cost.

For similar reasons, make sure that other people in your organisation do not use a specific handling house address automatically before quotes are obtained. It puts you in a very poor negotiating position if the first thing a handling house knows about an offer is when applications start pouring through their letterbox.

Use the checklist to help you to select. You will then need to agree the terms of business in writing. Consider all the points in this section that it will be appropriate to agree and cross-reference with the contractual section under sourcing.

Briefing

A handling house can only give a quotation if it has a fully comprehensive briefing. An effective briefing checklist is given in the Promotional Handling Code of Practice as issued by the Promotional Handling Association and available from the ISP. It has been reproduced here.

Quality handling houses will help you determine appropriate specifications for different jobs, for example warn you off datacapture for free prize draws if you have no database or profiling requirement. They will also help on such things as packaging requirements for mailed items and many have connections in the packaging industry and can devise special packaging for your needs.

Handling house selection checklist

☐ **Term of appointment:**
   - longer-term relationships will allow understanding of the client's needs and help provide a consistent quality service.

☐ **Staff quality/supervision:**
   - is it adequate?

☐ **Administrative abilities:**
   - can they supply the information you want in the form you want, when you want it?

☐ **Facilities:**
   - ensure they have adequate computer/technological facilities.

☐ **Alternative quotes:**
   - cast around for alternative quotes within your chosen supplier portfolio.

☐ **Price vs quality:**
   - do not simply accept the cheapest quote.

☐ **Reliability:**
   - ensure the supplier is reliable and can guarantee to deliver the type of service you require at a sensible price, seek references.

☐ **Agency appointments:**
   - where a promotions agency is appointing and working with the handling house on your behalf still ask yourself the same questions and insist on seeing the original quotations to ensure you are getting a good service.

☐ **Size:**
   - can they physically handle the job? Many handling houses have vast numbers of casual workers they can bring in at short notice to deal with peaks of activity.

☐ **Storage:**
   - can they offer adequate space, security and storage conditions?

☐ **Insurance:**
   - are your goods ensured by them or you? Coverage might include, fire, theft, goods in transit, business interruption and the liability of employees of the handling house.

☐ **Financial stability:**
   - consider how long they have been around and get bank references.

☐ **Membership of the Promotional Handling Association (PHA):**
   - this should guarantee compliance with the Promotional Handling Code of Practice (copies available from the ISP).

☐ **Data protection and usage:**
   - a handling house will normally be registered as bureau, the client as ultimate list holder should be registered as appropriate with the Data Protection Registrar (see the database management section in Chapter 10).

☐ **Confidentiality:**
   - handling houses may use aggregated data relating to response rates, type of promotion and seasonal variations for its own internal or commercial purposes, but should not reveal details on individual consumers,clients or products.

Briefing prompt list

❒ **Description of promotion:**
- incentive offered/instructions to applicant/special instructions (ie one per household).

❒ **Handling requirement:**
- handling mechanic/turnaround time.

❒ **Promotion duration:**
- start date/close date.

❒ **Response forecast:**
- anticipated volume/response pattern.

❒ **Promotion media:**
- on-pack/off the page/TV/direct mail etc.

❒ **Application format:**
- coupon/leaflet/plain paper/telephone.

❒ **POP requirement:**
- number/type tolerances/count procedures.

❒ **Payment requirement:**
- amount(s)/coins/cheques/postal orders/credit cards/charge cards/tolerances/await cheque clearance.

❒ **Bank account:**
- client's or handling house: if latter specify charges levied by bank for a) paying in and b) clearance of cheques.

❒ **Postage and dispatch:**
- first class mail/second class/rebate/Trakback (recorded delivery)/registered mail/carrier/postage float/direct charge to client's own postal account.

❒ **Packing materials:**
- delivered pre-packed/envelope/padded bag/carton/other.

❒ **Storage requirements:**
- quantities/period/security or general.

❒ **Insurance of goods:**
- handling house or client.

❒ **Capture and production of application details:**
- manual or computer/fields required/deduplication/selections/ sortations.

❒ **Reports and analyses:**
- type/frequency/period covered.

❒ **Consumer relations:**
- procedures for incorrectapplications/correspondence/ complaints/returns/exchanges/refunds.

❒ **Audit:**
- POP and application retention/record dispatch date.

❒ **Stock control:**
- reorder levels/returns/final disposal.

❒ **Goods inwards:**
- delivery date(s)/counting in procedure/advice of receipts to clients.

❒ **Security/confidentiality:**
- special requirements.

The brief will be followed by a response. This should be written and should include:

- ❏   duration of validity of quote;
- ❏   clarity on what is included or excluded;
- ❏   details of costs that may vary over the period of the promotion;
- ❏   administration costs, note minimum weekly charges that may apply for the tail end of the promotion;
- ❏   stationery costs;
- ❏   costs for special computer tasks;
- ❏   postage costs;
- ❏   details of any cash floats required, eg for refunds or postage;
- ❏   storage costs (remember to dispose of residuals swiftly at the end of a promotion to minimise these).

Administration and reportage

Depending on the offer you will need different frequencies of reportage, from daily, or even hourly, to monthly. You may want special analyses done, as well as the basic facts of how many applications have come in. Reportage should come in writing in the format and at the times you have agreed. Consider the following inputs:

- ❏   offer details;
- ❏   start and end dates;
- ❏   number of applications this time period;
- ❏   cumulative applications;
- ❏   number of applications fulfilled;
- ❏   number awaiting fulfilment;
- ❏   date of oldest unfulfilled application;
- ❏   details of queries/errors;
- ❏   stockholding;
- ❏   number of weeks stock at current redemption rate;
- ❏   postal/cash float held/used/needed;
- ❏   special analyses, eg phasing of applications, profiling the applicants against a database to see what type of people have responded or sorting redemptions by media.

It is sensible to check handling houses are doing their job properly, so send in your own test applications as well as having known test mailings agreed with the agency. Consider test mailing throughout the whole activity. Audits and spot checks on the premises may also be appropriate.

Remember, handling houses are often small businesses and may not have the financial back-up to stand high levels of credit. Ensure you pay bills on time, and that floats for post and cash refunds are promptly paid. Failure to do this will simply put the quality of response to your customers at risk.

Sending promotional material

The usual medium is post via the Royal Mail. There are many options, and most promotional goods go by ordinary mail, but sometimes special requirements are appropriate and the carrier can advise. A publication called *Mailguide* is available from the Royal Mail's local customer service centre. This offers guidance on postcodes, postal packaging, insurance, special delivery services, international mailings, ways to pay and so forth. The main options relevant to the promoter are noted below, along with details on the importance of postcoding and how postal savings can be made.

Inland letter mail types include the following.

- ❐ Ordinary letter post:
  first or second class. Low compensation for loss, damage etc.
- ❐ Special delivery:
  guaranteed next day delivery.
- ❐ Recorded delivery:
  for special messages, queries and where a record of delivery is important.
- ❐ Registered mail:
  for secure mailings where compensation considerations are important.
- ❐ Freepost:
  first or second class. Envelopes pre-printed to a specified design can be used for first and second class replies. If consumers are asked to write out the address on their own envelopes it can only be used as second class. There is a nominal handling fee of 0.5p per mailing. Discounts are available for big users. Payment is made only for the replies received. A response service licence (RSL) available at a nominal charge is required. Freepost can be combined with Admail, a redirection service that enables replies to be automatically redirected to a different address, eg a handling house.
- ❐ Business reply service:
  Primarily for business-to-business use, a RSL is required. Reply

cards and envelopes are preprinted to a specified design, reply-paid for first or second class post. Payment is only for those replies made.

☐   Priority response service:
for an extra 0.5p your first class business reply or freepost mail can be targeted for the first scheduled post of the next day.

Whatever postage device is used for customer replies it is important to get it right. The last thing you want is the recipient to be asked to pay a surcharge.

Dealing with money

Cash in
Do not ask for cash as it is unwise to post this. Normal payment methods will be by cheque or credit card. With cheques it is best not to bank them until goods are about to be dispatched. Credit cards do carry a cost with charges being levied by the credit companies, but it is worth considering this route as it so easy for consumer to respond by mail or telephone. Handling houses can easily arrange the administration.

Cash out
It is rare that cash will be sent to consumers, but if you do make sure a robust opaque envelope is used that disguises the contents. If coins are being sent, use a coin cards to disguise contents. Cash is cheaper to send than other forms of refund, but in many cases the value of the refund will vary, and for this and security reasons cheques are normally used. These can be personalised to the offer. One company got a celebrity to sign and so consumers didn't even bank the cheque, preferring to keep the autograph.

Postcoding and mailing economy

The composition of postcodes was explained in the section on targeting, above. Postcode information is available on over 24 million household and business addresses in the UK via the Royal Mail's Postcode Address File (PAF). It is available on computer tape, CD and various other formats to suit the application. PAF can help to postcode addresses or work out addresses from limited information, eg when only part of the address is available or legible.

Postcodes can provide cost savings to the promoter in a number of areas.

❐   *Database accuracy*:
     databases with postcodes provide more information and allow
     easier de-duping of databases.
❐   *Savings on postage*:
     There is a specialist type of Mailsort RSVP available
     for posting fulfilment items. Savings in excess of 20 per cent are
     possible, depending on the exact specifications of the individual
     job, if mailings are:
     - pre-sorted to suit the Royal Mail's task;
     - at least 90 per cent correctly postcoded;
     There are three levels of service:
     - Mailsort 1: targeted for next day delivery;
     - Mailsort 2: targeted for delivery within three working days;
     - Mailsort 3: targeted for delivery within seven working days.
❐   *Targeting*:
     postcodes can be used to profile promotional prospects and
     respondents using geographic and geodemographic databases.
     These can identify types of respondents, useful in evaluation,
     potential new customer types, or customer locations.
❐   *Rapid addressing*:
     using the PAF system rapid addressing is possible from as little
     information as just the postcode and the house number. This can
     save a lot of time in sorting mailings or operating a telemarketing
     service.

It is important to note that postcode geography is dynamic and changes. This
will have particular bearing on database and direct mail users who will need
constantly to update records to ensure their targeting systems do not call up
postcodes which have moved and to ensure the mail can be suitably sorted for
Mailsort discounts. The PAF is regularly updated and can assist.

The redemption package

This should be thoughtfully put together. It is how the applicant will receive
and view your offering. Test mail before you go live to ensure the packaging
does the job intended.
     Redemption packages being sent will need to include:

❐   the reward;
❐   a compliment slip from the right source, eg the brand for

consumer offers or the company for most business offers;
- [ ] instructions, guarantees and service or repair details as appropriate;
- [ ] good packaging;
- [ ] possibly further offer (known as a 'bounceback' offer), eg another reward offered for further purchases or a coupon off another brand or item in your range.

Stock control

Ensure you have set up a system with the handling house and have agreed responsibilities in terms of who is going to flag up reorder requirements in good time.

Graphing redemptions over time will reveal a pattern of redemption. Comparing this to evaluations of past activities can help in predicting sensible reorder levels.

Queries and complaints

Complaints

The majority of aggrieved customers will do business again if dealt with efficiently so plans need to be laid down for any problems that might arise. Such problems need to be dealt with swiftly, ideally within three working days. There has been too much bad press from consumer watch-dogs on the failure of companies to fulfil their promises on offers.

Complaints should always be dealt with in a quality way and you should agree specifically what handling houses can and cannot say on your behalf. Anything falling outside this should be referred to the client for a decision.

It is important to pick up on complaints about poor-quality promotional goods quickly and try to rectify the matter. Refunds and replacements should always be made promptly with all costs being carried by the promoter.

Invalid applications

Occasionally there will be people who try to cheat on offers and sensible measures need to be taken to deal with these too.

Invalid applications need to be dealt with. These are normally of three types:

- [ ] those applications that will be honoured;
- [ ] those that will not be honoured;
- [ ] those that cannot be honoured.

The first type might include no or insufficient POPs or postage. You need to make it clear to the handling house whether you will or will not honour these. If you decide not to honour, eg if no cash is included on an SLP or multiple applications are received on a restricted offer, then it is normally appropriate to write back to the applicant and politely explain why not. If it is just not possible to honour, eg the address has been left off then these applications need to be kept on one side for subsequent claims.

Delays

Delays are a special case and if items to be sent out are unavoidably delayed then the BSCCP obliges you to write to the customer within the offer redemption period (normally 28 days), explaining the problem and giving a realistic estimate of when they will receive the goods. Do not be over-optimistic or you may have to write again! Where money has been sent in refunds should be offered.

Complete unavailability of items

Applicants should be offered alternatives to the equivalent or greater value. Refunds should be offered to those who have sent in money. Advertising for the offer should be withdrawn. Considering the applicant's feelings and best interests will ensure they are dealt with in the best way possible.

INSURANCE

Apart from statutory requirements such as employer's liability, promotional insurance is optional. You need to asses the risk versus the cost.

Many aspects of promotions can be insured and the decision on which to insure is up to you. My personal view is that it is the real uncertainties of life that need insuring, eg against the weather if running an event on one set day, or third party protection if running a roadshow in case someone trips over a prop and sues you.

When you do insure, treat it like any other commercial contract, and make sure you have the best deal, make sure the quality is good and look carefully at the small print. Your cover will need to be adequate or you may find yourself subject to a restricted payout, so ensure you have full indemnity.

Types of insurance that may be appropriate to promotions include the following.

❏ *loss of trade and the cost of the promotion*:
eg if you are let down by circumstances beyond your control;

❏ *public liability*:
ie indemnity against injury or loss/damage to the personal property of third parties. This should be high, probably £1,000,000 plus;

❏ *goods in transit*:
do not rely on supplier or haulier insurance unless you know it to be adequate;

❏ *the weather*:
eg for events;

❏ *people*:
eg non-availability of staff for an event and also personalities, both against non-appearance or worse still if they get involved in scandal and damage your reputation;

❏ *over- or under-redemption*:
in case your offer comes in much higher or lower than expected;

❏ *money*:
eg if you are selling product at a promotional site;

❏ *premiums/products in storage;*

❏ *professional indemnity insurance*:
eg where an agency is insured against making mistakes:

❏ *errors and omissions insurance:*
eg where printers are insured against printing errors. These can be very costly, eg scratch card promotions.

One other form of promotional insurance is the 'fixed-fee' or 'buy-out' promotion as covered in Chapter 8.

Having looked at implementation processes we can now go on to more specific checklists.

12
Implementation Checklists

This chapter provides a series of checklists, notes and copy guides for key promotional offers and practices. Use of these checklists should cover most of the issues concerning promotional implementation but there will inevitably be some situations where further checks and actions are required.

The following elements are covered:

❐ General checklist and notes:
  - overview;
  - restrictions and conditions;
  - protection against copying;
  - proofs of purchase;
  - application forms.
❐ Specific activity checklists:
  - price promotions;
  - coupons;
  - sendaways;
  - gifts with purchase and container premiums;
  - banded packs;
  - prize promotions;
  - joint promotions;
  - press promotions;
  - sampling;
  - direct marketing;
  - database building;
  - telemarketing;
  - door drops;
  - charity promotions;
  - in-store demonstrations, roadshows and exhibitions.

GENERAL CHECKLIST AND NOTES

Overview

In addition to the specific checklists by promotional type as detailed below, all promotions should be cross-referenced with the general implementation checklist and notes below.

Overview promotional implementation checklist

☐   *Cross-reference to Chapter 10.*

☐   *Adherence to the general codes of practice, eg:*
- the British Code of Sales Promotion Practice (BCSSP);
- the British Code of Advertising Practice (BCAP).

☐   *Adherence to any special codes or sections of above codes, eg:*
- product type;
- promotion type;
- intended audience;
- promotional medium;
- distribution channels.

☐   *Adherence to any data protection regulations.*

☐   *Communicate widely:*
- ensure everyone who needs to know about it, knows about it;
- seek input from experienced colleagues;
- use a timing plan.

☐   *Simplicity and easy understanding of the offer.*

☐   *Ensure it does not mislead in any way.*

☐   *Clarity over restrictions:*
- ensure any restrictions or conditions, eg geographical, age, number of applications per household etc, are clear and on the outside of the pack, leaflet or other promotional material;
- if these include closing dates, proofs of purchase, till receipts financial contributions, or if it is a sendaway, these:
- must be on the front and outside of the pack;
- should allow adequate time for product sell through;
- should feature on any advertising for the promotion;
- closing dates should be on pack outers;
- closing dates should ideally not be before sell by or best before dates or careful stock management will be required;
- any other special restrictions and conditions (see below).

☐   *Comparisons and worth:*
- ensure comparisons and statements of value (especially of worth) are in the copy and supportable.

☐   *Legality:*
- ensure the principles, words and design are legally acceptable;
- do not accept copy suggestions included here verbatim, check every one.

☐   *Agreements:*
- ensure formal arrangements are made with all external parties (see Chapter 11).

☐   *Ensure it is designed and structured well:*
- be happy with your offering.

☐   *View the promotion from a practical, customer perspective.*

Restrictions and conditions

Date restrictions

Date restrictions on offers do not normally legally invalidate a pack as being saleable once past. However, it is not Total Quality and any intermediaries, eg retailers are hardly likely to be pleased at the idea. If you want to avoid having redundant stock make sure closing dates leave adequate time for stock to sell through in all, even the smallest of, outlets. You should not be selling stocks to the trade that you do not expect to sell through before the offer expires.

Ensure the offer is of sufficient length for customers to buy requisite packs to have enough POPs.

Geographical limitations

Make sure these are clear, eg the British Isles includes the Republic of Ireland, Great Britain is England, Scotland and Wales only, the UK is England, Scotland, Wales and Northern Ireland but not the Channel Islands or the Isle of Mann.

Age

Be sure the prize or reward is suitable for anyone who might win or apply for it. Consideration should be made to cash alternatives and the gaining of parental or guardian consent where appropriate.

Cars should not be offered as prizes to persons under 17 years. For performance cars and potentially hazardous prizes act responsibly and consider some sort of training as part of the prize.

Alcohol and tobacco promotions should only be offered to people over 18. Where children are involved pay especially careful attention to the BCSPP. Parental or guardian approval should be obtained. Any promotion where a contract is formed with young people can only be binding if a parent or guardian signs to confirm acceptance.

Pack outers

Show offer details and closing dates. Offers should ideally last at least as long as best before dates. Otherwise careful stock management will be required and there may be a risk to listings.

Restrictions on copy, design and print
Living persons

Under BCAP promoters and advertisers cannot portray living persons without their consent except in certain circumstances. Such use, even if within the guidelines, runs the risk of being withdrawn if any person used complains.

Two areas that are likely to be encountered in promotions are crowd shots and the use of personalities. In general terms crowd or background shots are not a problem as long as there is no defamation, offence or humiliation. In terms of individuals, they may sometimes be used providing the advertisement does not contain anything which is inconsistent, or likely to be seen as inconsistent, with the position of the person referred to, and when it does not abrogate the person's right to enjoy a reasonable degree of privacy. From this it follows that people in the public eye should be all right as long as no commercial involvement inconsistent with their position is suggested or if it restricts how they might exploit their name commercially.

Since many people, particularly those in the public eye, are used to throwing law suits around I would recommend close scrutiny of BCAP and legal consultation at an early stage before using any likeness or reference to an individual without their permission.

Royalty

Great care must be taken in the use of photographs and illustrations of the monarch or royalty. It is not normally acceptable to use their likeness on promotional goods. Guidance can be obtained from the Lord Chamberlain's Office (see Useful Organisations).

Royal Warrant

Even for Royal Warrant holders special rules apply over its use and the use of Coats of Arms. The Royal Warrant Holder's Association can advise (see Useful Organisations).

Banknotes

Banknotes must not be the same size as the real thing and should be made different in some way, eg partially shown as a fan of notes. It is prudent not to show the monarch's head. The Bank of England (see Useful Organisations) can grant approval and can give guidance notes. If you wish to use foreign notes contact the respective embassy or high commission for guidance.

Coins

The Royal Mint can offer guidance (see Useful Organisations).

Stamps

Copyright lies with the Post Office, but in general it is permissible to reproduce stamps if their use is incidental to main advertisement theme. Guidance notes are available from the Post Office (see Useful Organisations).

Protection against copying

It is frequently necessary to take steps to avoid being copied or to be sure you are not copying someone else. There are a number of different legal devices to protect against this. Protection on an international basis is much harder and more complex than local protection. Specialist legal advice should be sought.

Trade marks: might be brands, names, words, labels, letters, numerals or combinations of these and they can be registered at the UK Trade Marks Registry. The main legislation is the Trademarks Act 1938. A trade mark:

- ❐ is owned by the person who registers it, not the first user, ie ensure you are registered and protected and ensure you are not infringing anyone else's mark;
- ❐ protects brands from counterfeiting by registering their trademarks;
- ❐ will be registered by product providing there is genuine intention to use it in the course of trade on the goods for which it is registered, otherwise it will lapse;
- ❐ cannot be ascribed to products which are free, eg free giveaways;
- ❐ does not protect slogans, container shapes (eg bottles), products similar to but not exactly the same as the registration.

There are two types of trade mark, Part A where distinctive marks are registered (denoted 'R' in a little circle) and Part B where full registration is not possible because the mark is not distinctive enough, at least at this point in time, (marked 'TM'). Service marks showing the origin of services can also be registered (Trade Marks [Amendment] Act 1984).

When referring to competitors it may be possible to refer indirectly or by implication or to the corporate body supplying the product.
NB it is prudent to check the latest position with your legal advisor as EC harmonisation may affect the situation.

Passing Off: Protects designs, trade marks and slogans. Slogans need a reputation attached to them to ensure such protection, which is not guaranteed. Protection cannot be extended to cases of satire or parody or use in relation to different products.

Copyright: this is the exclusive right assigned by law to the originator of a piece of work. Copyright:

- ❐ is owned by the creator rather than the first user. Copyright may be owned by the employer. Promotionally it is important to clarify with your agency, before the event, who is to own copyright;

❏   can cover slogans, (not conventional word marks or single words, unless a logo)

❏   can cover design (including logos). This is a good way of preventing people stealing your name and for example using it on T-shirts, ie by linking it tightly to a logo protected by copyright. It it important to keep original dated designs and the designer's particulars.

Proofs of purchase

Proofs of purchase:

❏   should be unique, consider using bar codes or special tokens;

❏   should be simple to use;

❏   should be clear and easy to identify;

❏   should not be repeated on a pack if you are to avoid mis-redemption;

❏   removal must not remove warnings/instructions relevant to product;

❏   removal must not make the product harmful or useless;

❏   should be easy to remove but not so easy as to be pilferable;

❏   should be mailable where appropriate;

❏   should be clean and safe to handle;

❏   should not always be the same, or people will collect pack tops knowing they will come up as requirements for a future offer;

❏   the number required should be clear and flagged on the front of any pack or other promotional material.

With the large numbers of itemised till receipts available, they are becoming viable as POPs and the consumer should be asked to ring the item(s) bought in ink. However, remember consumers may want to apply to more than one offer from the shop and they may lose the receipt, ie slippage is likely.

Technically proofs of purchase can easily fall foul of the Trading Stamps Act if they are going to be exchanged for cash voucher. In reality this is not an issue, although some people do print a value on their proof of purchase tokens to be safe.

Application and entry forms

Application forms are technically company order forms (Companies Act 1985). Therefore they should carry the company's place of registration, registered address and registration number.

Things to ensure about the application or entry form for an offer:

- ❐ that you can write on it, beware plastic and glossy materials;
- ❐ it is not tainted by product;
- ❐ it removes easily;
- ❐ it is simple to use and has plenty of space for application details;
- ❐ ask for key information in block capitals and use tick boxes where possible;
- ❐ removal must not remove warnings/instructions relevant to product;
- ❐ removal must not make the product harmful or useless;
- ❐ the application address appears on the form and on the part of the promotional material retained;
- ❐ it is easy to send;
- ❐ it is easy for the handling house to extract the data needed;
- ❐ restate the POP and any contribution requirements on it.

Plain paper applications are not illegal but rarely work well in practice.

SPECIFIC ACTIVITY CHECKLISTS AND NOTES

Price promotions

Copy claims
There are a large number of different possible copy claims for price promotions. Some of the more common acceptable ones are:

'XXp off normal in-store price'

'XXp off recommended retail price'

'XXp off RRP'

'XXp off manufacturer's recommended price'

'XXp off MRP'

'Previous price XXp, offer price YYp'

Price marked pack (PMP)

'XXp'

'Price XXp'

'Only XXp'

While you cannot specify a comparison on a promotion, try a special qualifying statement, eg 'A hot price XXp'.

Extra value, ie extra fil free (EV)

'XXml Extra free. YYml for the price of ZZml'

'XXml Extra free. YYml for the RRP (or MRP) of ZZml'

PMP EV

'WWml extra free. XXp. YYml for no more than the previous price of ZZml'

Launch offers

'Introductory offer ....(offer details), based on future in-store price'

Half price pack

'Half price trial offer, half normal in-store price'

Buy one get one free

'Two for the price of one. 2 x ZZml for the price of 1 x ZZml'

'Buy one get one free. 2 x ZZml for the price of 1 x ZZml'

Buy two get one free

'1 pack free. 3 x YYml for the price of 2 x YYml'

'3 for the price of 2. 3 x YYml for the price of 2 x YYml'

Price promotion checklist (discount off retail/selling price)

☐   *The overview implementation checklist.*
☐   *The checklist for any offer run at the same time.*
☐   *Make price indication meanings clear:*
  - do not compare value or worth without a justifiable comparison;
  - consumer prices should include any VAT;
  - trade prices need not include VAT as long as this is clear;
  - comparisons to previous prices should state what they were;
  - do not use initials to describe higher prices in a comparison, except RRP (recommended retail price) or MRP (manufacturer's recommended price);
  - do not describe a price as normal or regular unless it applies to at least half your customers.
☐   *Conform to timing constraints:*
  - previous prices must have been available for at least 28 consecutive days in the previous 6 months in the same retailer. The onus is on the retailer to ensure this happens;
  - it should be made clear to the consumer if prices only apply for a limited period;
  - introductory offers should not run for an unreasonably long period;
  - future prices should only be indicated if you are certain that the product will be available at the higher price for at least a 28-day period in the 3 months following the offer.
☐   *Do not exploit the goodwill of others:*
  - by naming names in making offers targeted at competitors (this is not the same as comparing offers, eg prices, made by competitors, which is permissible).
☐   *Agree funding arrangements up front:*
  - agree how discounts are to be funded to retailers and other outlets, ie discounting the cost to maintain the outlet's percentage margin (on the principle that increased sales will ultimately provide more profit) vs (more expensively) funding the discount at the out-price to maintain their cash margin.
☐   *Capture all costs:*
  - some may be hidden or from different budgets, eg trade support costs.
☐   *Bar codes:*
  - packs with a volume or physical size change to the retail unit, eg EV, will require new bar codes on the retail unit (known as consumer unit codes or CUCs) and also on the trade's bulk pack (trader unit codes or TUCs);
  - even if the contents have regular CUCs, trade offer outers quoting a price or discount, eg '12 for 11 packs', or when there is an outer size change, will require a new TUC.

Coupons

Coupons come with a wide variety of values, mechanics and tasks to perform. The coupon implementation checklist should capture the majority of issues you need to cover off for an effective outcome.

However it does not go into misredemption which has been covered earlier.

Coupon design, format and layout is important and remember that design affects redemptions enormously, often more so than face value. Recommendations for design are detailed in the checklist below. This should be read in conjunction with the FDF/BRC/ISP notes for guidance referred to in the checklist.

Typical coupon copy

On/in-pack announcement

Coupon inside (on reverse etc). XXp off this (and/or next) purchase. Closing date xx/xx/xx (if applicable).'

Body copy

XXp coupon off this/next purchase of (brand, product, size, variant etc).

To the customer: This coupon can be used in part payment for (brand, product, size, variant etc). Only one coupon can be used against each of the products purchased. Please do not attempt to redeem this coupon against any other product as refusal to accept may cause embarrassment and delay at the checkout.

To the retailer: (Promoter's name) will redeem this coupon at its face value provided ONLY that it has been taken in part payment for (brand, product, size, variant etc). (Promoter's name) reserve the right to refuse payment against misredeemed coupons. Please submit coupons to (handling house address).'

Free product coupons

These should state the maximum redemption value for the coupon, taking into account price variances between retailers and price increases. A blank box should appear on the front of the coupon for the retailer to write the price in.

Coupon Coding

Inherent in coupon design will be a requirement for special identification codes:

- ❐ ensure all coupons have coupon bar codes on them (provides cheaper, easier handling);
- ❐ conceal coupon bar codes on on-pack offers;
- ❐ make sure bar codes have adequate light margins and are

sufficiently far away from the edge of the coupon to ensure good scanning;

❐ ensure the correct use of bar code colours for good scanning;

❐ a nine-digit NCH code should also be carried on coupons if they are providing coupon handling services;

❐ bar codes require films and a list of suppliers is available from NCH.

Coupon bar coding

Coupons should carry bar codes. These are similar to the 13 digit European Article Number (EAN) code structure for products. Taking the example code of which the first 12 digits are 997654321030, the number is calculated as detailed below.

Coupon identifier

The first two digits (99) identify the item as a coupon. If it is 99, validity is for the UK only, international ones would start 98.

The coupon issuer number

The next four digits (7654) represent the coupon issuer number allocated by the ANA. Membership of the ANA is required for the allocation of an issuer number. There is a small one-off fee payable to the ANA for this.

The coupon reference number

This is the next three digits (321). They identify that particular coupon activity for the coupon issuer. A thousand numbers are available per issuer, who can use them as they wish. There must be a three year gap before the same number can be re-allocated by the coupon issuer.

The coupon value

The next three digits (030) represents the coupon value in pence, ie 30p.

The check digit

The last digit (5) is the check digit. Calculation is as follows.

Step 1. Starting with the digit on the right of the number (excluding the check digit) sum all the alternate digit values, reading from right to left.

Step 2. Multiply the result of Step 1 by three.

Step 3. Sum all the remaining digit values.

Step 4. Add the result of Step 2 to the result of Step 3.

Step 5. The check digit is the smallest number which when added to the result of Step 4 produces a multiple of 10.

The calculation for the example above is shown overleaf.

Step 1.	$0 + 0 + 2 + 4 + 6 + 9$	$= 21$
Step 2.	x 3	$= 63$
Step 3.	$9 + 7 + 5 + 3 + 1 + 3$	$= 28$
Step 4.	$63 + 28$	$= 91$
Step 5.	Check digit	$= 9$

$$\overline{}$$
$$100$$

The complete number is therefore 9976543210309.

Coupon design checklist

❐ *Size:*
   - coupons should be sensibly sized and shaped to fit in the till;
   - minimum 4cm x 8cm;
   - maximum 7cm x 13cm.

❐ *Identification and removal:*
   - ensure the print position is convenient for removal;
   - ensure an obvious border or cut lines;
   - ensure the reverse does not carry another coupon or bar code;

❐ *Design:*
   - impart value through the use of design;
   - include a pack shot to make brand identification easy;
   - include a brand logo to aid recognition;
   - check with handling and trade customers before embarking on the use of unusual materials.

❐ *Bar Codes:*
   - the bar code should be at least 10mm from the lower right-hand corner of the coupon. Allow 26.26mm height x 37.29mm width, to include a light margin around the code.

❐ *Offer clarity:*
   - make close dates bold and clearly visible;
   - the usage occasion, eg 'off this/next purchase' should be clearly and boldly stated with equal colour and size emphasis on each word;
   - offer value should be clearly visible and boldly stated once only on the front of the coupon, with the word 'coupon' or 'voucher' by it;
   - manufacturer, brand names and a redemption address should be clearly shown;
   - product/size/variant restrictions should be clear;
   - any store specificity should be clear;
   - do not have claims like '30p off Brand X' on other parts of the promotional material, or they will be cut out and used as extra coupons, eg if the message has to be repeated elsewhere, just say '30p off' without specifying off what. Think practically, say things like 'this is not a coupon' or 'coupon overleaf';
   - ensure double sided coupons have the values positioned so that they cannot be cut in half and used twice;
   - in-pack coupons should be announced on the outside of the pack.

Coupon implementation checklist

☐ *The overview implementation checklist.*
☐ *The checklist for any offer run at the same time, eg the price promotion checklist.*
☐ *Industry guidance notes:*
  - available free of charge from the ISP, these have been drawn up in conjunction with the manufacturer and retailer trade bodies. It is recommended you get a copy of the latest edition.
☐ *The coupon design checklist.*
☐ *Ease of use:*
  - coupons should be sensibly sized and shaped to fit in the till;
  - ensure they will not get damaged/dirty when removed from the pack or the pack is in use;
  - use suitable and robust materials for printing to ensure handling is possible.
☐ *Closing dates and timing:*
  - make close dates bold and clearly visible;
  - only use a closing date for the coupon user, not for the trade;
  - allow at least six months for trade redemptions after the consumer close date;
  - offer close dates for on-pack coupons should be after product use-by dates;
  - give on-pack coupons time to sell through, or preferably do not have a close date;
  - be wary of couponning on top of other concurrent offers.
☐ *Administration:*
  - advise your clearing house in advance, using established administration systems. Supply them with a sample. Most coupons go through NCH (Nielsen Clearing House).
☐ *VAT:*
  - there are normally no VAT implications on consumer coupons unless your goods bearing the offer are subject to a different VAT rate than the goods against which the offer is valid.
☐ *High value coupons:*
  - if the value is over £9.98 then the coupon value digits should be '999' and the value stated clearly on the coupon so that the checkout operator can pick it up directly from the coupon.
☐ *Free product coupons:*
  - free product coupons should use '000' for the coupon value code. This will act as a prompt for the retailer to write the price on it. The maximum redemption value for the coupon, taking into account price variances between retailers and price increases should be stated on the coupon. A blank box should appear on the front of the coupon for the retailer to write the price in. CONT...

Coupon implementation checklist (cont)

❑   **Store specifics:**
  - ensure conformity to any retailer guidelines, eg size, design;
  - use account bar codes not manufacturer bar codes on store specific coupons.

❑   **Product availability:**
  - ensure the product is in good distribution when using mass media coupons;
  - if cross-couponning ensure matched distribution or carrier product has smaller distribution base.

❑   **Trade notification:**
  - advise the trade of any planned coupon activity including free product coupons.

❑   **Redemption checks:**
  - cross-reference redemptions to stock sold in to specific retailers;
  - consider agreeing maximum redemption levels with retailers where misredemption is a concern;
  - do not pay retailers' claims if they do not stock the product, advise your clearing house in advance of known non-stockists;
  - check the retail value claims for free product coupons matches the known retail price by outlet.

❑   **Security:**
  - bar codes will in the long term enable in-store verification to product purchase;
  - ensure printers destroy plates, proofs and run-ons;
  - ensure distributors have good checks;
  - consider sequential numbering and asking distributors to sign for numbered boxes of coupons;
  - security printing is possible, eg ultra-violet inks that show a 'void' message when photocopying and ultra-violet codes or watermarks;
  - use more than one colour, try to avoid black and white;
  - consider personalising coupons when direct mailing;
  - ensure on-pack coupons are tamper-evident and not easily removable in-store;
  - name and address panels are of limited use but may help. Only around 40 per cent will complete these, even if linked to another offer, eg a competition;
  - ensure face value is less than the publication value for press coupons.

❑   **Payment:**
  - payment to most retailers is organised by NCH who receive, count and verify submitted coupons. NCH bills suppliers:
  1. the face value of coupons redeemed;
  2. a trade handling allowance (as agreed between the FDF and the BRC);
  3. postage costs in getting the coupons to NCH;
  4. a NCH fee.
  - NCH can provide weekly or monthly redemption figures by coupon, by retailer and various other special analyses;
  - note that some big retailers now scan coupons and deduct the money due direct from the trading account.

Sendaways

These will generally be of two types, free mail ins (FMIs) and self-liquidating offers (SLPs). They may be alone or combined, eg one POP to qualify for the SLP, more to qualify as a FMI.

FMIs
Typical FMI copy

'Send for Premium A.

2 Tokens and 40p postage required.

Offer closes xx/xx/xx.

(Full offer explanation and reward description, choice of colour/sizes etc)

(Full application instructions including address)

Promoter's address.

Rules (eg):
1. Offer applies to UK and Eire only.
2. Only one application per household (if applicable).
3. All applications must be on the application form.
4. Allow 28 days for delivery.
5. No responsibility accepted for applications lost or delayed in the post.
6. Closing date for applications is xx/xx/xx.

Application form:
To: Offer A, handling house address.

Please send me ... Premium As. I enclose XX proofs of purchase (specify tokens, till receipts etc) plus XXp postage (if applicable).
BLOCK CAPITALS PLEASE
Name...............
Address............
....
Postcode...........

(If you do not wish to receive details of future offers please mark 'x' in the box provided).'

Free mail in checklist

☐   *The overview implementation checklist.*
NB the special lists on:
- restrictions;
- proofs of purchase;
- application forms;
- insurance.

☐   *The checklist for any offer run at the same time.*

☐   *Full offer description:*
- do not overclaim;
- illustrate whenever possible;
- warn of any likelihood of variation, eg in size, colour or materials;
- offers for textiles should state their fibre content;
- say 'send for' on the main announcement if that is what must be done to get the goods.

☐   *Contributions:*
- at most only the actual, or a contribution towards, postage or delivery (not packing) can be requested on a FMI if the claim 'free' is to be made;
- requirements should be flagged on the outside and front of pack. Cheques or postal orders are preferable, coins may be easier but run the risk of being lost etc. Stamps are not desirable as they cannot normally be reused and may not be cashable, certainly not without extra charges being levied.

☐   *Closing date:*
- closing dates should be on the outside and front of the pack, leaflet or other promotional material;
- should be on pack outers;
- should allow time for product sell through;
- should not close before 'best before' dates if on-pack.

☐   *Premium availability and purchase:*
- any restrictions or risk should be clear. Exclusion clauses are not really valid unless circumstances make it completely impossible (not impractical or expensive) to fulfil the offer;
- ensure you have adequate supplies and contingency plans for over- and under-redemption;
- try not to buy too many expensive SLPs up front;
- refer to the sourcing section in Chapter 11.   CONT..

Free mail in checklist (cont)

☐ *VAT:*
- there are not usually any VAT implications on FMIs. VAT is payable by the promoter on the cost of the item. However this is recoverable if proof of purchase has been requested as it is looked on as a combined supply of goods plus an entitlement to the free item. If the offer was totally free, ie no POPs required, then business gift rules would apply.

☐ *Premium suitability:*
- must be suitable for likely applicants, especially where children are concerned.

☐ *Premium marking:*
- the country of origin of the premium should be included if tokens or vouchers are being exchanged for goods;
- consider personalising either to the consumer or subtle manufacturer branding, eg on a label;

☐ *Quality:*
- do not disappoint, ideally the consumer should get something a little better than they expected;
- ensure the premium meets all safety and quality requirements.

☐ *Contact/application address:*
- the promoter's trading address or registered office address and number should be on the portion of the promotional literature retained by the customer so they have a contact in case of complaint;
- put application addresses on the application form, make them bold or maybe a different colour, and keep promoter and fulilment house addresses separate and well defined to ensure applications do not all turn up at head office.

☐ *Fulfilment:*
- ensure offers are fulfilled within the promised time period, which should not normally exceed 28 days;
- ensure the redemption package does not let the offer down:
- ensure quality is good;
- packaging is secure (test);
- include instructions, addresses for service or repairs;
- include a compliment slip from the brand;
- refer to the handling and fulfilment section.

SLPs
Typical SLP Copy

' Send for Premium A

£5 (specify including VAT, postage and packing if applicable) plus 2 Tokens required.

Offer closes xx/xx/xx.

Full offer explanation and reward description, choice of colour/sizes etc. Country of origin of reward.

Full application instructions including address.

Promoter's address.

Rules (eg):
1. Offer applies to UK and Eire only.
2. Only XXX application(s) per household (if applicable).
3. Slight colour variations may apply from the premium illustrated.
4. All applications must be on the application form.
5. Allow 28 days for delivery.
6. No responsibility accepted for applications lost or delayed in the post.
7. Closing date for applications is xx/xx/xx.
8. Any limitations on availability.

Application form:
To: Offer A, handling house address.

Please send me ... premium A's at £... each (including postage if applicable). I enclose XX proofs of purchase (specify tokens, till receipts etc) plus £... for each item.

I enclose a cheque/postal order made payable to ... for £... and ... proofs of purchase,

or, please debit my Visa/Access (etc) account by £...

card number ..., expiry date ..., signature ...

Colour/size required is ...(or tick box).

BLOCK CAPITALS PLEASE

Name...............
Address...........
....
Postcode...........

(If you do not wish to receive details of future offers please mark 'x' in the box provided.)'

SLP checklist

☐   *The overview implementation checklist.*
☐   *The checklist for any offer run at the same time.*
☐   *The FMI checklist.*
Plus:
☐   *Country of origin.*
☐   *Payment issues:*
     - the VAT inclusive cost to the consumer of the item plus any postage and packing;
     - who payment is to be made to;
     - do not ask for cash;
     - consider alternative methods of application and payment, eg credit card payment, telephone application;
     - do not bank money if there is any delay to goods dispatch;
     - the dealing with money section in Chapter 11.
☐   VAT:
     - the promoter has to pay VAT on the higher of:
     a) the cost of the item + handling + postage + packaging + VAT on all of these;
     b) the sum obtained from the consumer including any charge for postage and packing.

Gift with purchase (GWP) and container premiums

GWP and container premium checklist

☐ *The general implementation checklist.*
☐ *The checklist for any offer run at the same time.*
☐ *Full offer description.*
☐ *Special merchandising requirements:*
- eg space, display, explanation of offer.
☐ *Special outer and shipment needs.*
☐ *Contract packing requirements.*
☐ *VAT:*
- *GWPs* - VAT on the cost of the gift is usually recoverable, although the rules are more complex if product and gift are subject to different VAT rates, or if the item costs over £10;
- *container premiums* - when containers are used as part of the retail line, the VAT implications need to be considered. If the product is normally zero rated, and if the packaging is seen as normal and necessary, the entire retail line will be zero rated. A special reusable container which entails an extra charge for the container will be subject to VAT on this part of the retail line in addition to any due on the product. Check individual situations carefully.

Banded packs

Banded pack checklist

☐ *The general implementation checklist.*
☐ *The checklist for any offer run at the same time.*
☐ *Full offer description.*
☐ *Special merchandising requirements:*
- eg space, display, explanation of offer, stability of pack.
☐ *Special outer and shipment needs.*
☐ *Direct product profitability (DPP) Issues:*
- are there unacceptable size changes?
☐ *Contract packing requirements.*
☐ *Bar codes:*
- packs with a volume size change to the retail product, eg banded packs be they product or gift will require new CUCs and TUCs.
☐ *Obscure CUCs on the single items in banded packs.*
☐ *Splitting packs:*
- consider labelling single items to render them unsaleable to avoid unscrupulous retailers splitting them down and selling at a higher price individually.
☐ *Safety:*
- give clear instructions on how the consumer should split the packs apart.

Prize promotions

General checklist for prize promotions

☐ *The overview implementation checklist.*
  in particular note:
  - restrictions;
  - POPs;
  - application forms.

☐ *The checklist for any offer run at the same time.*

☐ *Avoid complex rules.*

☐ *Customers should not be misled about the chances of winning.*

☐ *Closing dates:*
  - should have particular prominence;
  - should be fixed regardless of the number of entries, unless this has been stated as a condition at the outset or it is outside the control of the promoter, in which case entrants should be told.

☐ *Conditions and restrictions to entry;*
  - see general notes above;
  - any restriction to prizes that may be won;
  - number of entries allowed;
  - access to any supplementary rules;
  - alternative prizes, eg cash alternatives;
  - permissions, eg parent or guardian, employer;
  - abdication of responsibility for application lost or delayed in the post;
  - unacceptability of damaged, altered or defaced entries;
  - exclusions of employees of the promoting company and its agents;
  - that no correspondence will be entered into and the judges' decision is final.

☐ *Availability:*
  - entry forms and product (if proofs of purchase required) should be widely available for nationally advertised prize promotions.

☐ *Prizes:*
  - make arrangements in good time;
  - tie up third party contracts before artwork stage;
  - ensure liability restrictions are clearly set out in the rules, eg on making the arrangements for holiday promotions;
  - purchasing will be subject to VAT at normal rates;
  - refer to the checklist on agreements with other parties and sourcing sections in Chapter 11 when buying prizes. CONT..

General checklist for prize promotions (cont)

☐   *Judging and draw making:*
- should be fair, impartial and independent;
- allow enough time between close date and announcement date;
- the judges' identity should be available in advance or on request at the time of announcing the results.

☐   *Winner notification:*
- it must be clear how (eg by post) and when winners will be notified;
- allow enough time for notification.

☐   *Winner and solution announcement:*
- names and counties of winners should be made available;
- a list should be available once the judging has been completed, eg on sending in a stamped addressed envelope;
- winners should be published if cost is not disproportionate to the cost of the competition.

☐   *Respect for winners:*
- full addresses should not be published;
- steps should be taken to try and ensure winners are not subjected to any harassment as a result of winning;
- publicity for the winner (and/or outlet involved) should only be given if they have given written permission;
- consideration to training should be given for prizes that require special skills;
- consideration should be given to providing spending money for holiday prizes so that no embarrassment can result.

☐   *Ownership of copyright:*
- it should be clear who owns entries after the event.

☐   *Prize distribution:*
- prizes should normally be with winners within six weeks of the close date.

☐   *Records:*
- keep records for six years in case of challenges.

Competitions

Winning is dependent on merit resulting from the application of a substantial degree of skill by the entrant. Proof of purchase is allowed.

Typical competition headline copy

'Win ....(specify, including number of prizes).

YY proofs of purchase required (specify tokens, till receipts etc).

Closing date xx/xx/xx.

See back (side etc) for details.'

Competition checklist

☐   *Cross-check with the general prize promotion checklist.*
☐   *Proof of purchase:*
   - these are normally allowed;
   - particular prominence to requirements must be made on the outside and ideally front of the pack, leaflet or other promotional material;
   - trade competitions are restricted in that only sole traders and independent owners can enter when a proof of purchase is required (check carefully with your legal adviser to ensure bribery and corruption legislation is adhered to).
☐   *Judging criteria:*
   - should be made clear to the entrant;
   - ideally an original and unique answer is being sought;
   - gambling is not permissible, eg the prediction of actual sports results. Trying to match the results set by a panel of judges is acceptable.
☐   *Check the answers:*
   - check the answers before going to print;
   - ensure they are factually correct and the clues for and detective work on the entrant's part are robust.
☐   *Judging:*
   - whenever the selection of the winner involves subjectivity, a competent independent judge or a judging panel containing an independent judge is required.   CONT..

Competition checklist (cont)

☐ *Tiebreaks:*
- where there may be more than one entrant with the correct answer, a tiebreaker is recommended. This should provide an answer with two or more qualities, eg unique and original, that can be judged on merit;
- the requirement and judging criteria should be clear;
- if a tiebreaker has not been used to provide a unique answer, a postal tiebreak can be considered but is not recommended.

☐ *Returning entries:*
- state the position on this in the rules;
- returning entries is costly, rarely done and normally inappropriate except possibly for creative competitions such as painting etc;
- the winning solution should be made available unless it is against the legitimate interests of the prizewinner or promoter.

☐ *ISP registration:*
- consider using the ISP Standard rules facility to register the legal acceptability of your offer.

Free draws

Here entry is free, no purchase is allowed and the winner is picked at random.
Typical free draw headline copy

'Win ....(specify including number of prizes).

No purchase necessary.

Closing date xx/xx/xx.

See back (side etc) for details.'

Free draw checklist

☐   *Cross-check with the general prize promotion checklist.*

☐   *No proof of purchase is allowed.*

☐   *The draw date should be stated, along with how and when winners will be announced.*

☐   *An independent observer should be used at the draw.*

☐   *Free draws on coupons:*

- free daws are often run on coupons where the coupon is an entry form. Entry must be possible without using the coupon to make a purchase. The redeemed coupons are saved and any other applications (eg those from people who have not made a purchase and instead posted a filled in coupon or plain paper entry) are mixed in and the draw taken. It is important to ensure consumers know that they are reliant on the trade submitting their entry by a certain date. This should be clearly stated on the coupon for the benefit of all parties.

Games

Winning is based on chance, usually through the participant having a unique gamepiece, card or number. Winning may be by a variety of means, eg matching a single number, a series of numbers or symbols over time, or scratch off cards. Purchase cannot be demanded for entry.

Games checklist

☐   *Cross-check with the general prize promotion checklist.*

☐   *Proof of purchase:*

- not allowed;
- it should be very clear that no purchase is necessary;
- it should be very clear how to enter without purchase.

☐   *Free entry:*

- it must be sensibly possible to enter totally free;
- unlimited free entries should be allowed, eg by plain paper entry (although it is permissible to say only one free entry is allowed at a time).

☐   *All entries should have an equal chance of winning.*

☐   *Start and close dates should be clear.*   CONT..

Games checklist (cont)

☐   *Security:*
- care should be taken over the printing and distribution of winning gamecards etc;
- double check there is no artwork or printing error, as promotions have had to be pulled very expensively when vast numbers of winning game cards have been printed and distributed in error, or codes have been cracked;
- use printers and creative agencies experienced in these matters;
- check any odds calculations are robust;
- give careful consideration to the claims procedure;
- have hidden security codes on winning gamepieces;
- state that gamepieces which are damaged, altered, forged, illegible, tampered with or containing printing errors will be void.

☐   *Free checking of gamepieces:*
- where winning numbers etc are placed in a purchased item such as a newspaper, ensure a system has been established so consumers can check to see if they have won, free of charge;
- there is usually a phone in option available or winning answers are displayed in a public place.

☐   *Winning claims:*
- ensure claim instructions are clear, usually either by telephone or recorded delivery or a combination of the two. Think carefully about personal handing in of claims forms in case of complicity or dispute;
- ensure the handling system can cope with demand, including false or mistaken claims;
- ensure an independent observer is available for checking claims.

Instant win

Typically a winning symbol is concealed inside a pack or is on a gamepiece which has to be matched with the pack. Entry should not have to rely on product purchase.

Typical instant win headline copy

'Win ....(specify including number of prizes).

No purchase necessary.

Closing date xx/xx/xx.

See back (side etc) for details.'

Instant win checklist

☐   *Cross-check with the general prize promotion checklist.*
☐   *Access to winning symbol(s):*
      - ensure consumers cannot access without seriously tampering with the packs.
☐   *Security:*
      - care should be taken over the printing and distribution of winning packs etc;
      - double check there is no artwork or printing error;
      - use printers and creative agencies experienced in these matters;
      - check any odds calculations are robust;
      - give careful consideration to the claims procedure;
      - consider hidden security codes on winning gamepieces.
☐   *Free entry:*
      - it must be sensibly possible to enter totally free;
      - unlimited free entries should be allowed, eg by plain paper entry (although it is permissible to say only one free entry is allowed at a time).
☐   *All entries should have an equal chance of winning.*
☐   *Claims procedure:*
      - ensure claim instructions are clear, usually either by telepho or recorded delivery or a combination of the two. Think carefully about personal handing in of claims forms in cas complicity or dispute;
      - ensure the handling system can cope with demand, incl false or mistaken claims;
      - ensure an independent observer is available for check claims.

Lotteries:

Rarely used by commercial promoters.

Lottery checklist

- ☐ *The general prize promotion checklist.*
- ☐ *Registered with the local authority.*
- ☐ *Can only be run by registered charities and voluntary groups.*
- ☐ *Ticket sales must not exceed £180,000.*
- ☐ *Only 50 per cent of the revenue can be offered as prizes.*
- ☐ *The maximum cash value of a single prize is £12,000.*

Joint promotions

The principles of good communications become even more important in joint promotions where more than one party is involved. Good, shared information, goals and action plans are essential.

Joint promotion checklist

- ☐ *The general implementation checklist.*
- ☐ *The checklist for any offer run at the same time.*
- ☐ *Finding partners:*
  - this is very time consuming, so recruit suitable resource;
  - many will fall by the wayside, so have alternatives and leave time to implement them should negotiations fail.
- ☐ *Matching partners:*
  - partners should already have been established as needing complimentary positioning, objectives and ideally of similar stature;
  - the distribution of carried brands should be the same or greater than carrier brands (unless this is part of a realistic distribution drive strategy).
  - *Agreements:*
  - refer to the checklist for agreements with other parties.

Press promotions

- ❐ *The general implementation checklist.*
- ❐ *The checklist for any offer run at the same time.*
- ❐ *Creative:*
  - design does not have to be by an advertising agency. Promotional and direct marketing agencies are often better at generating response oriented advertising;
  - advertising agencies are often better at getting the branding across.
- ❐ *Agencies:*
  - encourage partnerships/liaison between promotion and advertising agencies to get the best results;
  - ensure fees are equitable to all parties to facilitate partnership building.
- ❐ *Barter deals:*
  - treat as joint promotions.
- ❐ *Advertorials/editorials:*
  - agree a word count with the editor before copywriting/designing;
  - get in the right profile publications;
  - consider run-ons for PR use.
- ❐ *Media planning and buying:*
  - ensure clarity on who owns what part of the process;
  - a full brief will be required and will include:
    brand and marketing background,
    promotional objectives,
    profile of target audience,
    regionality,
    competitive activity,
    why a specific media direction has been chosen,
    any special positioning needs,
    circulation, readership and coverage of target audience,
    how often they need to see it,
    dates,
    budget.
  - the response will include:
    rationale for media selected,
    flexibility in the timing or choice of the titles selected (should negotiations prove difficult or space be unobtainable),
    issue, publication and copy dates,
    cost estimate.

CONT...

Press promotions (cont)

❐ **Position, layout and size:**
   - which page and layout will work best for you? Generally right-hand pages are better than left-hand pages and it is better to face editorial, eg relevant articles, horoscopes, TV listings and other high-interest areas. Also the front of a publication tends to be better than the back.

❐ **Coupons and application forms:**
   - ensure they are easily accessible, eg the outside edge of a page is better than one near the spine;
   - avoid coupons appearing on the reverse of parts of the magazine that people will want to avoid cutting into.

❐ **Size of advertisement:**
   - influences are the complexity of the message, the impact and interest of the ad and the relationship between the frequency and coverage needed;
   - which is best will also depend on what you are paying for the space.

❐ **Buying space:**
   - specialist agencies perform this function. Ask your media department or agency;
   - a full brief will be required from the media planner;
   - big buyers get discounts, check for ways to tap into this;
   - discounts may also be possible for agreeing a series of ads, and last-minute discounts.

❐ **Agreements:**
   - refer to the checklist on agreements with other parties.

❐ **Timing:**
   - will people be interested in your direct response promotion when they are busy with other things, eg Christmas shopping or holiday planning?

❐ **Testing:**
   - if a direct response is expected.

❐ **Budgeting:**
   - capture the extra costs such as planning, production, media space and special treatments such as tip-ins (something stuck to the page) or bind-ins (something bound into the spine).

❐ **Sort codes:**
   - code each media insertion for evaluation purposes and collect this data whenever a response mechanism is included.

Sampling

Sampling checklist

☐   *The general implementation checklist.*

☐   *The checklist for any offer run at the same time.*

☐   *The checklists relating to the distribution medium, eg door drop*

☐   *Sample safety. It is paramount to ensure any sampling will not cause or risk causing problems in terms of:*
- safety, ie injury or harm;
- being a health risk from packaging, contents or hygiene;
- ensure suitable storage and safety checks have been carried out;
- ensure the product is distributed in packaging suitable for the use intended;
- ensure product usage instructions and warnings are included;
- provide a contact address and telephone number for queries;
- pay particular attention to the safety of children and animals;
- consider your liability in relation to solicited and unsolicited samples.

☐   *Distribution:*
- consider the safety of, and your liability towards, persons distributing samples on your behalf;
- ensure bulk outers are of suitable packaging and size.

☐   *Agreements:*
- refer to the checklist on agreements with other parties.

☐   *Design :*
- say 'free sample not for resale' if you want to cut down on the numbers appearing at car boot sales.

☐   *Press sampling:*
- cover mounts or press inserts of sachets, replica packs etc should undergo testing by the Printing Institute Research Association (PIRA).

Direct marketing

Direct marketing deserves more space than is possible here. The purpose of this section is to give some pointers to the key issues and to help promoters likely to use direct mail as a small part of their business in their dealings with the experts they will employ. It is not designed to give guidance to a business primarily driven by direct marketing.

The core of most direct marketing and especially direct mail is the establishment of a customer based database. Once established it can be used for, among other things:

❒   analysis - identifying specific respondents and their characteristics;

❒   prospecting - identifying new customers and worthwhile new lists, and modelling expected redemption rates from them;

❒   selling from - existing products or cross-selling by using the list for new business opportunities.

Many promoters will use databases for a limited period to make contacts for introducing products or services to new consumers, differing from direct mail companies which will use the medium on a long-term basis. However, along with database building the above three areas form the basic steps and these are looked at in more detail below.

Once committed to a database approach, the first decision is whether to manage the database internally. This will probably hinge on how important it is to your long-term plans and whether you have, or are prepared to buy in, the knowledge, resource and experience to do so. Many promoters think direct mail is easy and that they can just tap into it. It is a highly complex science.

Direct marketing checklist

❒   *The general implementation checklist.*

❒   *The checklist for any offer run at the same time.*

❒   *The database management section in Chapter 10.*

❒   *Data protection registration and principles:*
   - check the scope of your and your agent's registration with the Data Protection Registrar.

❒   *Selling off the page:*
   - mail order ads must have details of the company's registered name and address, and orders must to be fulfilled within 28 days;
   - note publishers associations' rules and guidelines.

❒   *UKDMA Code of Practice.*

❒   *The skill and experience to implement.*

Database building

Plan every use to help you develop the structure, before buying computer hardware and software. You will need expert skills or help to ensure you have a system and structure adequate and not excessive to your needs.

Lists may be:

- ☐   *cold* - ie lists compiled from information in the public domain, eg directories;
- ☐   *response generated* - from known responders. This is likely to give better response rates.

Sources include:

- ☐   listbrokers;
- ☐   directories;
- ☐   previous promotional responders;
- ☐   guarantee cards;
- ☐   friend get friend (member get member) activity;
- ☐   any other source in the company.

List quality

The quality of a list is paramount. Pareto's law is likely to be well in evidence with 80 per cent of business coming from the best 20 per cent of the list.

Questions you might like to ask a listbroker include:

- ☐   the source of the names;
- ☐   how old they are;
- ☐   when they were last cleaned and updated;
- ☐   who has used the list recently;
- ☐   what the result was;
- ☐   how often it has been used (good lists are used more often);
- ☐   how accurate the names/titles/addresses etc are;
- ☐   how many returns can be expected;
- ☐   will they accept payment only for those names you choose to mail?
- ☐   are they fully data protection registered;
- ☐   has the database been cleaned against the Mailing Preference Servic (MPS);
- ☐   whether they are members of the List and Database Suppliers Group (LADs);

Lists can be refined by a number of techniques. The records can be enhanced by software packages designed to rectify errors and supply missing bits of information, for example:

- ❑ name enhancement;
- ❑ address details;
- ❑ postcodes;
- ❑ telephone numbers.

Records can also be enhanced by:

- ❑ merging and purging - where lists are combined and data added together, surplus information being discarded;
- ❑ de-duping - where duplicate entries are deleted;
- ❑ cleaning - eg against MPS, county court judgements of bad debtors, people who have moved, deceased people.

List analysis

List profiling against consumer classification systems include:

Acorn;
PinPoint;
Mosaic;
Superprofiles;
Behavioural databases;
Psychographic databases;
Internally developed profiles.

Business addresses can also be identified and profiled, eg:
SiC code (industry classification)
company size, turnover,
number of employees.

Prospecting - list testing

List users will tell you time and again to test them. They believe strongly in complex testing procedures on samples from lists and scoring models to ensure the best mailing goes out to the best list. The principle that the list quality has primacy is based on the fact that even an average creative package will sell to an audience who is predisposed, but if the audience is not interested then nothing will work.

Some generalisms involved in direct mail that are crucial to testing include the following.

☐ ***Past behaviour predicts future behaviour:***
if we have a list of people who have bought before they are more likely to buy than people who have not bought before. Clearly this depends on the product on sale, but it may apply to similar products, and this leads to the next point.

☐ ***Refining:***
identifying those on the list who are the most important buyers and respondents, ie those who will buy the most. Direct mail can be expensive and, especially in fmcg, single purchases will rarely pay for the expense of the communication. Such activities will rely on the lifetime value of that customer. That is the value of all the purchases that communication will have generated in the long term.

☐ ***Profiling:***
by using profiling systems such as those above, the quality of a list can be improved by matching the profile of a new list to that of an old list of responders. Negative profiling can also be carried out, ie removing known non-responders.

☐ ***Caution:***
tests must be big enough to be statistically significant. The sample size required will be a function of the statistical confidence required, the response rate necessary and how far out you can afford to be on your response target. Ask the experts from your direct mail agency to work it out for you, do not guess.

Using and selling from databases
The format of the output from a database will depend on its end use.

☐ labels - may be used for direct application to mailers;
☐ discs - may be more appropriate if the information has to be sent to a fulfilment house to organise the mailing;
☐ typed lists - are more suitable if some telephone research has do be done before the mailing is made or as a follow up.

When mailing, note:

❐ do not over-personalise so as to be intrusive or condescending;

❐ consider the need for support offers, eg gifts, free draws;

❐ use the most appropriate envelope and message on the outside to encourage opening and not immediate binning of your offering;

❐ use a return address for undeliverables and update your database;

❐ use postcodes and mailsort for postal discounts;

❐ ensure the the label does not cover part of the promotional message;

❐ try the mailer out practically, this is very important if complicated paper engineering is involved.

❐ ensure the window in a window envelope is in the right place and the right size;

❐ ensure the reply envelope or paper engineered reply vehicle is the right size and meets fulfilment house needs;

❐ discuss your plans well with all involved and any experienced parties.

Telemarketing

Experienced telemarketers will learn little from this section. It is designed to flag some of the issues to promoters about to venture into telemarketing and who will be about to seek professional help.

Telemarketing may be inbound or outbound. Inbound calls from customers can use a variety of dialled service options, so choose the one appropriate to the task.

❐ *Toll free calls:*
The BT 0800 or the Mercury 0500 numbers. Expensive to the promoter but the caller is not charged, so they remove the risk to the consumer and encourage high level responses.

❐ *Freephone numbers:*
ie where the caller dials 100 and asks for 'Freephone Product X'. Benefits as above.

❐ *Local call rates:*
The BT 0345 and Mercury 0645 numbers. Wherever the caller is in the country they are only charged at the local call rate. This removes a lot of the risk to the applicant and and reduce costs to the promoter.

❐ *Normal Public Service Telephone Network (PSTN) calls.*

❐ *Premium call rates:*
The BT 0891 is the one the promoter is most likely to use. The caller is charged a premium rate and the promoter makes a profit. It is questionable whether this is a TQ approach. Also, many promotional responses are made from work and the premium call numbers are often unobtainable in this situation.

Telemarketing checklist

☐   *The general implementation checklist.*

☐   *The checklist for any offer run at the same time.*

☐   *Adhere to the ICSTIS Code of Practice.*

☐   *Visibility and awareness:*
- ensure prominence and strong visual aids to locate the telephone number in printed material;
- on radio, consider repetition and a memorable number;
- for direct response television (DRTV) ensure the number is of adequate size, is on screen long enough and is accompanied by a voice-over.

☐   *Inbound:*
- the merits of personal operators versus machine reception. Sometimes machines find accents hard to pick up. People generally prefer a personal operator;
- consider use of Automatic Call Distributors (ACD's). These can show operators which number is being called for which client, can direct the call to the right team and ensure the correct script is selected.

☐   *PAF:*
- consider using the Postal Address File (PAF), which can provide the full address from a name and postcode, or postcode an inadequate address.

☐   *Resource level:*
- can you cope with peaks?

☐   *Scripts*
- ensure they get interest to the target quickly;
- ensure one element follows on naturally from the previous one;
- ensure they are scripted to dealt with expected objections,
- unavailability and hurdles, eg secretaries;
- test them and monitor the reasons for failure;
- do not make them too long;
- do not pretend to be doing market research;
- get them written by an expert.

☐   *Bureau charges:*
- are they per hour, call, contact, completed script or sale?

☐   *Telephone Preference Service (TPS):*
- a register of people not wishing to be telephoned at home by companies they have not dealt with before;
- ensure you check any cold domestic lists against the TPS register.

Door drops

Door drop checklist

☐ *The general implementation checklist.*

☐ *The checklist for any offer run at the same time, especially the sampling checklist.*

☐ *Controls:*
  - have they permanent field staff checking up that the drops are made and at the time they are meant to;
  - go and see if there are any issues in the field, ask the teams and the houses who have been delivered to;
  - ask for copies of backchecks made by supervisors on houses dropped;
  - consider numbering bulk outers and getting teams to sign for specific consignments;
  - consider sequential numbering of coupons;
  - do the distributors always prosecute thieves?

☐ *Deliver the goods in time:*
  - significant expenses can be incurred if you do not deliver your items to the distributors in good time, usually two weeks before the drop.

☐ *Agree specifications:*
  - make sure the size and weight of outers for the items to be dropped is acceptable;
  - ensure they are labelled up to the distributor's needs;
  - note that there may be more than one delivery point;

☐ *Targeting:*
  - check what the distributor can offer;
  - allow time to do this;
  - getting in first on a shareplan will allow you more influence in targeting;
  - accept it is only an improvement. The quality of households will not meet your specifications by 100 per cent.

☐ *Agreements:*
  - refer to the checklist on agreements with other parties.

☐ *Coverage:*
  - some outlying rural areas are not covered by house-to-house distributors, so consider other means, eg direct mail or the Royal Mail's household delivery service if this is essential;

☐ *The item:*
  - make sure the brand recognition or message is almost instantaneous;
  - use colour and shape to provide strong, simple, visual cues;
  - teasers rarely work;
  - too much copy is a turn off, remember KISS (Keep it Simple Stupid!);
  - the more immediate the reward the greater the interest.

Charity promotions

Charity promotions checklist

☐   *The general implementation checklist.*

☐   *The checklist for any offer run at the same time.*

☐   *The BCSPP:*
     - this has a special section on charity promotions.

☐   *Agreements:*
     - refer to the checklist on agreements with other parties;
     - be cautious of your potential liability with open ended donation
       deals.

☐   *What the appeal is for:*
     - are the details of the charity and the specific appeal clear and on
       the outside of any pack?

☐   *Donations:*
     - how the charity gets the donation should be clear on the outside
       of the pack, including any proof of purchase requirement;
     - what the charity gets should be clear and the level and
       potential benefit should not be overstated, eg any ceiling on
       donations should be stated.

☐   *PR:*
     - what extra publicity can you get, eg by utilising the resources
       of the charity or the media?

☐   *Information:*
     - the BCSPP states that on request 'brief authenticated
       information on the benefit accruing to the cause concerned as
       a result of the promotion' should be provided;
     - consider also providing details of how to join, further help or
       contribute to the charity.

☐   *Good causes:*
     - if the link is with a good cause not a registered charity,
       ensure the nature and objectives of the good cause are defined.

In-store demonstrations, roadshows and exhibitions

Demonstrations, roadshows and exhibitions checklist

✕   *The general implementation checklist.*

✕   *The checklist for any offer run at the same time.*

✕   *Agreements:*
    - refer to the checklist on agreements with other parties.

✕   *Special merchandising requirements:*
    - eg space, display, explanation of offer.

✕   *Special transport or accommodation needs.*

✕   *Stock supply and storage.*

✕   *Briefing:*
    - brief staff well, provide an aide-memoire;
    - provide samples for the demonstrators to try;
    - are incentive schemes clearly understood and motivating?

✕   *Safety:*
    - ensure consumers and staff are not endangered in any way.

✕   *Hygiene:*
    - comply with hygiene requirements.

✕   *Security:*
    - is any stock or expensive equipment secure, eg overnight storage?

✕   *Services:*
    - eg electricity, water etc.

✕   *insurance:*
    - see Chapter 11.

13
Evaluation

Evaluation is the corner-stone to effective decision making.

In TQ terms, evaluation is the the final 'check' in the macro PDCA cycle of promotion. It is through evaluation that an organisation is able to make fact based decisions in the future and to improve the systems by which these decisions are made. The feedback loops that facilitate these improved systems and processes represent the final 'act' to complete the circle.

This chapter is about both the check and the act, how to evaluate practically and what to do with the learning. Figure 13.1 illustrates how this chapter fits into the macro PDCA promotional cycle.

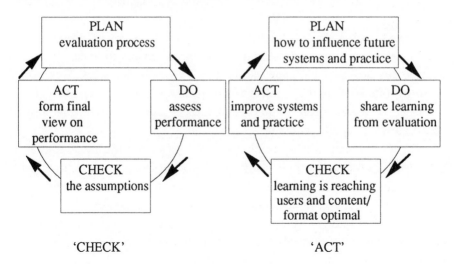

Figure 13.1 The 'check' and 'act' of the evaluation process

This chapter is short because the principles are simple. The practice is simple too, once the pain threshold of starting a comprehensive and co-ordinated evaluation process has been overcome.

The subject has been broken down into the following topics:

- ❒   the principles and scope for evaluation;
- ❒   the responsibility for evaluation;
- ❒   an evaluation checklist;
- ❒   evaluation measures explored;
- ❒   learning - completing the circle.

THE PRINCIPLES AND SCOPE FOR EVALUATION

The principles of evaluations are:

- ❐   they should be factual;
- ❐   they should offer a view from all involved;
- ❐   they should not be restricted to your own products, as you should also assess the total market performance and competitor activity;
- ❐   the cost of evaluation should be more than covered by the savings made (quality is free);
- ❐   the format and methodology should be common to allow comparisons;
- ❐   learning needs to be tempered according to the quantity and accuracy of data;
- ❐   the learning should be shared and actionable.

Fact based evaluations will enable a company to excel in running TQ promotions by making fact based decisions possible and to make cohesive plans to counter problem areas exposed by the evaluation work. Decisions made any other way will be subject to the disastrous course plotted by guesswork or, worse, the disinformation and forced decisions driven by strong personalities and political clout.

There is much to learn from both successes and failures. A true and balanced view is necessary, covering all types of performances and this means all activities should be evaluated. The tendency to look only at disasters on a witch-hunt to see who went wrong, or for a brand manager to crow about a success, will only distort perceptions and drive the company in erroneous directions. This also means that the inputs to the evaluation process should be from a wide base, all parties involved in the creation, implementation and results of a promotion will have a view on whether it was a success or a burden. Their views should count.

Restricting evaluation to your own activities is only part of the story. It is the most important element, but keeping a watch on competitor promotions can be extremely rewarding. It would be impractical to analyse them all, but you should note what activity competitors get up to, especially when you are promoting. The data at your disposal to analyse competitors are more limited, but there is information available, eg store surveys, retail audits, cost measures based on the scale of activity and continuous research panel analyses such as Nielsen and AGB. All of these can help divine what the competition is doing and how your offering compares to the rest of the market.

Initially the the amount of work in setting up an evaluation system may seem daunting, but once efficient systems are up and running it will become a simple and quick process. Once evaluation becomes part of the natural way of doing things, the cost of the resource will be more than paid back by the benefits in time and money spent on ineffective activities and promotional achievements will soar. Figure 13.2 illustrates.

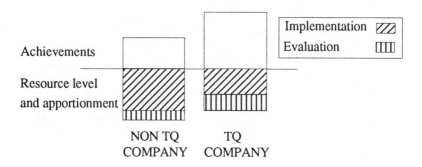

Figure 13.2 The relationship between resource, achievement and evaluation

Much reported analysis and research into the effect of promotions shows there is an enormous opportunity to improve performance efficiency and to reduce the cost of waste. The old Lord Leverhulme adage that half of his advertising was wasted (but could anyone tell him which half?) is an understatement for promotions.

In most companies, with the probable exception of mail order houses where response rates generate their revenue, I am sure promotional evaluation is studiously avoided or dealt with only superficially. Most companies may well take a cursory look at the sales effect and some at the profit effect, particularly on large or controversial activities. More need to look back to check against their 'SMART' objectives, more closely at the resource being tied up, and the true customer and consumer dynamics of who is responding and why.

Information technology - models and systems
The key to effective and easy analysis, and the retention and sharing of learning is information technology (IT).

Simple spreadsheet models can be used to cost out the promotional effects. The models described in Chapter 10 are as equally robust for post-evaluation as they are for pre-evaluation.

More sophisticated IT systems will allow common access of information.

Individual evaluations will reveal some useful learning, but the real value will come from the accumulation of many analyses. This is the route by which general truths will become visible, enabling swift and accurate decision taking on promotional proposals. This requires the adoption of standardised practices. Only by adopting a consistent methodology and format can comparisons be made.

Naturally pragmatism has to apply and if a particular promotion is only run infrequently then learning from many examples is not possible. In such cases the quality of evaluation will be even more important.

The information recorded needs to be sensible in its detail. Information is needed, not reams of data. It is easy to slip into immobility through 'analysis paralysis' where looking back takes precedence over getting on with business and the quantity of data prevents clarity in decisions.

Figure 13.3 showes the basic evaluation measures by the main promotional objectives. The measures will all need to be compared to the cost of the activity to get a scale to their efficiency.

Image	-	attitudinal measures
Awareness	-	recall (spontaneous vs prompted)
Trial	-	number of (new) people using
Volume	-	units sold (through)
Distribution	-	surveys of availability
Display	-	number/quality of features
Weight of purchase	-	number of items bought/occasion
Loyalty	-	purchase behaviour pattern
Expanded reasons for use	-	product usage research
Switching	-	purchase behaviour patterns

Figure 13.3 Basic evaluation measures by objective

THE RESPONSIBILITY FOR EVALUATION

Since decisions are the things that senior management like to make, it is self-evident that they should be genuinely interested in evaluation. In a TQ company they will appreciate its fundamental importance and the task will not be left to the office junior.

The table in Figure 13.4 shows who in an organisation should be participating in the evaluation process.

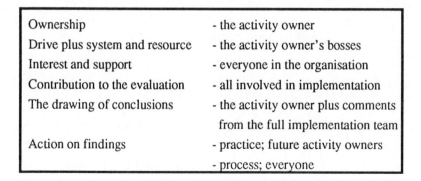

Ownership	- the activity owner
Drive plus system and resource	- the activity owner's bosses
Interest and support	- everyone in the organisation
Contribution to the evaluation	- all involved in implementation
The drawing of conclusions	- the activity owner plus comments from the full implementation team
Action on findings	- practice; future activity owners
	- process; everyone

Figure 13.4 Ownership in the evaluation process

Creative and implementation agencies will also wish to evaluate promotions. However they are not well placed to evaluate activities for the client for the following reasons:

☐ they may not have a sufficiently long relationship with the client, especially if the results are less than satisfactory;

☐ there may be confidential internal issues the client may not be able to share;

☐ they may be only a part of the support programme, and all costs and inputs may not be available to them;

☐ if they are one of a number of agencies there may be difficulties in developing common systems and sharing learning;

☐ there is a basic conflict of interest as the agency will not wish its creation to be seen as a failure.

It may well be possible to involve trusted agencies with whom there is a long-term commitment in the evaluation process. Certainly the agency will want to know if the promotion achieved its objectives and what the sales or redemption results were. This is only reasonable if the agency is to be able to judge its performance and build on it for the future. Subject to a formal confidentiality clause, the quality client should give its agency a full debrief after the event.

There are specialist consultancies who specialise in analysing promotional performance. These can certainly prove of value in thinly resourced organisations or those that need a helping hand to initiate change. However the ideal is for evaluation to be not an extra item tagged on to the end of an event, but part of the fundamental organisational culture, where it is the natural way of everyday working in the organisation. It should be seen as part of the whole operational process and not as a separate chore or specialist activity. Everyone should participate and be interested in what happens.

AN EVALUATION CHECKLIST

This section is designed to provide a skeleton checklist for an evaluation format. Different organisations will have different needs so this offers basic building blocks showing the type of information that may be appropriate. It is up to the individual organisation to put the flesh to the skeleton, although some suggestions are made.

The key is to end up with usable and actionable information that can easily be shared. It is worth having information in depth but when communicating findings brevity usually makes the learning easier to absorb. Many people will simply require extracts relevant to them, or a summary or overview from a number of evaluations.

The checklist has a two-tier structure. The headlines are mandatory building blocks for any effective system. The sub-sections are examples of the type of content and the issues which need to be considered. These will need to personalised to the organisation.

EVALUATION MEASURES EXPLORED

Getting the depth of analysis right is important. Depending on the activity, and the background work done in evaluating the particular type of promotion in the past, it may be that just sales or redemption information is adequate. More likely you will need greater detail, which could involve on-going monitoring and special ad hoc work.

Here we explore some of the ways some individual measures can be looked at in more depth. The basic measures covered are illustrated in the schematic in Figure 13.5.

These measures often need to be compared to one another and looking at them in isolation can be misleading. For example, if the brand share did not come up to expectations was it because the offer was not attractive enough or was it because the store went out of stock? If they went out of stock, why was this? Was it because of your failure to supply, because it was not merchandised or because a few people bought the lot? Comparing different measures will be very revealing and will help in the understanding of the promotional dynamics.

Evaluation checklist

☐   ***What it was***:
- as appropriate, a sample, copy or photograph of the item plus a copy of the artwork;
- a sample of any reward package;
- a simple and accessible description of the offer and how to participate;
- promotional volumes;
- details of any support package.

☐   ***When it happened***.

☐   ***Where it happened:***
- sales channels, eg any regionality or outlet restrictions;
- media used etc.

☐   ***The objective(s).***

☐   ***Performance against objectives.***

☐   ***What else happened:***
- other activity (by you or competitors) at the same time;
- sales effect;
- effect on other lines in the portfolio, did they gain or lose sales as a result?
- other learning, eg from continuous or special research and analysis;
- any information on participants.

☐   ***Financial indicators:***
- was it on budget?
- the breakeven point, the cost/participant or cost/incremental sale.

☐   ***Qualitative comments:***
- internal, from all involved departments, eg production, sales, commercial etc;
- external, consumers, customers, distributors and suppliers.

☐   ***Conclusions and lessons learnt***
- was it worth the time and resource?
- did it add value to the total brand proposition?

☐   ***Future recommendations:***
- practice;
- process.

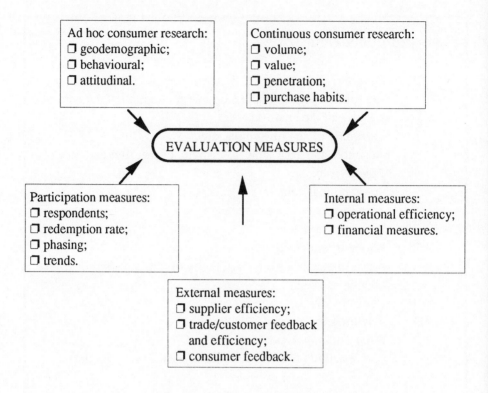

Figure 13.5 Evaluation measures

The list of evaluation measures above sounds comprehensive and straightforward but in reality the noise in the marketplace masks the effect of promotions and can make quantitative measures very difficult. When there is a lot of competitive activity, concurrent advertising and only small market movements it becomes difficult to strip away the layers of influence to reveal the baseline of non-promoted sales against which to measure your promotion's performance and any incremental sales.

Normally it is only by comparing the different measures available and by performing many evaluations that clear pictures of the effect of promotions will emerge.

Participation measures

This refers to learning about the number and nature of the response to the offer.

In price promotions where everyone gets the benefit of the discounted price, there is little to measure in terms of participation. What we can usefully measure is the respondent level to an offer.

Respondents and redemptions

Respondents are the number of people responding to an offer, for example the number of consumers (or customers) taking up either:

- ❏ a conditional offer, where the offer is awarded on condition of a qualifying purchase;
- ❏ any offer application or entry, eg a competition.

The number who apply or take up will be an easy measure which gives a very broad indication of success or failure. It is not accurate because of promotions where the wrong people apply and because of slippage. In most offers the degree of slippage cannot be determined without specific research and is rarely worried about.

It is important to be consistent in measuring participation and redemption, and it should be expressed as a percentage of the opportunities available, eg if an on-pack send-in offer requires three proofs of purchase, then the opportunities will be one-third of the packs available. In some types of offer there are two or more layers of involvement to measure, but the same principle applies.

For example, say 100,000 mailers were put out offering consumers the opportunity to telephone in for a free voucher for product X and 10,000 responded, of which 8,000 redeemed the voucher.

The redemption or participation rate for the voucher application would be 10 per cent. However, this figure alone would be of minimal value to the business, as it merely provides an upside risk to the cost of the offer. If we want to know how many voucher users we are going to get we need to know the redemption rate for the voucher. This is obviously 80 per cent of the applicants or 8 per cent of the opportunities to apply.

The 8 per cent is the key figure for the brand manager concerned about the number of trialists. If it is a constant value, the 80 per cent will be important for the accountant budgeting for redemptions on a subsequent offer where the applications are in, but the redemptions have not all come back yet.

The important factor is consistency and clarity. This can be illustrated by expanding on the offer above. If instead of a mailing a press ad is run, what basis do we use for our percentages? Many publications are read by more than one person, so do we take the circulation or the readership? As a telephone number is being used, anyone who sees the ad could apply, so the readership is the correct figure. If it were a coupon to clip then the circulation would be appropriate. Taking the wrong figure would confuse those planning future campaigns.

In addition to absolute measures of response, the quality of respondents is important. Specific research can be simply carried out to assess whether you have attracted the type of respondents you wanted. This would be done by ad hoc or continuous research methods (see below).

Other redemption measures include phasing and trends.

Phasing

Any patterns to redemptions will provide useful learning. Examples include the rate at which redemptions come in over time. This tends to be consistent within markets by different offer type.

All offers will have the basic 'S' shaped curve as illustrated in Figure 8.6. If the number of weeks by which the curve will flatten out can be determined as a standard, then calculating redemption rates can be done part way through a promotion. This can be of tremendous value when premiums have to be bought. Assuming lead times allow, they can be bought in batches during an offer to assure supply without expensive residuals. Coupons, in particular, show very marked redemption patterns by media type, and understanding this can help budget control. NCH can offer advice on this.

Phasing also allows fulfilment houses to ensure they have the right resource at the right time. This applies not only to sendaway offers, it is also illustrated by the phasing of telephone calls over the course of a single day for a call-in offer. There are dramatic peaks when respondents get home, the calls change to cheap rate or when there is a supporting ad on TV etc.

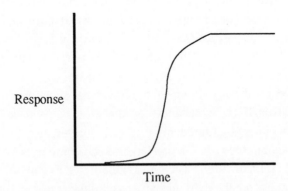

Response

Time

Figure 13.6   Offer redemption curve

Trends

Redemption trends are also valuable, especially over long periods. Comparing redemption rates to previous promotions and sales over promoted and non-promoted periods can give early warning signs of offer types failing to perform if they are inappropriate to the market conditions or if wear-out of a long-standing technique is occurring.

Continuous consumer research

Continuous panels are a rich source of data for most fmcg marketers. Here, individuals are recruited on to panels and they keep a diary of their purchase and/or usage habits. The use of scanning technology has increased the efficiency of these panels as consumers are given scanning equipment to record bar coded purchases on, largely replacing old style manual diary record keeping. The type of raw data, depending on the panel, include such information as:

- demographics;
- purchase made, brand, size, variant etc;
- quantity bought;
- price paid;
- where bought;
- awareness;
- usage.

The data are often available in basic tables providing instant information on, for example, market sizes, brand shares and penetration. It is also often possible to get special analyses done using the raw data, perhaps using filters to remove unwanted consumers from the panel. These allow more detailed information to be obtained on the dynamics of the market.

Things to beware of when using these measures include:

- concurrent activities;
- competitive action;
- advertising;
- distribution changes;
- gains and losses between brands including your own;
- seasonality;
- total market movements.

Volume and value
These are effectively brand share measures and look at what movements have occurred in total sales versus others in the market. Usually the source is a

continuous research panel such as AGB Homescan which records customers' purchases.

Questions that might be asked include whether you have benefited in general brand share terms, as well as more specific analyses.

What were the dynamic effects on volume (units or measure of fill) and value (cash) brand shares? For example, if the absolute volume of product sold (eg literage) has gone up, is it as a result of selling more units of product overall, or is it due to increased weight of purchase, ie selling more big packs at the expense of smaller ones? Is this the way you wanted the market to go?

Which is more profitable in the long run? Which do the trade want to see?

Penetration

This measures the number of people buying the product.

In the example above, volume increase due to more units being sold does not necessarily mean more people have bought your product. It could be that each individual is buying more units. It is therefore important to monitor penetration.

Penetration is a key measure in trial gaining activities. For example, measuring cumulative penetration during the course of a sampling campaign can show up the effects on consumer purchase.

Purchase habits

People buy products in different ways and continuous panel analysis can help reveal some of these.

Loyalty measures are valuable in showing whether you have retained a more dedicated purchaser base. Consumers of fmcg products tend to buy from portfolios of brands, and loyalty will show if you have increased your share of this. It is a measure of frequency of purchase of your brand within this portfolio. You may also wish to see if the frequency of purchase for the whole category has changed.

Tracking the aggregated purchase patterns of individuals to reveal the order, size and weight of purchase can also reveal a lot about their habits and the effect of promotions. Were they new buyers into the market category, had they bought your brand before, did they buy it again and so forth?

Ad hoc consumer research

Panel data are not available for all markets, nor for respondents to sendaway offers, and some brands are too small to show a statistically significant sample even if they are recorded on a panel. In these cases some special research is necessary. This could be a specific research programme commissioned through a a research house, or it might be as simple as a reply paid postcard with a few questions included in the response pack. Ad hoc research might include some of the areas covered under continuous research and the following.

Geodemographics
As discussed in the targeting section in Chapter 8, this looks at the places where people live and the type of person they are in simple measures such as sex, age, social class, household composition etc. Some limited behavioural information can be inferred. One use in evaluation is to profile names and addresses of respondents using one of the various geodemographic systems available and to see if the profile matches that which you were hoping to achieve. You may wish to compare to existing users or a database of competitors.

Behavioural and attitudinal
Specific research to ascertain any behavioural and attitudinal effects of the promotion using methodologies as described under the research section. This is often simple follow-up research, eg a telephone survey of a sample of respondents.

Post promotional research can be more detailed, eg what effect the promotion had in image terms. It may even be valuable to consider the effect on non-respondents and determine their reaction to the brand having seen the promotion - it should not have been a negative one.

Internal measures

There is a great deal of information internally held within an organisation that can contribute to evaluation and this needs to be captured.

Operational efficiency
Measuring operational efficiency runs right to the heart of evaluation. It is through this that you can not only improve the things you do but the way in which they are done. Measuring operational efficiency runs hand-in-glove with external measures to build up clear pictures of potential process improvements.

This will include soft measures from those involved in bringing the activity to life. Gaining comment from all departments on how a promotion went can contribute to the learning process. Care has to be taken to separate fiction and hearsay from fact and worthwhile opinions, but this is a useful source. If part of the supply chain is not happy there must be a problem to solve, even if it is only attitudinal.

Implementation is very difficult to do well and is under-rated. Many marketers love ideas, pretty pictures and flowery prose. Few enjoy the mundane implementation tasks such as ensuring the correct bar code is on a pack outer or that the offer rules are correct. However, these details can make or break a promotion and a TQ company will want to capture these problems.

Sales measures

There are often robust bookings or shipments data that can help. This is especially valuable when consumer or distributor data are unavailable.

Financial measures

Internal financial measures are necessary to contain costs and understand promotional profitability.

In the US research across 65 product categories (Abraham and Lodish, 'Getting the Most Out of Advertising and Promotion' , *Harvard Business Review*, May-June 1990) showed that only 16 per cent trade promotions were profitable. Not only that, the researchers found that for many promotions the cost of an incremental dollar's sales was greater than 1 dollar.

Just as the application of a financial analysis to consumer response is important, so it is necessary to monitor internal commercial issues to build the whole picture. Did costs come in as planned? If the offer over- or under-redeemed what was the effect on the profitability of the promotion. Did you have to fly in more premiums at extra cost because the offer was over-subscribed? Did extra sales give an unexpected profit boost via marginal sales?

The model in Figure 13.7 will help calculate the profit stemming from a promotion. Many promotions will show a loss. This is not a disaster as long as they can be shown to be achieving long-term goals that will yield profits in the future. Most trial gaining activities will run at a loss, they are an investment. The concern is if short-term switching promotions in mature brands are running at a loss.

STAGE 1
    income from baseline sales (the non-promoted alternative)
          less
    production and distribution costs
          less
    trade related costs
          gives

theoretical return if not promoting

STAGE 2
    income from promotional sales
          less
    production and distribution costs
          less
    trade related costs
          gives

return from promotional sales

STAGE 3
    return from promotional sales
          less
    theoretical return if not promoting
          gives
    incremental sales
    less
    promotional costs
    ❐ creation
    ❐ implementation
    ❐ fulfilment
    ❐ additional trade costs attributable to the promotion;
    ❐ additional support (eg promotional advertising)
    ❐ cannibalisation
    ❐ opportunity
          gives

incremental profit

Figure 13.7 Model to calculate incremental profit of a promotion

Some costs may be seen as lying elsewhere, eg promotional advertising may be seen as brand building as well and companies may sometimes wish to discount them from this calculation. Other costs included in the model need further comment.

Trade related costs

In both the promoted and the non-promoted alternative there will be additional trade costs. Some costs may be hidden in different budgets in the company, particularly trade related ones. To ensure a true picture of profitability, all these costs must be captured in any profitability model. If these costs are likely to increase in the promoted option, then this too should be captured. Such costs might include:

- discounts;
- advertising allowances;
- listing allowances;
- display allowances;
- merchandising allowances;
- coupons;
- display material;
- quantity discounts;
- over-riders.

Cannibalisation

Not all sales movements will be positive:

- some promotions may not sell as well as regular pack;
- others may result in lost sales to other brands or sizes from your portfolio;
- there may be a pre-promotional, eg dip where the trade know a promotion is on the way and so do not order;
- there may be a post-promotional dip, eg where the trade is left with residual stocks and do not order for some time after the promotion.

All of these costs eat into your regular sales and need to be accounted for as part of the cost of running the promotion.

Opportunity costs
The loss of profit from not doing something else that would have been more profitable.

While financial measures are essential, they are not necessarily the final word on evaluation. This is just as well as the short-term financial picture is often not a rosy one. Longer term there may be benefits from such things as protected listings, maintained or extended distribution and increased trial. There are many other soft benefits to promotion which cannot be easily captured in a financial model. These will include increased trade and consumer visibility, sales later due to increased awareness, defensive freezing out the competition and image effects.

External measures

These will include measures of the efficiency of suppliers generating promotional material and in some cases implementing activities, eg handling houses, sales demonstrators or roadshows. Also to be measured are how well any retailers or distributors put your promotions into effect.

In addition to looking outwards in these measurements the company striving for partnership relations will want to ask suppliers and recipients of promotions how they viewed your performance in the process.

Supplier efficiency
Continuous measurement of suppliers' performance is important to ensure the establishment of long-term partnerships. Quality audits can establish if a supplier has the potential to deliver, but what is important is to ensure they continue to do so. In some instances the performance measures can themselves be carried out by the supplier and reported back to the client. This is clearly a more efficient use of the client's time and quite feasible for long-term TQ partners and where quantitative measures are involved, eg faults in premiums supplied or merchandising efficiency.

Performance measures are best made objectively and quantitatively, but sometimes softer quality measures will also be involved, eg in the case of creative agencies where the supply of ideas, abilities, attitude and commitment will be key measures.

Trade/customer feedback and implementation efficiency
This is about looking at how well others involved in presenting the proposition to the target audience perform their part of the bargain and what they thought about the promotion.

In fmcg markets measuring different retailers' performance is likely to be implemented through continuous research, eg scanning information or in-store audits. This might measure whether the promotion has been effectively implemented in all intended stores.

External measures will include delivery data, distribution, pricing, shelf location, store/shelf out of stocks, stock levels, consumer offtake by brand/size/variant, eg EPOS data.

Comparison against expectation and also the performance compared to the presence in store can help refine future plans and expectations. For example, the correlation between shelf share and sales share can reveal optimum levels of facings to achieve the best sales.

Support should be measured as well as effect. I am aware of past studies which have shown levels of display feature as low as 20 per cent of that which the sales team negotiated with the account. I am aware of similar figures for the placement of agreed display material. Only evaluation can reveal these costs and allow the opportunity to plan a strategy to counter them. If a retailer does not deliver the promised support, then why pay? If they have a problem why not offer to help?

In the US it has been estimated that only one-third of the money spent on trade promotions is passed on to the consumer. I do not know what the figures are in the UK but I am sure they are significant. This is not just because of poor
implementation (indeed this is much improved), but because promotion support money is sometimes seen as a profit opportunity in its own right. Payment to go into a retailer's ad, door drop booklet or to pay for a feature is seen by some retailers as way of getting more money out of the manufacturer.

Many retail price promotions are unprofitable not only because of high entry costs or because the discount does not generate true incremental business, but because of trade bunce (selling without passing on the discount). Here the trade forward buys stock at cheap price. They will often sell on at regular price later when you should be selling them more profitable regular price stock.

Consumer feedback

Even without research the consumer is a valuable source of feedback. Comments, complaints and suggestions should all be welcomed and absorbed into your learning. Many manufacturers actively encourage customer feed-back. For example many carry toll-free telephone numbers on their packs to encourage consumers to contact them.

LEARNING - COMPLETING THE CIRCLE

Only through evaluation can the different dynamics of a promotion be explored and a balanced view on the effect of the activity made. Once this has been established measures can be taken to enhance the benefits and counter the problems.

The learning needs to be input into two areas, the practice and the process.

The practice

Learning can be used every day. For example:

- ❏   to determine the sales uplift associated with a specific type of promotion;
- ❏   to avoid unprofitable promotions;
- ❏   to estimate redemption rates and set budgets;
- ❏   to keep discounts down to the minimum necessary to get support and achieve your consumer objectives;
- ❏   to control trade buy-forward on discount;
- ❏   to assess the worth of feature and display costs.

The list goes on endlessly, but it is not the individual learning points that really add value. It is the aggregation of learning from different promotions and indeed other support, eg advertising that allows effective promotional planning. Establish systems in your organisation to capture and share your learning.

The process

This can yield even greater benefits than getting the practice right.

From evaluation we can not only learn about the consumer and customer dynamics, we can also understand how to operate with them and how to run our internal processes in the most efficient way. The application of TQ tools, as discussed in Chapter 2, eg fishbone analyses, Pareto charts, process mapping and error cause removal, will be particularly helpful to identify areas for improvement.

Encouraging TQ thinking in suppliers and trade partners will facilitate improvements in shared processes. Feeding learning back to them, thanking them when they excel and helping them when they have difficulty, will all help to build firm foundations for a long, profitable and efficient relationship.

It is only by understanding how to do things in a total quality way that all promotional activities can eventually be right first time, performed at minimum necessary cost and best meet the needs of the customer.

GLOSSARY

A list of terms used in promotions and related areas. The explanations are designed to give an indication of their meaning rather than a formal definition.

Above the line: paid advertising in the media.

Account specific: promotion designed for a specific customer.

ACORN: a geodemographic targeting system.

ANA: Article Number Association.

Article number: a specific and unique number ascribed to identify an item. See also under bar code.

Artwork: original material (eg illustrations, type, transparencies) prepared for print reproduction.

Bar code: representation of a number by a series of parallel lines of different widths with different spaces between them it is known as a bar code. In promotions these may be on products, coupons or other pieces of promotional material. Special ones may be produced on each piece of promotional support material to identify and track individual respondents.

BCAP: British Code of Advertising Practice.

BCSSP: British Code of Sales Promotion Practice.

Below the line: all marketing activity except advertising.

Bleed: a print term, where the print area extends beyond the edge of the area to be cut out and used.

Bold: a print term where a heavier typeface is used.

Bonus: usually an extra reward offered to the trade, eg discount or free stock, in exchange for a promotional order.

Bounceback: an offer to a promotional respondent, often included in the response package.

Bromide: a print term, out of date which refers to a black and white photographic print on paper. See also PMT.

Buy back: a refund offer where the product can be sold back to the supplier at a later date.

Character merchandising: where an established fictional character is used in the marketing of a product.

Chromalin: a print term, where an accurate proof is produced photographically without the preparation of printing plates. Good for checking detail but colour balance will usually be imperfect.

Clusters: various types of groupings of individuals made when targeting.

Cold list: database with no affinity or history in relation to the product.

Colour separation: a photographic film of one colour element of a piece of artwork, used in the preparation of printing plates.

Competition: where a prize is allocated according to merit. Success must depend to a substantial degree on skill and/or judgement.

Copy: the words used in a communication.

Coupon: a voucher exchanged for a cost reduction against goods or services. Sometimes used confusingly to describe an application or order form.

Covermount: item stuck to the front cover of a magazine.

Cross-promotion: where two or more brands are promoted together. Typically one brand carries an offer for the other. Often the offer is reciprocated.

CUC: customer unit code.

Customer unit code: the bar code on the unit the consumer purchases.

DAR: Digital artwork and reproduction, where artwork and repro activities are performed on computer.

Database: a file of stored information, usually on computer.

Dealer loader: a trade promotion designed to encourage an increase in stockholding.

De-duping: comparing two or more databases and removing duplicated data.

Demographics: a way of dividing and describing populations according to selected economic and social criteria.

Die-cut: a piece of print which has been cut to a special shape.

Dielines: the area used for artwork production, within which the printed message must appear if it is to be reproduced in the final printed item.

Direct mail: a part of direct marketing where the promotional message is mailed.

Direct marketing: any activity which creates and profitably exploits a direct relationship between you and the prospect.

Direct promotion: any promotional activity which works through direct contact with the current or potential customer.

Display outer: a construction which works both as a shipper for delivery and as a display unit.

Door drop: where a promotional item is delivered directly to individual homes by area (not by specific addresses).

Dupes: a print term, meaning duplicates usually of transparencies.

EPOS: Electronic point of sale.

Extra value pack: a pack containing extra fill free or at a special price.

Facings: the linear shelf space a product commands measured in packs.

Flash pack: where a pack or outer has a special message on it.

FMI: Free mail in.

Four colour print: the basic system of colour printing where magenta, yellow,cyan and black are used in various intensities and combinations to produce a full colour representation. There may be limitations to the colour balance that can be obtained in which case special colours will be used.

Free (prize) draw: where winners are determined purely by chance, product purchase must not be a prerequisite for entry. Free mail in: where a reward is given free to postal applicants, normally in exchange for proof(s) of purchase.

Free standing insert (FSI): a promotional communication loosely inserted into a publication.

Fulfilment house: another name for a handling house.

Games: a prize promotion where the prizes are awarded without the use of skill and judgement, and without demanding money or proof of purchase. Geodemographics: the combination of demographics with a geographic information system.

Gift with purchase: normally used to describe a promotion where the gift is awarded at the time and place of purchase.

GWP: gift with purchase.

Handling allowance: payment to an intermediary, eg the trade, or to a handling house for the handling and administration of promotional materials.

Handling house: a marketing services agency which handles, eg sorts, packs up and/or mails, promotional materials.

Incentive: a reward given to motiovate the purchase or use of a product or service.

Laser scanner: usually a device to read bar codes.

Lifestyle database: a system defining populations according to their behaviour.

List broker: an agency that selects, sells and rents lists.

List cleaning: correcting and/or removing incorrect names and adresses on a mailing list.

Lists: normally used to describe computer databases.

Lottery: the distribution of prizes by chance but where a ticket is purchased to qualify for entry.

Loyalty: a measure of the propensity for customers to continue to buy a product.

Lithography (litho): a form of printing most commonly used for promotions. Sheet litho is where sheets of paper are fed into the machine. Web litho is where the paper is in one continuous roll and is used for very big jobs.

Mail in: where the promotional participant mails in to gain fulfilment of the offer, normally a premium reward.

Mailing Preference Service (MPS): system by which consumers not wishing to receive direct mail are screened from mailings.

Mailsort: a system whereby promotional mailing are pre-sorted by postal areas to gain postal discounts.

Malredemption: fraudulent aquisition and cashing of coupons.

Mark-up: a written instruction on a piece of artwork to help the printer understand what is expected. Also the additional charge levied on a product or service bought in by a service company.

Merchandising: representing the product at point of sale, eg display material, display area and actually filling shelves.

Merge and purge: the combination of lists along with the removal of duplications.

Mock-up: a pre-production representation or model of what an item will finally look like.

Misredemption: where the customer uses a coupon but not for the product intended, or where an offer is applied for when the conditions have not been fully met.

Multi-brand: short for multibrand promotion where a number of brands participate in the same activity.

Multi-media: typically interactive technology based communications, eg interactive computer screens providing information and offers at the point of sale.

Multi-pack: a number of consumer units packed together to form a larger retailunit.

Origination: the pre-production stages, eg in printing.

Outer: the packaging that contains, protects and describes a number of items during distribution.

Overlay: a printing term where additional or alternative promotional messages are overlaid on piece of artwork using clear acetate sheets carrying the messagewhich can hinge in and out as required.

Overrider: additional payment made to a trade customer for acheiving pre-determined targets.

Overs: excess items from a print or production run.

Pantone reference: a numerical reference system linked to specifically defined colours. Used extensively to advise printers of the intended colour match.

Paste-up: assembly of the elements making up the final artwork.

Penetration: the degree to which an item or service extends into a population.

Photo mechanical transfer: PMT.

Plates: a set of colour specific representations of a piece of artwork in the physical form that the printer will use in the printing process.

PMT: black and white line or tone photographic prints used in artwork preparation, eg of a logo.

Point-of-sale: typically display or other promotional material physically at the point of sale.

POP: proof of purchase

POS: point-of-sale.

Premium: a promotional item of merchandise usually used as a gift or reward.

Premium offer: where a premium is offered to respondents.

Proof of purchase: evidence that a purchase has been made.

Prospects: potential customers.

Psychographics: a way of describing populations according to their psychological characteristics.

Redemption rate: the number of applicants or redemptions in relation to the number of opportunities to participate.

Registration: the accuracy or otherwise of two or more printing inks in a print job.

Repro: shortened version of reproduction, itself another term for origination.

Reverse out: a print term where the lettering is represented by the absence of ink rather than the printing of ink.

Rough: a drawing representing what the final item will look like.

Sampling: the free provision of goods or services to enable the customer to decide on their worth before purchase.

Scamps: a very basic rough.

Scanning: a print term for the filtering of an artwork into its component colours for the preparation of separations, also the reading of bar codes.

Self-liquidating promotion: typically where a premium is offered but the participant pays for the goods and thus funds the cost of the promotion.

Self-liquidating premium: a premium item funded by the participant.

Separations: colour separations.

Send in: where the promotional respondent has to send in to participate.

Shareout: where a prize, usually money is shared out between qualifying applicants.

Silk screen printing: a form of printing useful for printing on awkward surfaces, eg many premium items.

SLP: self-liquidating premium or promotion.

SKU: stock keeping unit.

Special colours: specified print colours produced by using a special ink to match the specification. Often given as Pantone references.

Stock keeping unit: the smallest unit for a product, eg size, colour, variant and some promotional packs.

Sweepstake: the allocation of prizes by chance, no POP is allowed.

Tailormade: a promotion designed for a specific customer but not always as unique as an account specific, eg the activity may only be a modified version of activities running in other customers.

Telemarketing: using the telephone for marketing purposes, may be inbound (customer to telemarketer) or outbound (telemarketer to customer).

Tie breaker: a technique to determine the winner in a competition where a number of correct answers have been received or are likely.

Trader unit code: the bar coding used on trade outers.

Trading stamps: special stamps offered to customers to collect and so qualify for rewards.

Trading up: customers buying larger or better products or services.

Traffic builder: a promotion designed to increase the number of people coming to an outlet.

UC: trader unit code.

Typeface: the named design of type.

Vignette: a print term where the image gradually fades away from a solid or dense colour to a light tint or no colour.

Voucher: an item that qualifies the holder to specified products or services.
Widget: another term for a premium item.

USEFUL ORGANISATIONS

Advertising Association (industry lobbying voice)
Abford House, 15 Wilton Road, London, SW1V 1NJ
Tel 071-828 2771   Fax 071-931 0376

Advertising Standards Authority (ASA) (adjudicators)
Brook House, 2-16 Torrington Place, London WC1E 7HN
Tel 071-580 5555   Fax 071-631 3051

Article Numbering Association (ANA)
11 Kingsway, London WC2B 6AR   Tel 071-836 3398

Association of Exhibition Organisers
417, Market Towers, Nine Elms Lane, London SW8 5NQ
Tel 071-627 3946

Association of Household Distributors (AHD)
3 Brunswick Square, Gloucester GL1 UG   Tel 0452 387070

Association of Mail Order Publishers (AMOP) (promoter's association)
1 New Burlington Street, London W1X 1FD   Tel 071-437 0706

Bank of England
Issue Office, Bank of England, London EC2R 8AH   Tel 071-601 4028

British Promotional Merchandise Association (BPMA)
BPMA Secretariat, Suite 12, 4th Floor, Parkway House, Sheen Lane,
East Sheen, London SW14 8LS
Tel 081-878 0825   Fax 081-878 1053

British Retail Consortium (BRC) (retailer voice)
Bedford House, 69 Fulhan High Street, London SW6 3JW   Tel 071-371 5185

British Standards Institute (BSI)
PO Box 375, Milton Keynes, MK14 6LL   Tel 0908 220908

Central Statistical Office
Press and Information Office, Room 65C/3, CSO, Great George Street,
London SW1P 3AQ   Tel 071-270 6363

Chartered Institute of Marketing (CIM)
Moor Hall, Cookham, Maidenhead, Berkshire, SL6 9QH   Tel 0628 524922

Committee of Advertising Practice (CAP)
Contact the ASA.

Confederation of British Industry (CBI)
Centre Point, 103 New Oxford Street, London WC1A 1DU
Tel 071-379 7400

Consumers Association
2 Marlebone Road, London NW1 4DF   Tel 071-486 5544

Corporate Hospitality Association (CHA)
PO Box 67, Kingswood, Tadworth, Surrey, KT20 6LG
Tel 0737 833963

Data Protection Registrar (DPR)
Office of the Data Protection Registrar, Springfield House, Water Lane,
Wilmslow, Cheshire SK9 5AX   Tel 0625 535777

Department of Trade and Industry (DTI)
1-19 Victoria Street, London SW1   Tel 071-215 5000

Direct Mail Information Service (DMIS) (industry information)
3rd Floor, 5 Carlisle Street, London W1V 5RG Tel 071 494 0483

**Direct Mail Services Standards Board (DMSSB) (run by the Royal Mail and
awards recognised status to suppliers)**
26 Eccleston Street, London SW1W 9PY   Tel 071-824 8651

**Direct Marketing Association UK Ltd   (DMA(UK)) (industry voice for DM advertisers,
agencies and consultants, list and database suppliers, also mailing and fulfilment houses)**
Haymarket House, 1 Oxenden Street, London SW1Y 4EE
Tel 071-321 2525   Fax 071-321 0191

Direct Marketing Centre (DMC) (training and education)
1 Park Road, Teddington, Middlesex TW11 8BR   Tel 081 977 5705

European Direct Marketing Association (EDMA)
34 Rue du Gouvernement, Provisoire, B-100, Brussels, Belgium
Tel 010 32 2/217 63 09

European Federation of Sales Promotion (EFSP)
Square Vergote 34, B-1040, Brussels, Belgium Tel 010 32 2/735 03 28

Food and Drink Federation (FDF) (manufacturer voice)
6 Catherine Street, London WC2B 5JJ   Tel 071-836 2460
Gaming Board for Great Britain (lotteries)
Berkshire House, 168-173 High Holborn, London WC1V 7AA
Tel 071-240 0821

Incentive Travel and Meetings Association (ITMA)
133A, St Margaret's Road, Twickenham, Middlesex TW1 1RG   Tel 081-892 0256

Incorporated Society of British Advertisers (ISBA) (advertiser's voice)
44 Hertford Square, London W1Y 8AE   Tel 071-499 7502

Independent Committee for the Supervision of Telephone Information Services (ICSTIS)
3rd Floor Kingsbourne House, 229-231 High Holborn, London WV1V 7DA
Tel (complaints line): 0800 500 212

Independent Television Commisssion (ITC) (controls and regulates TV advertisements and issues an advertising code)
70 Brompton Road, London SW3 1EY   Tel 071-584 7011

Institute of Grocery Distribution (IGD)
Letchmore Heath, Watford, WD2 8DQ   Tel 0923 857141

Institute of Packaging
Sysonby Lodge, Nottingham Road, Melton Mowbray, Leicestershire, LE13 0NU   Tel: 0484 500055

Institute of Practictioners in Advertising (IPA) (agency voice)
44 Belgrave Square, London SW1X 8QS   Tel 071-235 7020
Institute of Public Relations
The Old Trading House, 15 Northburgh Street, London EC1V 0PR
Tel 071-253 5151

Institute of Purchasing and Supply
Easton House, Church Street, Easton on the Hill, Stamford, Lincolnshire, PE9 3NZ   Tel 0780 56777

Institute of Sales Promotion (ISP) (industry voice)
Arena House, 66-68 Pentonville Road, London N1 9HS
Tel 071-837 5340   Fax 071-837 5326

ITV Network Centre (replaces ITVA, operates ITC code and vets TV ads)
200 Grays Inn Road, London WC1X 8XZ   Tel 071-612 8000

List and Database Suppliers Group (LADS)
Contact via the DMSSB

Local Authorities Co-ordinating Body on Trading Standards (LACOTS)
PO Box 6, Token House, 1A Robert Street, Croydon, Surrey, CR0 1LG
Tel 081-688 1996

Lord Chamberlain's Office
St James's Palace, London SW1   Tel 071 930 3007

Mailing Preference Service (MPS)
Consumer: Freepost 22, London W1E 7EZ
Industry: 1 Leeward House, Plantation Wharfe, London SW11 3TY
Tel 071-378 1625

Marketing Society
Stanton House, 206 Worple Road, London SW20 8PN   Tel 081-879 3464

Market Research Society (MRS)
The Old Trading House, 15 Northburgh Street, London EC1V 0AH
Tel 071-409 4911

National Consumer Council
20 Grosvenor Gardens, London SW1W 0BD   Tel 071-730 3469

National Postcode Centre
Fenton Way, Basildon, Essex SS15 6TY
Tel 0268 490571

Newspaper Publishers Association (NPA) (represents the national press and runs MOPS)
34 Southwark Bridge Road, London SE1 9EU   Tel 071-928 6928

Newspaper Society (NS) (regional press)
Bloomsbury House, Bloomsbury Square, 74-77 Great Russell Street, London
W1CB 3DA   Tel 071-636 7014

Office of Fair Trading (OFT)
Field House, 15-25 Breams Buildings, London EC4A 1PR   Tel 071-242 2858

Office of Population Censuses and Surveys (OPCS)
St Catherines House, 10 Kingsway, London WC2 6JP   Tel 071-242 0262

Packaging Industry Research Association (PIRA)
Randalls Road, Leatherhead, Surrey, KT22 7RU   Tel 0372 376161

Periodical Publishers Association (PPA) (consumer and business magazines)
Imperial house, 15-19 Kingsway, London WC2B 6UN   Tel 071-379 6268

Promotional Handling Association (PHA)
Tel 081-751 6373

Promotional Sourcing Association (PSA)
Adnac House, 6 Denton Drive, Newhaven, East Sussex BN9 0PT Tel 0273 515212

Public Relations Consultants Association
Willow House, Willlow Place, London SW1P 1JH   Tel 071 233 6026

Radio Advertising Bureau (an association of independent radio stations)
1 Euston Centre London NW1 3JG   Tel 071-383 3288

Radio Authority (government appointed regulator)
Holbrook House, 14 Great Queen Street, London WC2 5DG Tel 071-403 2724

Royal Mint
The Press Office, Royal Mint, Llantrisant, Pontyclun, Mid Glamorgan CF7 8YT   Tel 0443 222111

Royal Warrant Holders Association
7 Buckingham Gate, London SW1E 6JP   Tel 071-828 2268

Sales Promotion Consultants Association (SPCA)
Tel 071-702 8567

SOME USEFUL SUPPLIERS

This list does not include many valuable suppliers. It is restricted to some of those specifically mentioned in the text, especially where their details are not so easily accessible from the institutes or associations mentioned above. Those mentioned may provide other services and there are also many other suppliers of similar services. The ISP can sometimes help promoters with contacts.

AGB (market research)
Research Centre, West Gate, London W5 1UA   Tel 081-967 0007

BT Business Communications (use of the telephone)
Freepost BS 6259, Bristol BS1 2BR   Tel 0800 800 905

BT Connections in Business
Walpole House, 18-20 Bond Street, London W5 5AA   Tel 081-567 7300

CACI Ltd (targeting)
CACI House, Kensington Village, Avonmnore Road, London W14 8TS
Tel 071-602 6000

CCN Marketing (targeting)
Talbot House, Talbot Road, Nottingham NG1 5HF   Tel 0602 410888

CDMS (targeting)
PO Box 15, Crosby, Liverpool, L23 0UU   Tel 051-949 1900

Census Customer Services (targeting)
Scotland: GRO, Ladywell House, Ladywell Road, Edinburgh, EH12 7TF
          Tel 031-334 4254
Other areas: OPCS, Segensworth Road, Titchfield, Fareham, Hants. PO15 5RR
          Tel 0329 42511

CMT Data Corp Ltd (targeting)
Teddington House, Broad Street, Teddington, Middlesex, TW11 8QZ
Tel 081-943 5511

FRS (targeting)
Tower House, Southampton Street, London WC2E 7HN   Tel 071-836 1511

Chas E Goad Ltd (targeting)
8-12 Salisbury Square, Old Hatfield, Herts AL9 5BR   Tel 0707 271171
ICD Ltd (targeting)
29 Corsham Street, London N1 6DR   Tel 071-251 2883

Infolink Ltd (targeting)
Coombe Cross, 2/4 South End, Croydon CR0 1DL   Tel 081-686 7777

Mercury Communications Ltd (use of telephone)
90 Long Acre, London WC2E 9RA
Tel 071-528 2000 or Mercury Free Call 0500 500 415

National Postcode Centre (use of postcodes)
4 St George's Business Centre, St George's Square, Portsmouth PO1 3AX
Tel 0705 870307

NCH (Nielsen Clearing House) (coupons)
Corby, Northamptonshire, NN17 1NN
Tel 0536 400123

NDL International (targeting)
Port House, Square Rigger Row, Plantation Wharf, London SW11 3TY
Tel 071-738 0522

Nielsen Marketing Research (market research)
Nielsen House, Headington, Oxford OX3 9RX   Tel 0865 742742

NRS Ltd (targeting)
Garden Studios, 11-15 Betterton Street, Covent Garden, London WC2H 9BP
Tel 071-379 0344

Ordnance Survey (mapping)
Romsey Road, Maybank, Southampton, Hants SO9 4DH   Tel 0703 792683

Pinpoint Analysis (targeting)
Tower House, Southampton Street, London WC2E 7HN   Tel 071-612 0568

Royal Mail
Headquarters: Royal Mail House, 148 Old Street EC1V 9HQ   Tel 071-490 8837
Letters: try the local Royal Mail customer care centre, in your telephone
directory. Parcels: try your local Royal Mail Parcelforce customer care unit, in your
telephone directory.

Target Group Index (TGI) (targeting)
BRMB, Saunders House, 53 The Mall, Ealing, London W5 3TE
Tel 081-567 3060

FURTHER READING AND USEFUL PUBLICATIONS

CODES AND INDUSTRY GUIDES

The British Code of Sales Promotion Practice
Available from the ISP

The BSI Suppliers Guide (lists companies with BS5750)
from BSI Quality assurance, PO Box 375, Milton Keynes, MK14 6LL

Market Reasearch Society Yearbook
Contact the MRS for information on a wide range of research publications, annuals and serials.

Lotteries and the Law
published by the Gaming Board of Great Britain

Foresight (future events directory)
Profile Systems Ltd, 32-38 Saffron Hill, London EC1N 8FN

The Marketing Handbook (directory of suppliers)
Reed Information Services Ltd, Windsor Court, East Grinstead House, East Grinstead, West
Sussex RH19 1XA

The Promotional Handling Code of Practice
available from the ISP

Code of Practice for Traders on Price Indications
available from the Consumer Affairs Division of the Department of Trade and Industry

ITC Code of Advertising Standards and Practice
contact the ITV Network Centre

The DMA Code of Practice
from the DMA(UK)

British Code of Advertising Practice
contact CAP

The Creative Handbook (directory of suppliers)
Reed Information Services Ltd

Mailguide (information on the postal system)
Springfield House, West Street, Bristol BS3 3YY   Tel 0272 535342
(or contact your local customer care centre)

Article Numbering and Symbol Marking Operating Manual
contact the ANA.

The Letterbox Marketing Handbook (information on door drops)
available from the Association of Household Distributors

Magazines and periodicals

Campaign
Haymarket Campaign Pulblications Ltd, 22 Lancastre Gate, London W2 3LY

Incentive Today
Langfords Publications Ltd, Ridgeland House, 165 Dyke Road, Hove, East Sussex, BN3 1TL

The Journal of Targeting, Measurement and Analysis for marketing
Henry Stewart Publications, 2/3 Cornwall Terrace, Regents Park, London NW1 4PQ

Marketing
Haymarket Business Pulblications Ltd, 30 Lancastre Gate, London W2 3LP

Marketing Business
HHL Publications, 3rd Floor, Greater London House, Hampstead Road, London NW1 7QQ

Marketing Week
Centaur Publishing Ltd, St Giles House, 50 Poland Street, London W1V 4AX

Precision Marketing
Centaur Publishing Ltd, St Giles House, 50 Poland Street, London W1V 4AX

Promotion News
Langfords Publications Ltd, Ridgeland House, 165 Dyke Road, Hove, East Sussex, BN3 1TL

Promotions and Incentives
Haymarket Business Publications Ltd, 30 Lancaster Gate, London W2 3LP

Sales Promotion
Market Link Publishing, Market Link House, Elsenham, Bishops Stortford, Hertfordshire, CM22 6DY

What's New in Marketing
Morgan-Grampian plc, Morgan-Grampain House, 30 Calderwood Street, London SE18 6QH

Books and other publications

Commonsense Direct Marketing
by Drayton Bird, published by Kogan Page

Crackingjack
by Alan Toop

The Exhibitor's Handbook
by John Northgover, published by Kogan Page

A Handbook of Market Research Techniques
edited by Robin Birn, Paule Hague, Phyllis Vangelder, published by Kogan Page

Handbook of Telemarketing: Strategies for Implementation and Management
by Michael Stevens, published by Kogan Page

How to Get Sponsorship
by Stuart Turner, published by Kogan Page

An Introductory Guide to The 1991 Census
edited by Barry Leventhal, Corine May, James Griffin, published by NTC Publications Ltd

Marketing Pocket Book
NTC Publications Ltd

The Practicioner's Guide to Direct Marketing
Published by The Direct Marketing Centre, 1 Park Road, Teddington, Middlesex, TW1 0AR

Retail Pocket Book
NTC Publications Ltd

Sales Promotion - How to Create and Implement Campaigns that Really Work
by Julian Cummins, published by Kogan Page

The Sales Promotion Casebook: Europe's Great Campaigns
by Alan Toop, published by Kogan Page

Sales Promotion Law; A Practical Guide
by Philip Circus and Tony Painter, published by Butterworths

Targeting Customers (how to use Geodemographics and lifestyle data in your business)
by Peter Sleight, published by NTC Publications Ltd

Index

accreditation 25
ACORN classification system 147
action plans 214
advertorials 63
anti-competitive pricing 57

banded packs *checklist* 262
bar coding 150, 253–4
Boston Square 38–9
brainstorming/idea selection 169–70
brand image 105–10
  service 110
  sponsorships/link-ups 106–8
brand life-cycles 38–41
  the Boston Square 38–9
  declining brands 40
  established brands 40
  growth brands 39–40
  summary of objectives by position
    40–1
brand loyalty/switching 31–3, 129
breakeven analysis 200–1
budgeting 50–2
  promotional reviews 190–3
    checklist 192–3
buy one get one free (BOGOF) 86
buy-outs/fixed fee promotions 161–2

cannibalisation 298
cashbacks 83–4
census geography 141–2
character merchandising 107
charity link-ups 107
  checklist 281
checking promotions *see* reviews,
    promotional
checklists
  agreements with other parties 229
  banded packs 262
  competitions/contests 265–6
  coupon design 254
  coupon implementation 255–6
  coupon redemption rates 161
  design brief 217–18
  implementation 243–82
    general 243–9
    specific activities 249–82

joint promotions 270
order specification 227–8
promotional briefing 167–8
promotional budgeting 192–3
promotional expression 186
promotional implication 183
promotional redemption levels 156
  influences on 161
promotional sourcing
  briefing suppliers 222
  premium suitability 221
promotional standards 196
promotional technique *vs* objective
  163–5
  supplier quality 225
redemption levels 156, 161
cinema promotions 121
clubs, marketing to 134
codes of practice/legislation 18, 53–64
  advertorials 63
  competitions/lotteries 58
  database management 58–60
  general standards/supervision 54–5
  international promotions 61–2
    legal promotions by European
      country 62
  mail order 60–1
  pricing/trading issues 56–7
  radio promotions 63–4
  specialist trade codes 63
  telemarketing 61
  television 64
collector schemes 99–100
complaints, dealing with 240–1
consumer research
  ad hoc 294–5
    behavioural/attitudinal 295
    geodemographics 295
  continuous 293–4
    penetration 294
    purchase habits 294
    volume/value 293–4
container premiums 99
conversion analysis, sampling activities
  199–200
copyright 246–8
corporate hospitality 109

couponing 71–83, 158–61, 252–6
  advantages/disadvantages 80–3
  bar coding 150, 253–4
  coupon abuse 77–9
  design *checklist* 254
  frequency of use 75
  how do consumers like to receive
    coupons? 76
  how many at a time? 75
  implementation *checklist* 255–6
  malredemption 77–8
  misredemption 77–8
  redemption rates 158–61
    checklist 161
  retailer perspective 79–80
  scale of 73
  typical copy 252–3
  what value to offer? 77
  who redeems? 76–7
  why consumers use coupons 73–4
  why coupon? 72–3
  why some consumers do not use
    coupons 74–5
creative briefing 167–8
creativity 43–4, 166–80
  brainstorming/idea selection 169–70
  the brief 166–8
    checklist 167–8
  buying in 170–3
    pitching 173
    required services 171
    selecting agencies 171–3
  executional tips 178–80
    design 179–80
    good copy 178–9
  managing resources 174–8
    agency remuneration 176–7
    assignment of responsibilities 174–5
    briefing 174
    contact reports 176
    contracts/terms of trade 177
    dealing with clients 178
    feedback 178
    response 175
cross-purchase coupons 82
customer, knowing your 44–5
customer types, identifying 128–30

database management 58–60, 148, 238–9,
    275–8
dealer loaders gifts/incentives 57
decision-making process, the 42–64
  budget setting 50–2

choosing the right promotion 52–3
creativity 43–4
dynamics of participation/response
    48–50
five promotional drivers 45–7
knowing your customer/the
    environment 44–5
planning 42–3
promotional law/codes of practice
    53–64
definitions
  awareness 30
  display 33
  distribution 33
  image 31
  multiple purchases 33
  repeat purchase 31–3
  socioeconomic targeting 145–6
  stock loading 34
  switching 31
  trial 30–1
demonstrations, roadshows and
    exhibitions 282
  budgets 192–3
  charity promotions 281
  door drops 280
  evaluation 288, 289
  exhibitions 282
  free draws 266–7
  free mailings 258–9
  games 266–7
  gift with purchase 262
  handling, briefing 235
  handling, supplier selection 234
  instant win promotions 269
  in-store demonstrations 282
  lotteries 270
  press promotions 271–2
  prize promotions 263–4
  roadshows 111–12
  sampling 273
  self-liquidating offers 261
  telemarketing 278–9
demonstrators/tastings 113
  checklist 282
design, artwork/print 216–19
  basic process 216
  design briefs 216–18
    checklist 217–18
  progression tips 218–19
desk research 205–6
direct marketing/promotions 113, 127–8,
    131–4

direct mail 131–3, 160
    consumer direct mail 131–2
    response rates/costs of 132–3
direct response marketing 133–4
discounting 68–89
    coupons (money off) 71–83
        checklists 161, 254–6
    price off single purchase now 67–71
display 33
distribution 33
door drops 114–18, 160
    checklist 280
    information/offers 115–17
    samples 117–18
    targeting 230–1
    types of 114–15
DRTV Direct Response Television 133

economic climate 17
Electronic Shelf-Edge Labelling (ESEL)
    151
electronic shopping trolley screens 152
emotional benefits, rewards and 105–10
    service 110
    sponsorships/link-ups 106–8
environmental issues 19, 193–5
    importance of 193–4
    opportunities 195
    packaging 194
    supplier choice 194
established brands 40
evaluation 283–302
    ad hoc consumer research 294–5
    checklists 288, 289
    continuous consumer research 293–4
    external measures 299–300
        consumer feedback 300
        supplier efficiency 299
        trade/customer feedback 299–300
    internal measures 295–9
        financial measures 296–9
        operational efficiency 295–6
        sales measures 296
    learning 301–2
        the practice 301
        the process 301–2
    participation measures 290–3
    principles and scope for 284–6
    IT models/systems 285–6
    responsibility for 286–8
events, sponsorship 106–7
everyday low pricing (EDLP) 68–9
exhibitions 112–13

checklist 282
extra fill packs *see* extra value (EV) packs
extra value (EV) packs 57, 84–5

fixed fee promotions 161–2
free draws *see* games
free gifts 90–100
    free item 96–100
        collector schemes 99–100
        container premiums 99
        free money 100
        gift with purchase 97–8
        sendaways 98–9
    free product 91–5
        on approval 95
        completely free 95
        as gift 94
        giving away product 91–3
        sampling 93–4
        try me free 94–5
Free Mail Ins (FMIs) 257–9
    checklist 258–9

games/game card promotions 101, 104–5
    checklist 266–7
geodemographics 295
    geographic targeting 141–2
    targeting systems 146–8
gift vouchers 83
Gift With Purchase (GWP)s *checklist* 262

handling/fulfilment
    dealing with fulfilment houses 233–7
        administration/reportage 236–7
        briefing 233–6
        briefing prompt *checklist* 235
        choosing/appointing 233
        supplier/selection *checklist* 234
    dealing with money 238
    postcoding/mailing economy 238–9
    queries/complaints 240–1
    redemption package 239–40
    sending promotional material 237–8
    stock control 240

implementation process 211–42
    agreements with other parties *checklist*
        229
    design, artwork/print 216–19
    general notes/*checklists* 243–9
        applications/entry forms 249
        overview 243–4
        proofs of purchase (POPs) 248

protection against copying 246–8
  restrictions/conditions 245–6
handling/fulfilment 231–41
  briefing prompt *checklist* 235
  handling house selection *checklist* 234
  insurance 241–2
  planning 212–15
  sourcing 219–29
  specific activity notes/*checklists* 249–82
    charity promotions 281
    coupons 252–6
    database building 275–8
    direct marketing 273–4
    door drops 280
    joint promotions 270
    press promotions 271–2
    price promotions 249–51
    sampling 273
    sendaways 257–70
    telemarketing 278–9
  targeting systems 230–1
in-, on-, or off-pack gifts 97–8, 159
in-store demonstrations
  checklist 282
  multi-media 151
Information Technology (IT) 19, 149–52,
    284–6
  IT led promotions 149–52
    electronic shopping trolley screens
      152
    ESEL 151
    intelligent packaging 152
    interactive TV 152
    multi-media 151
    smart cards/other plastic cards
      149–51
    models/systems 285–6
insurance 241–2
integrated communication package 15–16
intelligent packaging 152
interactive TV 152
international promotions 61–2
investment strategies/brand life-cycles
    38–41
  the Boston Square 38–9
  declining brands 40
  established brands 40
  growth brands 39–40
  summary of objectives by position 40–1
investments 57

joint promotions 152–5
  advantages/disadvantages 155

  checklist 270
  free/part-funded 153–4
  issues relating to 154–5
  types of 152–3

legislation *see* codes of practice/legislation
lifestyle/behaviourgraphic targeting
    systems 148–9
link-ups 106–8
local store marketing 137
lotteries 58, 101, 104
  checklist 270

mail order 60–1
malredemption, coupon 77–8
mass communications 114–22
  cinema/video 121
  door drops 114–18
    checklist 280
  press promotions 118–19
    checklist 271–2
  public relations 121–2
  radio 119–20
  television 64, 121
    DRTV 133
  third-party links 122
misredemption, coupon 78–9
modelling redemption costs/efficiency
    197–201, 285–6
  breakeven analysis 200–1
  conversion analysis, sampling activities
    199–200
  cost per new user 198–9
  redemption or cost to trial 198
money back guarantees/challenges 109
money off next purchase (MONP) 81
money off this purchase (MOTP) 80
more product free offers 84–5
MOSAIC classification system 148
multiple purchase price discounts 33, 86–7
  banded packs (same product) 87
  EPOS type offers 87

networks 24, 213–14

objectives, setting 27–41
  planning promotional strategy 35–41
  promotional goals/objectives 27–35
  promotion types to match objectives
    162–5
    checklist 163–5
one-to-one contacts 111–13
  demonstrators/tastings 113

checklist 282
exhibitions 112–13
personal direct selling 113
personal recommendation 113
roadshows 111–12
opportunity costs 299
organisations, marketing to 134
outlet led/preferred activities 125–6

PAF Postcode Address File 238–9
Pareto charts 24–5, 37
partnerships 25–6
passing off 247
PDCA (plan/do/check/act) cycle 24, 41, 43, 211
planning promotion implementation 212–15
   action plans/timing plans 214
      sample plan 215
   communication 214
   design, artwork/print 216–19
   process maps/networks 212–14
   sourcing 219–29
   see also strategy, planning
point of purchase promotions 122–6
   outlet led/preferred activities 125–6
   product as communication vehicle 122–3
   retail promotions 123–5
postcoding/mailing economy 142, 238–9
premiums 96–9, 219–29
   disposals 229
   orders 227–8
   quotations 224
   suitability 220–1
      checklist 221
   suppliers 221–5
      checklist 224
   the last check 226
pre-promotional research 201–10
   inputs 202
   limitations 204
   planning research/pre-tests 204
   research/pre-testing qualities 203
   types of research/pre-testing 205–10
      desk research 205–6
      qualitative research 206–7
      quantitative research 207–9
      testing 209–10
   what can research/pre-testing offer? 202–3
   see also consumer research
press promotions 118–19

checklist 271–2
price promotions 56–7, 67–71, 249–51
   after effects 32
   checklist 251
   copy claims 249–50
   price off single purchase now 67–71
      consumer reaction 68–9
      controlling prices 69–70
      discount level/offer type 67–8
      European perspective 70
      price elasticity 69
      price off single purchase, regular stock 70–1
      single pack discount via offer packs 71
   pricing/trading issues 56–7
prizes 100–5
   checklist 263–4
   competitions/contests 101, 103–4
   expectations 102
   games 101, 104–5
   legality/ethics 101
   lotteries 58, 101, 104
      checklist 270
   share-outs 105
   what prizes? 102–3
process mapping 23–4, 212–13
product or service support schemes 110
promotions
   choosing the right 52–3
   five drivers of 45–7
   goals/objectives 27–35
   law/codes of practice 53–64
   planning strategy 35–41
   and Total Quality (TQ) 13–26
proofs of purchase (POPs) 47, 248
public relations 121–2

qualitative research 206–7
quality see Total Quality
quantitative research 207–9
queries/complaints, dealing with 240–1
questionnaire based targeting systems 148–9

radio promotions 63–4, 119–20
raffles *see* lotteries
redemption levels, promotional 156–62, 189–90
   buy-outs/fixed fee promotions 161–2
   checklist 156
   coupons 158–61
      checklist 161

media comments on 159–60
  speed of redemption 160
information sources 156–7
redemption package 239–40
truisms 157–8
redemptions,
  evaluation of 291–3
    phasing 292
    trends 292–3
repeat purchases 31–3
research *see* pre-promotional research
respondents/redemptions, evaluation of
    291–3
  phasing 292
  trends 292–3
restrictions/conditions on promotional
    offers 245–6
retail promotions 37–8, 123–5
  tailormades/account specifics 25
reviews, promotional 181–210
  budgets 190–3
    checklist 192–3
  company policy 188
  customer effect 185
  environmental issues 193–5
  key questions 181–5
    promotional implication *checklist* 183
  modelling redemption costs/efficiency
    197–201
  pre-promotional research 201–10
  promotional expression *checklist* 186
  redemption history 189–90
  resources 191
  safety 193
  standards *checklist* 196
  taxation 195
  timing 188–9
  trade effect 187–8
rewards
  introduction 65–6
  better value without discounting 90–110
    emotional benefits (image) 105–10
    free gifts 90–100
    prizes 100–5
  price-based techniques 66–89
    cashbacks 83–4
    coupons (money off) 71–83
    credit deals 89
    more product free offers 84–5
    multiple purchase price discounts
      86–7
    price off single purchase now 67–71
    trader offers 87–9

roadshows 111–12
  checklist 282

safety, promotional 193
sales away from trade premises 57
sales promotion 13–16
  defined 13–14
  integrated communication package
    15–16
  transformation 14–15
sampling 93–4
  checklist 273
  conversion analysis 199–200
  door drops 117–18
Self-Liquidating Offers (SLPs) 108–9,
    260–1
  checklist 261
sendaways 98–9, 257–61
  FMIs 257–9
    checklist 258–9
  SLPs 260–1
    checklist 261
share-outs 105
slippage 47
smart cards/other plastic cards 149–51
societies, marketing to 134
socioeconomic targeting 144–6
  census definitions 145–6
  IPA social grade 145
sourcing, promotional 219–29
  accepting quotes 227–8
    order specification *checklist* 227–8
  briefing suppliers 220–2
    checklist 222
  choosing items 219–20
  choosing suppliers 222–4
  disposals 229
  getting quotations 224–6
    supplier quality *checklist* 225
  the last check 226–7
  premium suitability 220
    checklist 221
specialist trade codes 63
sponsorships/link-ups 106–8
  character merchandising 107
  charity 107
    checklist 281
  events 106–7
  exploitation of 108
  money back guarantees/challenges 109
  personalities 108
  product or service support schemes
    110

self-liquidating promotions (SLPs)
108–9
trade relations/staff incentives/
corporate hospitality 109
staff incentives 109
standards, promotional 196
stock control 240
stock loading 34
strategy, planning 35–41
inputs to strategy 36–7
investment strategies/brand life-cycles
38–41
promoting via retailers 37–8
retailers/service company promotions
38
short- *vs* long-term promotions 38
strategic hierarchies 35–6
suppliers, choosing 222–4
going it alone 222–3
sourcing houses 224
using promotions agencies 223–4
sweepstakes *see* lotteries

tailormades/account specifics 25
targeting 140–9
base data for 142–3
for door drops 230–1
geodemographic systems 146–8
geographic 143–4
geographic building blocks 141–2
individuals 231
lifestyle/behaviourgraphic systems
148–9
producing profiles 230

socioeconomic 144–6
types of 143
tastings 113
taxation 195
telemarketing 61, 134–7
advantages/disadvantages 136–7
charges 135–6
checklist 278–9
inbound 135
linking to direct mail 135
outbound 135
television 64, 121
DRTV 133
interactive 152
testing, promotional 209–10
third-party links 122
timing plans 24, 214
Total Quality (TQ) 13–26
a changing world 17–19
principles of TQ promotions 20–6
benefits of TQ to promoters 21–2
cost of quality 23
customer/supplier chain 23
goal of TQ companies 21
partnerships 25–6
practical TQ tools/methods 23–5
TQ defined 20–1
trade marks 246–8
trader offers 87–9
trading stamps 57
trialing 30–1
trial gaining 138–9

video promotions 121